## An IDENTIFICATION and VALUE GUIDE to

# VINTAGE CAMERAS AND IMAGES

## by JOHN F. MALONEY

BOOKS AMERICANA

ISBN 0-89689-017-1

# TABLE OF CONTENTS

(continued)

# ACKNOWLEDGMENTS

This guide for collectors would not have been possible without the gracious help of numerous collectors, dealers and auction firms. Special thanks go to dealer and collector David Silver of San Francisco, and to Graham Pilecki of Pilecki's Antique Camera and Image Exchange of Albany, Calif. Among the many others who supplied data, checked facts or otherwise helped in the production of this book are Anne Horton of Sotheby Parke Bernet New York, Frank D. Guarino, Dave Wheeler, John S. Craig, Alan Sessarego, George M. Rinsland, Ben Corning, Robert D. Connolly, Connie Meyer, Cori Cooper, Christie's East, Phillips, California Book Auction Galleries, and Sotheby Parke Bernet Los Angeles. The author is also indebted to those who pioneered price guides and reference works on antique cameras and images, for without those early efforts, compiling the listings would have been a far more intimidating task. Among those whose published data was especially helpful are George Gilbert, Myron Wolf, James M. McKeown, and Margaret Haller.

# INTRODUCTION

In the early days, camera collecting was easy. You went to flea markets, antique shops, some camera stores, the newspaper classified ads. You found lots of old cameras and a good selection of old images offered, usually at reasonable prices. Outstanding bargains were not unusual. The reason was simple: not many people were interested in those dusty leather-covered box cameras, those slightly-warped sets of stereo cards, those antiquated folding cameras, those old stern-faced portraits.

Collecting old cameras and images—even as recently as 10 or 15 years ago—was a breeze. Because hardly anybody did it.

Today, it's a different picture. Call it a "photographica boom" if you want to (the hype really isn't necessary). One fact can't be denied—there are more collectors today, the competition is tougher, prices are higher and still rising, and the buyers are far more savvy when it comes to knowing what's on the market and what it's worth.

It used to be possible to scan the classifieds for antique and classic cameras and images in collector-oriented publications such as **Shutterbug Ads** in a few minutes. Today it's a healty 60-70 page tabloid listing hundreds of antique cameras and accessories.

It used to be that auction houses shunned photographica as junk. Today some auction firms—including prestigious Christie's and Sotheby's—devote entire sales to nothing but.

It used to be that antique cameras were inexpensive outdated equipment, oddball antiques that puzzled most dealers (most of who had no way of figuring their real worth). Today, any antique dealer in his or her right mind who acquires an old camera is careful to check out its value before pricing it, since many have brought truly amazing prices.

It used to be that photography magazines in the U.S. could entirely ignore the small group of photobuffs interested in antique cameras and images. No more. Many magazines, including **Popular Photography** and **American Photographer**, feature frequent or regular columns on old equipment and images, as well as coverage of photo auctions and, increasingly, exhibitions of vintage photographs.

And, perhaps the ultimate test of the growth of any collectibles market, there are more fakes for collectors to contend with—fake photos, fake cameras, fake accessories and even fake darkroom equipment.

Thus, today's collector finds himself confronted with a far more complicated hobby than his counterpart of a decade earlier had to deal with. Some lament the changes in the photographica hobby. Others rejoice. Either way, reality demands that today's collector know his stuff better, including prices.

Just what to pay, just what to ask, how much latitude to expect for bargaining. We hope this book will be a helpful aid for the collector faced by such hobby decisions which may cost or earn him dollars. That is what a price guide is for.

But remember, it is only a guide. Prices for images are so volatile that we can hardly keep up with them. A single auction can radically alter the price structure for some categories of images, and some prices for cameras can change just as quickly.

John Maloney

**To my wife, Betty, who not only helped but was patient above and beyond the call of duty**

# A BRIEF HISTORY OF CAMERAS:

You can't be a serious camera collector without having a good understanding of the evolution of early photographic equipment. The many model variations resulting from technical developments can make significant differences in a camera's price, and many cameras are difficult to identify without at least some familiarity with various model changes and technical modifications.

People collect old cameras mostly because they are pieces of photographic history. There's a certain thrill in owning a camera that is just like the one Erich Salomon used to capture his images of famous statesmen, or like the one grandpa used to photograph the family's turn-of-the-century picnic.

History adds greatly to the enjoyment of any antique, of course. But also important, from the pragmatic standpoint of the collector, is the way in which knowing a camera's identy and place in history can radically affect its market value.

Try reading the classified ads for old cameras in **Shutterbug Ads,** for example. This is the chief mail order marketplace nationwide for old cameras. An ad reading: "No. 3A Autographic Special, f6.3/170mm anastigmat, Ilex shutter to 1/1000 B&T," for example, presumes the reader knows that the camera is a Kodak model and that it's "autographic" feature made it possible to write notes directly on the film when the picture was taken. It takes a bit more knowledge—that of an active collector— to know that the camera is worth today approximately what it was worth in 1930—$50 or so.

A working knowledge of camera history is even more vital to those who collect earlier cameras—the wood and brass beauties that served photographers such as Mathew Brady or Alexander Gardner. Fake versions of these cameras do exist. They're easy to fake, since they are basically nothing but wooden boxes with a hole for a lens, and often only the most knowledgeable collector can spot them.

Those old wooden boxes may be humble affairs, but there's a certain thrill that comes when you realize the magic they worked, producing man's first fixed images of reality. German monk Johann Zahn is generally credited with building the first fully portable camera in the early 1800s, a nine-by 24-inch wooden box with a moveable lens (for focusing), an adjustable aperture to control the amount of light, and a mirror that projected the image into a screen on top, where it could be viewed from outside the box.

Does that sound a bit like your run-or-the-mill view camera, or even a modern single-lens reflex camera? It was—except for one thing: Zahn didn't have any kind of light-sensitive plate or film to record the image. Nothing was known about photographic chemicals at the time. It wasn't until 1826 that Joseph Nicephore Niepce, a French lithographer with an inventive mind, applied recent discoveries about light-sensitive compounds to supply the element missing from Zahn's wooden box.

Niepce, who must share with Daguerre the title "Father of Photography," coated a sheet of pewter with an asphalt-based solution, inserted it into a camera obscura much like Zahn's, and set it on his windowsill. Eight hours later he removed the plate, having produced the world's first real photograph: a fuzzy image of his farmyard.

It was a humble beginning indeed.

Louise Jacques Mande Daguerre, a Parisian scenery designer, later joined Niepce in attempts to perfect the invention and capitalize on it. More sensitive chemicals were found, but the Niepce camera continued to be troublesome. In 1839, after Niepce's death, Daguerre announced to the world his system of producing "daguerreotypes," which required exposures of about half an hour but were incredibly sharp if the subject didn't move. The problem turned out to be the lens Daguerre was using—it was far too crude, rated at about f/17 by modern standards. A better lens (about f/3.6) was soon developed by a University of Vienna professor and optician Peter von Voigtlander, who built a

4

camera to hold it. Exposure time was reduced to less than a minute, permitting photography of people as well as stationary building and still lifes.

The new lens was known as "the German lens," and it formed the cornerstone for German domination of the market for early cameras. It spurred the immense popularity of the box-like view cameras in which the lens slid in and out in a sort of wooden drawer, later refined to a flexible leather bellows.

While most early view cameras are museum pieces, they are the starting point for a multitude of other types which reflected the continued improvement of the photographic instrument. With the introduction of faster plates during the late 1870s, the camera needed a dependible mechanical shutter that could produce faster and faster exposures, down to fractions of a second. The cameras were often crude affairs. The one Edweard Muybridge used to photograph a horse in mid-gallop in the mid-1880s had a simple shutter, a guillotine-like blade that dropped in front of an opening in the wooden camera. It produced shutter speeds ranging from about 1/500 to 1/2000 of a second, quite fast for those days. By 1861 the focal plane shutter was perfected, and the leaf shutter was introduced by Edward Bausch about 1887.

Faster shutters were matched with faster plates in the late 1870s, when multi-lens cameras first appeared. These could record many small portraits on a single plate. Double-lens cameras produced stereo images which, later viewd through lenses in special holders, produced startlingly three-dimensional effects. Gigantic cameras produced giant prints long before enlarging was practical. Panoramic cameras took in broad views thanks to a swiveling lens which swept around a scene, "wiping" a continuous image across a daguerreotype plate of unusual length.

More efficient cameras, better images, and the proliferation of photographers soon had customers flocking to newly established daguerreotype studios to have their portraits made. As they became familiar with the photographic process, they began to demand cameras of their own, turning what had been a highly technical profession into a widespread hobby. The public, of course, would need smaller, less cumbersome equipment. The first person to understand the advantages of smaller cameras was a contemporary of Daguerre, an English scientist named William Henry Fox Talbot. He fitted microscope lenses—the best available at that time—to small boxes of wood, making cameras that measured as little as two and a half inches on a side. His wife contemptuously dubbed them "mousetraps." The little pictures they produced displeased Talbot—he had no way of enlarging them. So he abandoned his "mousetraps" and worked on producing faster chemicals for the standard cameras of his time. But his idea of a small box camera would eventually revolutionize photography when George Eastman introduced his simple box camera in 1888.

The early experimental years produced scores of novel, interesting cameras, almost all of them sought by today's collectors. Perhaps the most ingenious advancements, and the darlings of many collectors, are the small "detective" cameras disguised as handbags, books, shoeshine boxes, walking-stick handles or even revolvers.

Since many collectors specialize in certain types of cameras, such as detective cameras or stereo cameras or folding cameras, the following sections will provide a look at these in greater depth.

# STEREOSCOPIC CAMERAS

"Two-eyed" stereo cameras form a collectible group in which many collectors specialize. They are, according to British camera authority Cyril Permutt, "the happy coincidence of the almost simultaneous invention of the stereoscope by Sir Charles Weatstone in 1838 and the announcement a few months later of the invention of photography by Daguerre and Fox Talbot." By the 1860s stereoscopic photographs were a fad in Europe and

America. The paired pictures, viewed through a twin-lens device called a stereoscope, merge into a single view that seems amazingly three dimensional. The photographs were taken using both the calotype and daguerreotype processes. The first real improvement in stereoscopic viewing was Sir David Brewster's box type refracting stereoscope of 1849; the three and a half-by seven-inch slide that it used was to become the first standard size for stereograms. Best suited to landscapes, stereo cameras were soon used to take thousands of images of landmarks around the world, and viewing them became the passion of "armchair travelers" in parlors throughout America. There, friends and family gathered to view the pyramids of Egypt, views of European capitals, sites in the Holy Land, and exotic scenes from the mysterious orient.

Among the first to make a camera specifically designed for stereoscopic images was an English optical instrument maker named John B. Dancer, who in 1856 patented a camera with two lenses about two and a half inches apart—about the distance between the pupils of a person's eyes. The camera duplicated the slightly different images received by each eye; the stereo viewer, like the human brain, reunited them into a single, three-dimensional image. Treasured for nearly a century, Dancer's camera was destroyed by bombs during an air raid in World War II.

Early stereographic cameras are extremely rare. Only one camera was needed to produce thousands of images, which were in turn reproduced for use in millions of viewers. The rarity accounts in part for their popularity among collectors. An 1860 wet-plate stereo camera made by Morley of London with a pair of Negretti and Zambra lenses sold, with a packet of stereo pictures, for $2,127 at a 1973 Christie's sale in London. At that time it was the highest price ever paid in Britain for an antique camera. Another rare early stereo camera is the Ives Kromscop, first produced in 1892. This was the first natural color stereoscopic viewer. Today, it rarely appears on the market.

After the turn of the century, Kodak helped popularize stereo cameras with the introduction of the Stereo Weno Hawkeye in 1902. This had a pair of rapid rectilinear lenses and a Bausch and Lomb shutter (the Stereo Hawkeye No. 1 of 1904 has a Stereo Automatic shutter with five-inch rapid rectilinear lenses, and the Stereo Hawkeye No. 2 was fitted with even larger lenses). A 1917 Stereo Kodak No. 1 was produced with a pair of Kodak anastigmat f7.7 lenses with a Stereo Automatic shutter, and an updated version two years later had a Stereo No. 2 Ball Bearing shutter. Despite the various models, stereo cameras sold in comparatively small numbers, adding, naturally, to their rarity today.

What thrilled the public was not so much **taking** stereo views of their own, but seeing the mass-marketed views three-dimensionally in the viewers.

A number of French firms also produced stereoscopic cameras sought by today's collectors. Mackenstein of Paris was one, and Cyril Permutt notes that one of the most interesting cameras was "the La Francia produced in 1900. It had a wooden body with a pair of f4.6 lenses—which could be stopped down to f192!"

Jules Richard of Paris and H. Bellieni Fils of Nancy are other French makers whose stereo cameras are highly prized. The Goerz Photo-Stereo-Binocular, introduced in 1899, is a German stereo camera worth noting, as is the Zeiss Stereo Palmas, made in 1908. Voigtlander also produced several fine stereo cameras before World War I, most notably the Stereo-Panoram-Alpine and the Stereophotoscope, introduced in 1907.

Many of the stereoscopic cameras from the early part of the 20th century were produced in limited numbers, sometimes as few as 20 or 30 cameras, often with the slightest modifications.

A Leica prototype stereoscopic camera, the Dopple-Leica, made by combining two Leicas into one body, was never produced. The prototype is in a German museum, but rumors persist that a few others were produced. If found, such a camera would bring an incredibly high price from a Leica buff. Leica buffs and stereo camera collectors are probably the two most "serious" groups of camera collectors, and a camera that appealed to both groups would be a real prize indeed.

Novelty stereo cameras were also produced, such as the

1930 Robin Hood plastic camera which used cut film.

Another popular British stereo camera is the Stereo Puck introduced in the late 1920s by Thornton-Picard Mfg. Co. of Altringham, England. A cheap rollfilm box camera using 120 film, it had Meniscus lenses and a simple shutter. Far from rare, it is still worth $60 or so to collectors. Another popular stereo box camera which used 120 film is the German EHO.

By the 1930s stereo box cameras were fairly common, and these and folding stereo cameras from the post World War I period are the models collectors most frequently find. Among the stereo cameras prized by collectors are the folding Weno Stereo Hawkeye, the Premo, the Korona, and the rare Stereo Auto Graflex (1907-1922) which exposed on a five-by-seven-inch plate and projected one stereo image on the ground glass plate. With Bausch and Lomb Tessar f4.5/135mm lenses, it sells today for $1,300 to $1,500, considerably more than the $290 it sold for in 1910. On the other hand, the Stereo Kodak No. 1, first offered in 1917, is easy to find at about $190.

Reflecting the wide popularity of stereo camera collecting is the National Stereoscopic Association. Only 18 months after it was founded in January 1974, it had a membership of over 450.

# PANORAMIC CAMERAS

Panoramic cameras, which produced the ultimate in wide angle shots, have inspired less enthusiasm than stereo cameras among collectors, but their place in photographic history nonetheless makes them valuable additions to any collection, and their rarity gives them plenty of value. While cameras in the mid-1800s usually had a viewing angle no wider than 45 degrees, Friedrich von Martens of Paris built a camera in 1844 that could photograph an arc of 150 degrees, thanks to a swiveling lens and a daguerreotype plate a full 17-½ inches long. Such cameras were ideal for cityscapes and landscapes and were later used to photograph groups of people, including the entire student bodies of schools. Thomas Sutton's panoramic wet-plate camera made by T. Ross of London in 1861 used Sutton's patent spherical water lens of 1859 and had a curved focusing screen, four curved wet plate backs for curved glass plates (and even a curved tank for sensitizing the plates!). One of these cameras sold at Christie's in January 1974 for a record $25,360. Only two other versions of Sutton's camera are known to survive.

The Al-Vista Panoramic camera marketed by the Multiscope and Film Co. of Burlington, Wisc., is easier to find. Patented in 1891, it came in various models which have an average value of about $150 today.

By far the most popular collectible panoramic cameras are the Kodak Panorams, a series of roll film cameras which had an angle of view of as much as 142 degrees and produced negatives measuring 3½ by 12 inches. They were fitted with f10 rapid rectilinear lenses, and today they usually sell for about $100.

The No. 1 Panoram, produced from 1900 to 1914, turned out a seven inch wide exposure on No. 105 rollfilm for an angle of 112 degrees. It originally cost $10, and today models are worth $125 to $160. The No. 3A is the least common of the series, having been made for only two years. It sells for $160 and up among collectors.

# BOX CAMERAS

Nothing popularized photography more than George Eastman's introduction of the simple box camera in 1888. Still, his was not the first "box" camera. The camera which Nicephore Niepce used in 1816 was a box, and so was the first commercial camera which made its debut in 1839. Even the camera's predecessor, the **camera obscura**, was a mere box.

Although many collectors prefer the flashy wood-and-brass view cameras or the classy Kodaks with red bellows or the eye-catching novelty cameras, a truly representative camera collection must, by definition, contain a lot of rather drab, seemingly boring black boxes. Even the first detective cameras were large wooden boxes made to look like workmen's tool boxes.

While most box cameras have only sentimental value, those made before World War I are often highly valued by collectors. Included are models specially created for tintype making, plate-loading cameras (from 1886 to the early 1900s), and, of course, stereo and panoramic box cameras.

Actually, the category covers a wide variety of simple "lens-in-a-box" affairs. A mahogany sliding box camera with Petzval-type lens by Lerebours et Secretan of Paris, 1855, sold for $1,932 at Christie's in 1974. A Conley Camera marketed by Sears & Roebuck, on the other hand, sells for $7. In between are hundreds of non-Kodak box cameras of interest to collectors. A Blair Hawkeye Junior, a 4x5 box for rollfilm or plates, c. 1895-1900, brings $90. The most common of the Weno Hawkeyes, the No. 7, dating from about 1897, sells for about $40. Rochester's Cyclone Junior, a plate box camera, is worth about $25. An unassuming wooden box camera dating from about 1870, made in Germany for use with glass plates and with a brass barrel lens, is worth $600 or more.

But among box cameras, Kodaks steal the show.

The box camera George Eastman's company announced in 1888 was unusually small, and early Kodak literature called attention to its size, only 3¼ by 3¾ by 6½ inches. "It is a magazine camera," said one advertisement for the camera, "and will make 100 pictures without reloading. The operation of taking the picture is simply to point the camera and press the button. The picture is taken instantaneously on a strip of sensitive film, which is moved into position by turning a key."

It was the instamatic of its day—with one notable exception. The Kodak No. 1, as it was called, didn't require the user to fumble around with plates. It was the first camera designed to use roll film, and it came loaded with enough film to make 100 exposures. The user didn't even have to worry about the unfamiliar—at the time—process of developing and printing. He paid $25 for the loaded camera, including shoulder strap and leather case. The price also covered the cost of processing the first roll of film. When he had made his 100 exposures, the owner mailed the unopened camera to Eastman's plant in Rochester, N.Y., where the negatives and prints were produced. "You Press the Button, We Do the Rest"—the camera lived up to its advertising motto.

To get the camera back fully reloaded and ready for another 100 shots, the customer mailed an additional $10 with the camera. The fee also prepaid the processing cost for the new roll.

Twenty-five dollars was a lot to pay for 100 photos in 1888—that was about two and a half weeks salary—but the lure was irresistible in a world of words but few pictures (mostly woodcut illustrations in magazine, an occassional painting or pastel, or lithographed posters). It didn't take long for the camera and the photographs it produced to become on of the chief amusements in an age dedicated to amusing itself with modern gadgets, leisure-time hobbies, and flashy world fairs and expositions.

It is difficult to overestimate the importance of Eastman's little black box camera. Only recently have scholars such as Susan Sontag begun to really scrutinize the impact of the visual image on our civilization. But collectors have for years realized the importance of the Kodak No. 1, That, combined with its rarity today, enables the humble camera to command a price of anywhere for $2,500 to $3,000 or so today. The Kodak No. 2 (1889-1897), by comparison, sells on the collector market for less than $500.

The first-model Kodak camera took round pictures, each 2½ inches in diameter. The size of the image increased with the Kodak No. 2—to 3½ inches—but the camera came loaded with enough film for only 60 exposures. The early Kodaks were evidently used to the hilt, as it is fairly easy today to find the circular photographs in antique shops and at flea markets, selling for $1 to $2, ocassionally more.

Later Kodak box cameras took square or rectangular

photographs. At first they had no "aiming devices", making focusing a hit-or-miss proposition and causing many to agonize over whether the pictures would actually turn out. Highly desirable among the early Kodaks are those which incorporate a string-set shutter, with the string emerging from a hole in the top of the camera. The string was pulled to cock the shutter mechanism. Finding brass string pull knobs and Kodak winding keys has proven so difficult for collectors that replicas are being marketed, with winding key **replicas** now costing about $25—the same as the whole Kodak box camera cost in 1888!

According to George Gilbert, author of "Collecting Photographica," the Kodak factory preloads rank today as "the **piece de resistance** of any collection of American or box cameras."

With the camera market expanding rapidly, Kodak soon marketed folding cameras as well as box cameras. The first Kodak folding camera was the No. 4, introduced in 1890. But box cameras continued to be made, evolving eventually into the familiar Instamatic. Through the years, a bewildering number of makes and models of folding and box cameras were produced—enough to keep even the most serious collector a bit confused as to which model is which.

Around 1888 plate holders started to become obsolete, thanks to box cameras incorporating such features as the drop-down plate system in the Improved Magazine Cyclone, made by Western Camera Mfg. Co. of Chicago.

In 1892 the Boston Camera Co. introduced the Bull's-Eye camera, the first to load with a numbered roll of film. It has a little red window at the back to guide film advance. George Eastman later bought the Boston Camera Co. so he could obtain the Bull's-Eye patents and so Kodak could offer cameras with this feature. In 1895 Kodak introduced its own version of the Bull's-Eye, the Bullet.

By 1900 the box camera was as common as the bicycle, the typewriter, binoculars and other family-owned luxuries. And from the turn of the century onward, larger box cameras were the province only of professional photographers; families were content with the less bulky models of box cameras.

The success of the Kodak quickly brought competition into the marketplace. Eastman Kodak introduced its own competition to the Kodak line with the Flexo and Bullet cameras. E. & H.T. Anthony marketed a family camera called the Buck-Eye, which used rollfilm on a transparent base, while glass-plate box cameras continued to be popular too. The latter included the Anthony Magazine camera of 1892, which took 4x5 inch pictures, and the Magazine Cyclone cameras produced from 1898 to 1907 (for a mere $6 to $10). The early Velox camera had to be turned upside down after each shot to "drop" the plate into position. The Blair Co., meanwhile, marketed its Hawk-Eye Jr. (introduced in 1896) for $8, and Kodak's own glass-plate-loaded box cameras, such as the Eureka No. 2 (1897) for $4, continued to sell well.

No survey of box cameras would be complete without some mention of the Kombi, which George Gilbert notes is "one of the most remarkable and smallest of the box cameras produced in those years." A black metal camera loaded with enough film for 25 exposures, it sold for a mere $3, later $3.50, and gave the user a choice of round or square photos. It was the marvel of the decade and could even be used in reverse as a closeup magnifying viewer (hence the name "Kombi"). Its manufacturer, Alfred C. Kemper, claimed in his ads that 50,000 Kombis sold in one year. Although not really rare today, they are still favorites among collectors. The usual price is $100 to $125.

Perhaps the best known of all box cameras—at least to the general public—is the Brownie, introduced in 1900 and named for the little mythical Scottish elves popularized by Palmer Cox in his Brownie cartoons and stories. The camera cost only $1 and, according to an early Kodak advertisement, "was originally produced for children, but the results were so good as to excite the interest of grown-up people."

Imitators followed: the Ansco; the Kewpie from Sears, Roebuck & Co.; the Buster-Brown; the Zar; the Mystic; and Little Puck. But the No. 0 Brownie outsold the all—with the result that the cameras are so numerous today that they are worth only $10-$13. The No. 1 Brownie, also introduced in 1900, was made to take a new-size film, No. 117 for 2¼ by 2¼-inch pictures. It lasted only four months before production was halted and the back redesigned. The Improved No. 1 was then marketed, with great success. The few Brownie's from the four-month production era today command about $250 apiece, while the Improved No. 1 sells for $30.

The Brownie had the great advantage of being a camera that could be loaded in broad daylight, just like the Blair Baby Hawk-Eye of 1897, marketed for children. But another development came in 1903, when the Rochester Optical and Camera Co. introduced a new concept: the film pack. This was a flat canister holding flexible film in sheets, thereby doing away with wind knobs and rollers. The system was used in the Cartridge premo cameras, as well as later camera such as the Plaubel Makina, Graflex, and Kodak's Recomar. Such film-pack-loaded cameras today sell mostly in the $5 to $25 range, including the Premos (the Premo line was taken over by Kodak in 1903.)

A popular box camera from the 1906-1911 era is the Quick Focus Kodak (No. 3B) which originally cost $12 and, unlike other box cameras, could be focused for more than just the "middle ground." The focus knob on the side of the camera was set to proper focal distance. When the button was pressed, the camera opened, with the front popping straight out, focused and ready to shoot. Today these cameras sell for about $90 to $100.

During the first three decades of the century, Kodak's Brownies dominated the box camera market, while inspiring hundreds of imitators. Sears, Roebuck & Co. sold one of the popular imitations (under the Seroco name and also without any identifying name). The cameras were made for Sears by the Conley Camera Co. of Rochester, Minn.

A special edition of the No. 2 Brownie Kodak was issued to commemorate the 50th anniversary of Eastman Kodak Co. in 1930. About 400,000 were given away to children that year, so they are far from rare. Covered with a tan-colored reptile-grained paper covering with a gold-colored foil seal in the upper rear corner of the right side, they're now worth about $10 to $15 if in mint condition.

Besides family box cameras, larger box cameras continued to be used, especially by the street photographers who, in the years before World War I, carried not only a box camera but also the chemicals needed to produce a print right there in the street or wherever the picture (usually a portrait) was taken. Most street photographers, according to George Gilbert, used box cameras made by the Mandel brothers of Chicago, readily identified by their labels (Chicago Ferrotype Co.) and by the design features that incorporated the developing process. The in-camera processing system is one of the features that endears these cameras to collectors. A typical prize is the PDQ, a 1930s version of the street photographer's box camera now worth about $90-100 (not to be confused to an earlier PDQ by Anthony, America's oldest manufactuer of cameras and photographic supplies—the circa 1890 PDQ detective plate box camera is worth $500). A Mandel brothers camera, the Mandel No. 2 post card box camera made between 1913 and 1930, brings about $125, and the smaller Mandelette, a direct positive street camera with sleeve at rear and a tank below, sold for $10 in 1929 and now brings about $80 from collectors.

# FOLDING CAMERAS

Long before Kodak's box camera of 1888, there were folding cameras, which today form an important category for many collectors. These cameras appeared in great numbers soon after the Daguerrean era (1840-1855), thanks largely to the development of the wet-plate collodion process, which made outdoor photography lightweight and compact equipment. The folding camera came into its own during the years after the Civil War, when the optical industry was eagerly devising improvements upon improvements to cameras and lenses—better shutter mechanisms, sharper and faster lenses, more durable housings and, of course, better film systems. Thus, folding cameras are a fascinating chapter of photographic history, and as such are beloved by many collectors. Wet-plate type cameras, the earliest folding cameras, were widely used between 1855 and 1880. They consisted of wooden frames with leather or canvas bellows enabling the lens to be extended. Most have a ground glass plate in the rear and a brass-mounted lens in front.

Popular into the mid-1870s, wet-plate cameras were loaded with freshly-made plates still wet with the collodion and silver nitrate that made the image on the plate. Inevitably, the chemicals dripped—were it not for the mess, photography might have become widely popular a lot sooner — and many of the cameras found today bear chemical stains in the woodwork along the back bottom edge.

The simple-in-design cameras were usually full-plate models (making an image 6½ by 8½ inches) but came smaller or larger—as large as 24-by-27-inch monsters, in fact, which loaded a 14-by-17 inch sheet of glass. There were no shutters; the lens cap was simply removed for the desired duration of exposure.

These cameras are often difficult to identify, since they seldom carried a maker's name, and some simply can't be identified accurately. To confuse things a bit more, some carry the name not of the manufacturer but of the retail store that sold the camera. Serial numbers, lenses, or nameplates help the collector identify some models, especially those made after 1880.

Wet-plate cameras in the 4x5, 5x7 or 6½x8½ (view camera) size by E. & H. T. Anthony or Scovill are eagerly sought by collectors. An 1886 Scovill Mfg. Co. (New York) detective 4x5 camera with red leather bellows commands $850, while a more common Anthony folding plate camera like the Ascot Folding No. 30 commands $80.

Dry-plate folding cameras are easier to find. They date from the early 1880s and 1890s when the dry-plate photographic negative made the process easier and more popular (it was during these years that the first camera clubs began to appear). Some were larger models intended for studio use, and a few, like the Scovill 5x8 camera of 1885, had an interchangeable lens board so they could be used for stereo photography too. For a few years Anthony Camera Co. marketed Ascot folding cameras, with a side door for loading and storing plate holders. Today Ascots sell in the $50 to $80 price range. Another kind of early folding camera is the satchel-style which, when not in use as a camera, could be unobtrusively carried like a satchel on straps slung over the shoulder. Kodak's early glass-plate folding Kodaks were of this type.

Soon after folding cameras appeared, technological developments enabled smaller versions to be made. An economy folding Kodak appeared in 1894. It was called the Kodet and sold for $12 to $15 new. By comparison, Kodak's larger folding No. 4, No. 5 and No. 6 were selling for $60, $75 and $100 respectively.

Kodak's small No. 0 folding camera, made from 1902 to 1906, was similar in style to the 1898 original and took 1-5/8 by 2½-inch exposures on No. 121 film.

To compete with Kodak's folding cameras, Blair Camera Co., makers of the Hawk-Eye Detective camera, introduced the Tourist Hawk-Eye for a mere $9 in 1898. A smaller and much plainer version of Blair's various folding Hawkeye models, it could nonetheless take a picture as large as the 4x5 inch size. One Blair folding camera, the Lucidograph, is especially prized by collectors. Produced circa 1885-86, it was a plate camera with all-wood body and a tapered black bellows. Made in several sizes, it sold only on a limited basis. Today the Lucidograph is worth $700 or more.

During the 1890s a wide variety of folding plate cameras made their dubut. Besides names like Premo, Ascot and Seneca, collectors look for such names as Conley, Ray, Poco and Graphic—and, for a new market of bicycle-riding photographers, the Cycle Poco and the Cycle Graphic.

Few of these early folding cameras had shutter speeds faster than 1/100 of a second; subjects were still required to remain still lest they turn out blurry in the image. Aiming was basically of two types. One viewed the subject through the ground glass before inserting the plate, or one looked through the tiny viewer built onto the camera bed, usually near the lens. By 1900 Kodak folding cameras had done away with the ground glass system and, to focus, owners had to guess the distance to the subject.

Throughout the early years of the century, folding cameras were sold along with box cameras at prices the public could afford. Sears, Roebuck & Co.'s Fall 1900 catalog offered seven pages of camera equipment (each sold with a complete "Instructions in Photography" booklet). For $15.35, one could buy a complete mahogany camera with tripod and plate holders, or for $34.65 the buyer could have the snazzier Empire State Photographic Outfit. In 1908 Sears offered the Conley Improved Compact Camera, a 4x5 with plate holders and a rapid rectilinear lens (f8) for $6.95. Today it is the most commonly found size of the Conley folding models and sells for under $50.

By 1927 the Sears catalog was selling "Kodaks and Eastman Cameras," including the Brownie box and such folding models as the Vest Pocket Kodak Autographic for as little as $4.45 and the Hawkeye roll-film camera for even less. The No. 2 Folding Hawkeye was priced at $6.45.

But while the Kodaks had an immense public following, thanks largely to the marketing genius of Eastman, other folding cameras were catching the attention of serious photographers—a growing group of image takers who were not professionals but wanted something more than mere snapshots. One of the favorites of this group was the Speed Graphic, which after World War I became the darling of the press photographers. Successor to the Graphic folding plate camera of the 1890s, it was made by Folmer & Schwing in a variety of styles. Folmer & Schwing was eventually absorbed by the growing Kodak empire of Rochester, N.Y. The pre-1940 Speed Graphics, which had a hinged "sportsfinder" and a wooden bed with a single focus knob, tended to be heavily used and are often found in poor condition today. Models in good shape sell for about $70.

Roll film had an enormous impact on the folding camera market, and it quickly made folding plate cameras obsolete. Kodak had introduced the first cartridge Kodak in 1897, a camera which could be loaded in broad daylight and sold for a mere $10. "The Folding Pocket Kodak means a full realization of the charms of photography without the drawbacks of burdensome apparatus, without bulky plate holders or heavy, fragile glass plates," read a Kodak ad of 1900. It was indeed a revolution in picture taking. Kodak's No. 2 folding Pocket Kodak cost only $15 in 1900. A couple of years later one could buy an elegant No. 2 with silk-covered bellows and silver details for $75.

Smallest of the folding pocket Kodak cameras was the No. 0, made from 1902 to 1906 and similar in style to the Original of 1898-1904 but made for No. 121 film (introduced in 1902) rather than the earlier 105 film. Today it sells for about $75, while the No. 1 sells for about $25 and the No. 1A (1899-1904) brings even less. By far the most common of the folding pocket Kodak series is the No. 3A, made from 1903-1908 for use with No. 122 film—typical of the red-bellows beauties that grace many private collections. It is usually offered for $20 to $40, having originally sold for $20 in 1910, when it was billed in Kodak ads as "the most popular of all cameras; takes the full size post card picture, 3¼ by 5½ inches."

Most folding cameras had the shutter system located in front, up with the lens. The Speed Graphic of the 1900s, however, had a different type: a focal plane shutter built in toward the back of the camera. It consisted of a curtain with a thin slit in it which was made to roll quickly past the film, "painting" the image across the film as it went. With such a shutter, it was easy to achieve shutter speeds up to 1/1000 of a second, and it make it easy to design cameras whose lenses could be changed. Cameras of this type were popularized by Folmer & Schwing Mfg. Co., which marketed the Graflex with built-in focal plane shutter and, later, the Graphic, which became the standby camera of press photographers.

Today the folding pocket Kodaks are an inexpensive series for collectors on tight budgets. Most models can be found (especially at flea markets and garage sales) for prices in the $10 to $25 range. Many of them work as well today as they did more than 70 years ago.

During the years immediately after the turn of the century the welter of camera designs became especially confusing. Mergers melded various companies under a variety of corporate umbrella names and, compounded by the number of models marketed by major makers, the result was a torrent of types, models, brands, identifying numbers, and imitations.

Among folding cameras especially, collectors must be careful to know exactly which model they are buying, since values can vary considerably. A Kodak No. 3A might be priced at $20, but if it is one of Kodak's special camera series fitted with better lens or shutter, it might still be a 3A but be worth as much as $50. The 3A cameras marketed from 1900 to 1903 were made for 188 rollfilm, while those made later required 122 film.

A shrewd inventor made a quick fortune when, in 1913, he sold a single idea to Eastman Kodak Co. for $300,000. It was simply this: a method which enabled the photographer to write on the edge of the film while it was still in the camera. The idea had its merits, since it meant one could date and title negatives immediately after taking the picture. But Kodak was willing to pay a high price for the idea for another reason: it offered the perfect solution to the problem of differentiating Kodak's folding cameras from everybody else's.

The result was the Autographic Kodak, which had a little trap door built into the back and a writing stylus which could be removed from the camera. Kodak billed it as "the greatest photographic advance in 20 years"—pure hyperbole in light of the many real advances in camera technology which had taken place during the previous two decades.

The autographic feature was available only on Kodak and Brownie cameras, but so many sold that they are relatively inexpensive collectibles today. Among them are the No. 1A for 2½ by 4¼ exposures, worth about $15; the No. 3A, circa 1914-1924, for postcard size pictures on 122 film, worth $20; and the Autographic Kodak Junior No. 1, worth about $10.

The No. 3A Autographic Kodak Special, 1916-1933, is worth about $50 today, largely because it lived up to the word "special." A landmark for Kodak, it was the world's first camera with a built-in range finder, an invention made necessary by the faster lenses bing used on cameras at that time (at wide-open apertures, the in-focus zone was often measured in inches, not feet).

In 1905 Folmer & Schwing was absorbed by the Eastman Kodak empire, and by 1908 Kodak was marketing cameras using the high-speed focal-plane shutters that Folmer & Schwing had originiated. They were the 1A and 4A Speed Kodaks, each of which had a moderately fast f6.3 lens. Since they were roll-film cameras, they provided no precise means for focusing or viewing—and these drawbacks kept them from being very successful in the marketplace (they were discontinued in 1913, soon after the introduction of the No. 0 Graphic). Fairly rare today, the 1A and 4A Speed Kodaks sell for $100 to $200, with the 4A sometimes priced as high as $350.

One of the great collectible cameras of the 1920s is not quite like Kodak's folding camera, but it does have a collapsible bellows. Made by the German Ernemann Co. after about 1924, and originally called the "Ernox," it could hold plate-loaded holders of various sizes. The smallest version—about the size of a cigarette package but sporting a focal-plane shutter and a large, super-fast f1.8 or f/2 Ernostar lens—introduced the world to an era of "candid photography," since its high-speed lens permitted indoor photography without a flash. It was a sort of detective camera, made famous by journalist Erich Salomon. The three and a half-pound camera had a four-inch lens which focused from five feet to infinity. Today these cameras are highly prized, valued as high as $1,120 for the 4.5 x 6cm model of 1924.

Miniaturization seemed to be a preoccupation of camera makers almost from the start, but it became especially relevant in the years just before World War I, when roll films, especially 127 film, made truly smaller cameras possible. These were the cameras that went into action with the doughboys in World War I. Among them were vest-pocket cameras from Kodak, which are easy-to-find items for today's collectors. Kodak's vest pocket camera of 1912-1914 is available today for a mere $20, sometimes even less, and autographic models from 1915 to 1926 are also inexpensive. A Seneca Camera Co. vest pocket model for 127 film commands $30 or less.

The sucess of vest pocket cameras eventually lead to the marketing of various other designs, especially from Germany, mostly in the form of boxy-looking metal cameras with pull-out lenses. Early models were set up for plates; later models could accept roll film. Fine optics were the main sales points, especially high quality lenses by Zeiss or the highly desirable Compur lens. In the 1930s, these German cameras began to challenge Kodak's domination of the market.

Kodak's executives were not the kind to slumber, however. Sensing the challenge to their leadership, they shrewdly hired a leading industrial designer, Walter Dorwin Teague. His assignment: design more appealing cameras, especially some models in a new series aimed at women, who had become a new force in the camera market.

Teague's efforts resulted in a variety of new models in the Kodak line. The Kodak Vanity of 1928, for example, sold in an ensemble which included lipstick, compact, mirror and coin purse. Somehow, cameras like the Vanity sold fairly well even during the Depression, when photography was a welcome diversion from the economic gloom. Today the Kodak Vanity is worth about $30. The 1929 Petite was available in blue, green, gold, rose, lavender and grey (at a time when Ford Motor Co. was just beginning to consider the possibility of marketing cars in something other than black). In 1930 Ansco also introduced a ''Photo Vanity''—a rarity today which in 1977 brought a whopping $600. The camera was designed to look like a lady's purse.

In 1931 Kodak unveiled the Rainbow Hawkeye cameras, both box and folding type, again in colors. Due to large quantities produced, they seldom sell not for more than $20.

After World War I, Kodak's main competitor was a new giant named Ansco, formed by the merger of E. and H.T. Anthony and Scovill & Adams in 1902, and merged with Agfa in 1928. This firm produced many collectible cameras, ranging from the inexpensive Buster Brown cameras—widely sold by mail order and seldom worth more than $15 today—to the highly desirable 35mm Memo of 1927 and the Automatic Ansco, with an automatic film-advance mechanism, worth about $150 today. "No more double exposures," promised ads for the Automatic Ansco, which could fire off six shots in six seconds.

By the mid 1930s German cameras such as the Leica, the Ikonta line, and the Zeiss Contax proved the superiority of European optics and designs. The Zeiss Super Ikonta (Models B, VX, C and D) today sells for $100 to $150. The Zeiss Contax I of 1932 is now worth upwards of $200.

In the late 1930s Kodak introduced the ultimate in folding cameras—the first camera with coupled electric eye for automatic exposure setting. Using 620 film, it was called the Super Kodak Six-20 and took eight pictures to a roll. It cost a painful $250. Production came to an end with World War II, and today rare Super Six-20s sell for $800 to $900.

Another revolutionary folding camera was introduced in 1948—the Polaroid Model 95, precursor of the "picture-in-a-minute" cameras using the patented process of Dr. Land. (Let us at least give a tip of the hat, however, to an earlier inventor of in-camera development, Jules Bourdin, who invented a simple in-camera system in the 1860s.) There is little collector demand yet for Polaroids, but with the success of the SX70, Polaroid's role in camera history is assured, and collector interest will undoubtedly increase. The Model 95 today bring about $20-$30, and other less common Polaroid models bring upwards of $100. A recent ad for the Model 180 listed a price of $127.

# NOVELTY CAMERAS, DETECTIVES, SUBMINIATURES

Camera collecting would be a rather dry, technical sort of hobby were it not for a group of unusual cameras which collectors find highly interesting primarily because they are so odd, at least when compared to the staid mahogany and brass box camera or the somewhat mechanical-looking folding camera. These oddball cameras are primarily three types: novelty cameras which reflect the whims of inventors, detective cameras used for surreptitious photography, and tiny cameras that tell of the camera manufacturers' dream of ever-smaller equipment to produce images on ever-smaller film.

The desire for smaller cameras dates back to Niepce himself. His first camera, according to British camera authority Cyril Permutt, was a six-inch wooden box made in 1816. When the lens of that camera was accidentally broken, he fashioned a second camera using a little jewel box that measured about an inch and a half by an inch and a quarter, fitted with a microscope lens. "This," says Permutt, "was surely the world's first sub-miniature camera." Although Daguerre worked with fairly large wooden cameras, Fox Talbot's cameras were so tiny his wife dubbed them "mousetraps." Many of Talbot's early paper negatives measure no more than one inch by one inch.

As early as 1883, a patent was issued in the U.S. for an undersized camera—Schmid's Patent Detective Camera, a box camera loaded with a glass plate holder. "Anyone provided with this instrument can take photographs while walking along the street without attracting notice from the curious," boasted **Anthony's Photographic Bulletin** that year. Marketed by E. & H.T. Anthony & Co., the camera was, surprisingly, a success despite its high price of $55. With no protruding lens, no bellows, no ground glass, it was unlike most other cameras of its day. One simply carried it at waist level and peered down into a tiny window to aim and shoot. Today Schmid's Detective Camera is worth $2,000 or more on the collector market.

E. & H.T. Anthony & Co. saw the success of Schmid's Detective Camera and followed it up with the Anthony Satchel Detective Camera in 1887, a box camera fitted inside an alligator-skin hand satchel. It was a rather snazzy unit and it has strong appeal for today's collectors. According to George Gilbert, the satchel alone would bring more than $2,500 today. New models cost a mere $35 to $95.

Inside the satchel was an Anthony Climax camera, worth

about $1,200 today. Together with the case—and in good condition—a complete Anthony Patent Satchel Detective Camera would command about $6,000 or $7,000. The cameras are quite rare, however, largely because the Anthony Climax was discontinued by 1893 and the Satchel Detective Camera by 1896.

What was the big appeal of a camera-in-a-satchel? It wasn't a small piece of equipment, but it **was** hidden, and the idea of "surreptitious negatives" held immense appeal in the 1880s. The decade saw the introduction of a variety of disguised cameras, with the trend toward miniaturization. It wasn't long before cameras were being produced which would serve quite well for espionage purposes but which were marketed to a public which felt no qualms about using such voyeuristic equipment. Thus, some of these cameras were at once **detective** cameras, were **novelties**, and were **miniatures**—the three categories blending to produce truly fantastic collectible cameras.

During the years they were popular, detective cameras came in some very sneaky forms. They were disguised as handbags, shoeshine boxes, cravat pins, brown-paper packages tied with string, walking stick handles, binoculars, and giant pendants.

In 1890 Anthony marketed the PDQ. The initials stood for Photography Done Quickly. Marketed for only a year or two, the $20 plate box detective cameras was not a smashing market success. The result is that the PDQ is today a $500-and-up rarity for collectors.

Even rarer is Scovill's 1890 4x5 box detective camera, which sells for $725 when offered for sale, and Scovill's Knack Detective Camera of 1891, now worth $600 or more.

Scovill produced a variety of detective cameras, including the 1886 Scovill Detective (which took 4x5-inch plates and is now worth $850), the Waterbury Detective Camera of 1888 (now worth about $500), and the 1892 Triad Detective, (which could use sheet film, roll film or standard plates and now brings about $450).

Other firms' detective cameras included Blair's Detective and Combination Hawkeye box camera for 4x5-inch plates in the 1890s and the Boston Camera Co.'s Hawk-eye

"Detective" box camera of 1892. These are worth about $125 and $50 respectively.

The ingenious detective cameras soon spawned novelty cameras, such as the tiny Kombi, the mini-marvel of the 1890s. Made to take 25 exposurers 1-1/8 inch square on roll film, it weighed a mere four ounces. The Kombi could also be used as a transparency viewer (the combination of uses gave it its name). The Kombi sold for $3 and ads by its manufacturer, Alfred C. Kemper of Chicago, claimed that "50,000 sold in one year." Today the Kombi is not all that rare, but good examples of this camera still bring $100 or more.

One of the great novelty cameras was C. P. Stirn's 1886 Vest Camera, which hung around the neck on a string and could be worn under a vest with only the lens protruding through a buttonhole in the photographer's coat. The disc-shaped camera cost $10 new and took six photos, each one and three quarter inches in diameter, around the edge of a five-inch diameter glass plate. Over 15,000 were sold in the first three years, according to Stirn's ads. Today the camera is worth about $1,000.

The Expo Camera Co. of New York made another popular disc-shaped camera. The Expo Watch Camera, introduced in 1905, was produced for about 30 years. Disguised as a railroad pocket watch, it took pictures through the "winding stem," with the "winding knob" serving as a lens cap. Today it is worth about $125 to $150.

Less rare than Stirn's Vest Camera but similar in appearance is the British Ticka pocket-watch-shaped camera. Since it was manufactured under license from the Expo Camera Co., it is identical to the Expo. Today it is worth about $100. The Expo company also made a tiny roll-film police camera which is among the smallest known box cameras. Introduced around 1915, it took 12 exposures on special Instamatic-like casettes. Today it is worth $200 to $225.

Far more rare and valuable is the 1897 Photake, a tiny disc-shaped gadget from the Chicago Camera Co. Loaded with glass plates, it sold for $2.50, and advertising for it presented the Photake as simply a good-quality camera that

27

happened to be round. Today it commands a price of $700 to $800.

Sleuth-oriented photographers had a variety of other ingenious detective cameras to choose from. One was Dr. Krugener's Patent Book Camera of 1892, which had a lens in the "spine" of the book; another was the Photorevolver of 1882, which took 10 postage-stamp-size pictures. Another was the Pocket Presto, just over three inches long and two inches wide, today worth $700-$800.

Miniature novelties continued to be made long after the turn of the century, and there are so many that some collectors specialize in these off-beat cameras. Mention must be made of the Compass, a Swiss camera of the 1930s made for plate or roll film. Fine optics and multiple functions (including built-in exposure meter) are combined in a camera no larger than a package of cigarettes. Only about 5,000 of these ingenious devices were produced and sold by Compass Cameras Ltd. of London. It takes more than $700 to buy one today.

Another tiny miniature is the Minox "subminiature" designed by Walter Zapp in 1937 in Riga, Latvia. The original stainless steel body model, with f3.5 Minostigmat lens, sells today for about $350. Worth a bit more is a Minox camera "Made in USSR"—the same camera but made between Spring and Fall 1940 when the Russians held Latvia before the German occupation.

Other novelty cameras include the Mickey-Mouse-shaped Mick-A-Matic, a 126 cartridge camera with, yes, two large black ears and a Meniscus lens in the nose (today it's worth $15); an Echo 8 Japanese cigarette-lighter-shaped camera of the early 1950s (it looks like a Zippo but sells for $225 or more); the c. 1888 Photosphere, one of the first all-metal cameras, worth nearly $1,000; the Ansco Photo Vanity, a folding novelty camera for women introduced in 1926 and concealed inside a vanity case with lipstick, mirror, etc., and worth as much as $700; and the Kraus Photo Revolver of 1921 (not to be confused with other novelty cameras actually shaped like pistols), which was a sort of elongated box which held a magazine for 48 plates or roll film for 100 shots and is today worth $1,500: the German Steineck ABC

Wristwatch camera of 1949, which took eight tiny exposures around a one-inch disc of film, now worth $300; and the 1955 Stylophot from France, which was designed to be clipped into a pocket like a fountain pen, worth $75 to $100 to $150 or more.

# TWIN-LENS
# REFLEX CAMERAS

Known to collectors by the initials TLR, the twin-lens reflex camera can be a bit confusing, and many camera experts are at a loss to explain why anybody bothered to invent it in the first place. Bascially, the TLR is nothing more than a camera atop a camera, with a viewing system set on top of the picture-taking lens system.

Yet some of the most cherished collector cameras—such as the Rolleiflex, Contaflex, Pilot and Zeiss Ikoflex—fall into this category.

The advantage of the TLR was that one could view the subject, focus and compose the picture with the camera below already loaded and ready to shoot quickly. In the U.S., three cameras of this type were offered before 1900; Folmer & Schwing's Graphic Twin-Lens camers now worth upwards of $2,000, the Carlton by Rochester Optical Co., and G. Gennert's Twin Lens Montauk—the latter now so rare that no examples are known to survive. Only old advertisements for these cameras tell us what they were like. Find one and you'll make camera collecting history.

Many collectors seek the good TLRs that **can** be found, such as the 1937 Pilot Reflex ($65 to $85), the 1937 Contaflex from Carl Zeiss Inc., ($700 or so), the 1932 Fothflex ($40 to $60), the Zeca-flex of 1933 ($200), or the Rolleicord of 1932 ($60).

European manufacturers seemed to turn out the most desirable TLRs. Besided those listed above are the Franke and

Heidecke Co. of Germany, which produced the Rolleiflex in 1929 ($100 and up), and Voigtlander, whose 1933 Brilliant was an inexpensive Depression-era camera with little to recommend it to the serious photographer ($10 to $15).

This is one area of collecting in which the name Kodak does not loom large. The twin-lens design seems to have never intrigued Kodak's designers, who were busy dominating just about every other segment of the camera market.

Probably the biggest name in TLRs is Rollei, and in the 1920s and 1932s, the German Rolleiflex provided photographers with a high quality workhorse camera. Although the six pre-1939 Rollei models do not inspire much excitement among collectors, interest in them is growing. These cameras, after all, were used by some of photography's greatest names, including Alfred Eisenstadt and Henri Cartier-Bresson. Today many photographers happily buy old Rollei models not as collectibles but as working equipment for studio photography. That adds to the demand for old Rolleis, and collectors would do well to consider them as long-range investments since they are sure to rise in value over the years.

# SINGLE-LENS REFLEX CAMERAS

A single mirror did away with the necessity for the cumbersome twin-lens reflex camera and enabled manufacturers to produce the SLR models that rule the roost on today's camera store shelves.

With these cameras, the photographer could look into the camera viewer and see the subject right side up. When he did so, he was viewing through the same lens that recorded the image, exactly as he saw it. When he pressed the shutter, a spring flipped the mirror out of the way and at the same time released the shutter. Press photographers (as well as art-oriented photographers like Edward Weston) siezed upon this design as the most desirable tool for their trades. Although many fine examples have come from Europe's factories, it was American cameras—particularly the Auto Graflex of the early 1900s—which first popularized the single-lens reflex camera.

Using a design devised by artists in the 17th and 18th centuries, England's William Sutton patented the first SLR design in the 1860s. Then only known example of the first American-made SLR, the Monocular Duplex of c. 1885, is in the collection of Matthew R. Isenberg.

By 1898 there was a Reflex Camera Co. at work in Yonkers, N.Y. Its rare wood-finished New Patent Reflex Hand Camera is today worth $375 without a lens.

Probably the earliest SLRs in most collections are the Graflex cameras made in the first quarter of this century. Produced by Folmer & Schwing and later by Kodak, Graflex cameras came in a wide variety of models, including the Auto Graflex Junior (c. 1915), Compact Graflex, the RB Graflex, the National Graflex series, the Press Graflex of 1907-23, and the top Graflex collectible, the 1907-21 Naturalist's Graflex Camera, with a long body able to accommodate lenses up to 26 inches in focal length and now worth about $4,500 to $5,000. The Stereo Auto Graflex of 1907-22 enabled the photographer to compose his picture while viewing a **stereo** image on the ground glass viewing screen—the ultimate luxury for stereo photographers. Today it is worth $1,300 to $1,500.

A cheaper camera from the Rochester Optical Co., makers of the popular Premo folding and box cameras, was the Premograph, introduced in 1906 with a f/11 lens that had no provision for focusing. The Premograph was among the least successful of all Premo cameras, and its rarity puts it in the $150 class today. Even rarer is the Premo Reflecting Camera of the same year, worth upwards of $800 today.

Many SLRs of the 1920s and 1930s are European makes, such as the Pilot 6 from Guthe & Thorsch of Dresden, Germany, with a metal guillotine shutter (worth about $40 today); the tiny Paff from Germany's Ihagee Camera Co., also of Dresden ($55 today); and the Vest Pocket Exakta from Ihagee (worth about $100).

# 35MM CAMERAS

When a single-lens reflex camera was developed with the capability of loading standard-size 35mm movie film, it was a marriage made in heaven.

Today, prices reflect collectors' esteem for the first still cameras which used 35mm film. The French Homeos of 1914, made by Jules Richard of Paris, was the first stereo camera for 35mm film. One sold for $800 in 1975, and current value is probably close to $2,000. The 1920 Minnigraph is worth about $1,500. The 1914 Tourist Multiple from the short-lived American Camera Mfg. Co. Inc. is worth upwards of $3,000, and early Leicas can bring as much as $7,000!

The Ansco Memo, introduced around 1927, was the first mass-produced 35mm camera in America. In good condition, it sells today for $50 to $60. The Memo is also available in an official Boy Scout Memo Camera, painted olive-drab and with scouting insignia on it. Rarer than the standard model, the Boy Scout Memo sells for $100 or so today.

One of the most intriguing 35mm cameras was the French Sept, a combination motion picture and still camera which could convert to a projector as well. Made by Debrie of Paris during the 1920s, it was a forerunner of today's motor-driven 35mm cameras. Collectors now must pay about $125 to acquire a Sept.

It wasn't until the 1930s that 35mm cameras really came into their own. The cameras of Ernst Letiz GmbH of Wetzlar, Germany, are today the most highly prized of all 35mm cameras. In 1925 Letiz introduced the Leica A, which was made until 1930. Only 100 to 150 were made with the f3.5/50mm anastigmat lens and today they command prices of $5,000 and more from "Leicamaniacs," who specialize in collecting high quality Leicas. Faster lenses were soon to come.

Leicas were costly even when new. During the Depression they cost an average $100 to $300 apiece—the latter price being nearly as much as a good new car cost then.

Various models of the Leica command startlingly divergent prices today, with rare and unusual models easily the top prizes for Leica buffs. The rarities include the 1934 Leica Reporter (which newspaper reporters shunned almost en masse). Just the camera body commands up to $3,000 today—without any lens! Fewer than 1,000 were made.

The 1926 Leica B—a dial-set Compur model—brings $4,000 or more since only about 1,500 were made in two variations, both with Elmar f3.5/50mm lenses. The rim-set Compur (1929-30) brings almost as much. The Single-Shot Leica of 1936 sells for about $1,500, and a wartime Luftwaffe or Wehrmacht model of the Leica IIIc sells for more than $1,000. Also rare is the Leica IIIa, a postwar model manufactured in the French-occupied state of Saarland in very limited numbers. "Monte en Sarre" is engraved on the top of the body of this camera, which brings $3,000 or more when offered for sale, which is rarely.

Leica lovers, however, can find less expensive models with all the virtures of Leica workmanship. The Leica C of 1930, the first Leica with interchangeable lenses, can be bought for a mere $270, and the Leica D and E models are even less expensive. Leicas from the 1940s such as the Leica IIIc, with f3.5 or f2 lenses, are in the $100 to $120 range.

The success of the Leica 35mm cameras quickly brought competitors into the marketplace, mainly Zeiss and Ihagee. Zeiss introduced the Contax in 1932 (it's now worth about $180), and prices for the 1930s-era Contax cameras that followed are now inching toward the $150 mark. The Contax III offered shutter speeds up to 1/1250 of a second—an example of the innovations that were offered in hopes of stemming the Leica domination of the market. Leica continued to outsell Zeiss and Ihagee, however.

The Exakta, Ihagee's entry into the 35mm war, was dubbed the Kine-Exakta, since 35mm film was designed for movies. The best of the Exaktas was the Night Exakta, with a fast Biotar f/2 lens, today worth $200 or more.

While the expensive European 35mm cameras battled it out in the marketplace—selling mostly to professionals—Kodak was working up a new film that would revolutionize the 35mm market in America. It was called Kodachrome.

Suddenly photography was no longer a black-and-white affair; even amateurs could produce vivid color images of their loved ones, snapshots of colorful Mother Nature, and delightful special effects.

In the late 1930s, cheap plastic (Bakelite) cameras were marketed which could use the new Kodachrome film. Their impact on the market tells the whole story. According to George Gilbert's "Collecting Photographica," "In the first few weeks, the makers of the (Bakelite) Argus A sold as many cameras as the number of Leicas sold in the prior ten years."

The millions of Argus cameras produced and sold, of course, means they are commonplace collectibles today. It's hard to find a buyer for most Argus models, widely advertised in the $10 to $20 range, although the Argus K of 1939 had a coupled extinction meter which intrigues collectors and makes it worth about $130 today. Some ads refer to the "Brick" Argus—the Model C and C2 of 1938-1942. It sells for about $15. The brick-shaped model CC "Colorcamera" with non-coupled selenium cell meter instead of extinction type sells for $40.

Kodak's entries into the 35mm camera market are lightweights among collectors today, but they are frequently offered in ads and at flea markets. Among them are the Bantams, introduced in 1935 and produced for the next 21 years. The only Bantam that really lures collectors is the 1936-48 Bantam Special with Compur Rapid shutter or, later with Supermatic shutter. These sell for $100 or slightly more. Part of the lure of this camera, too, is that it was designed by Walter Dorwin Teague. The Kodak Retina, with which Kodak entered the 35mm field in 1935, lacked the speed and the Teague design and today sells in the $50 to $75 range. The Retinas were made for Kodak in Germany —a fact that does little to impress today's camera experts. experts.

Other inexpensive collectible 35mm cameras include the Zeiss Tenax, the Robot (especially the rarely seen Luftwaffe Robot made from 1940 to 1945), the German Bolta Photavit, the Balda Baldina and Baldinette, Universal Camera Corp.'s Mercury, Candid Camera Corp.'s Perfex

Speed Candid and other Perfex models, and Kodak's Ektra (production of which was halted by World War II).

Since World War II, Japanese cameras have dominated the 35mm camera market. While many of them will no doubt become valued collectibles in the future, today's collectors prefer to look for earlier cameras—the classics, the great innovations, the unusual, the historic, the colorful, the rare, the intriguing.

There are hundreds of cameras we've had to ignore in this brief survey of camera history, many of them eagerly sought as collectibles. Any collector who is serious about his hobby will want to research deeper into the background history of the cameras he collects, the companies that made them, and the features that make them collectible. Camera collecting is a hobby of fine points—and knowing how to distinguish between one model and other, or how to determine which firm made which camera, can make an enormous difference in the enjoyment of the hobby and the dent it puts in the collector's pocketbook. In short, a good working knowledge of camera history is the first step in collecting wisely.

# THE COLLECTING GAME

Look at a publication such as **Shutterbur Ads**, the Titusville, Fla., monthly publication which features a large selection of collectible cameras, and you step into a world of strange names. Like a menu in a ritzy restaurant, it sometimes seems to be speaking a foreign language—at least to the layman or the neophyte collector.

Offered in a single recent issue were the following delectibles: a B&H Fonton, a Goerz Tenax, a Wing Camera, a Certo Super Dolina, a Trumpfreflex German TLR, a No. 4 Bullseye Model C Box Camera, an A&G Taylor One-Half Plate View Camera, a Boots Special 5x7 View Camera, a Robot Luftwaffen-Eigentum, a Pony Premo No. 2, an early Scovill Tailboard Camera, a Palko and lots of others (surprisingly, no partridge in a peartree). Despite the sometimes bewildering names, these classified ads give a good idea of what items are being offered on the collector market.

A look at various collections provides a slightly different view of what's considered collectible. Besides the kinds of cameras offered in **Shutterbug Ads**, one finds that most collections feature all sorts of accessories such as camera advertising from the past, old promotional items, assorted stray parts such as lenses and filters, and frequently an assortment of darkroom equipment.

A look in an antique shop gives on yet another entirely different view of the camera collecting hobby. One gets the impression here that cameras aren't collected at all. The reason is that antique dealers seldom know much about cameras and therefore tend to avoid stocking them. They do, however, offer plenty of old photos, mostly in the form of postcards, stereo views, cartes de visite and the like, as well as an occasional camera, usually the type that's far from rare.

Flea markets, on the other hand, usually offer a nice selection of old cameras and accessories—the kind that are beginning to pour forth from the nation's attics as word spreads that there are actually people who want those old pieces of equipment.

So what is collected? The answer is everything—any camera or accessory you can name is a potential collectible, especially in view of the growing demand for old cameras and the shrinking supply of them. But some of those "collectible" cameras are so common that it may be nearly impossible to find a buyer willing to pay more than a few dollars. Even a colorful camera like the Kodak Rainbow Hawkeye vest pocket camera fails to bring a substantial price. It's just not rare enough.

Which brings us to our main topic: prices. Obviously, the camera market is a supply and demand situation, and any camera is ultimately worth whatever someone is willing to pay for it. If you want to know which cameras are the most "collectible"—because of rarity, technical features, history, etc.—you can simply look at which cameras command the highest prices. In general, you'll find that the big price-getters are the super-rarities. That means that, while there are some collectors willing to pay top dollar for them, they are also hardest to find or to buy. For many collectors, that means they're actually the opposite of "collectible," that they are unattainable or nearly so. In the long run, therefore, the term "collectible camera" is a bit fuzzy in meaning. Some collectors go after rarities, while others seek complete series, which include some of the most common models.

But one factor renders all such hair-splitting meaningless. It's the gleam in the collector's eye when he speaks of Anthony's Satchel Detective Camera, or the Luftwaffe Leica, or Stirn's Vest Pocket Camera, or the No. 1 Kodak camera. Landmark cameras such as these—even if extremely difficult to acquire for your own collection—keep alive the essence of the collecting urge, the collector's ability to dream. On any level, the collector has cameras he dreams of finding, and the young hobby of camera collecting offers a good chance that the dream may come true. Old cameras are probably the last great category of collectibles to be discovered by the public, and untold thousands of good collectible cameras still gather dust in attics, cellars, antique shop shelves, even in museum storage rooms, unknown, unidentified.

What cameras are collectible? Every camera that some collector somewhere dreams of finding. And, in the long run, that means almost every camera ever made.

# HOW TO COLLECT

Besides mastering the subject of cameras, the shrewd collector masters the subject of collecting. The best way to do that is to look at the top collectors and see how they go about building their collections.

They tend to collect mainly in three ways: by beating the bushes during their free time, by cultivating plenty of contacts among other hobbyists, and by plugging into the postal system.

Beating the bushes takes a bit of stamina. It means attending flea markets, strolling through antique shows, checking out camera stores which sell used equipment, pouring through classified ads in the local newspaper, perhaps even attending estate sales, police auctions, and so forth. For the most part, these efforts produce few tangible results. A collector might visit five flea markets before finding a single piece he wishes to acquire, and some antique shows may turn out to have no camera equipment at all. Yet some of the best finds come from first-hand hunting of this sort, and it's also the best road to bargains, such as the rare model offered by an antique dealer who doesn't know what he has on his hands and therefore underprices it (of course, he might also **over**price it). There are countless stories of remarkable finds at old flea markets and garage sales—and those tales keep collectors hunting despite the bad odds.

It is usually more fruitful to locate other camera buffs in your area—through dealers, want ads, swap meets, word of mouth—with whom you can deal or trade. Fellow hobbyists will share information as well as equipment, they'll offer duplicates or buy yours, and they'll keep an eye out for your wants while they pursue their own prizes. And the friendship born of mutual interests is one of collecting's greatest rewards.

Plugging into a postal system can be rewarding or it can be frustrating. Almost any camera you want is on the market at one time or another. The trick is finding it offered when you want it and at the right price. The best bet is camera-oriented publications—the many camera magazines, the tabloid **Shutterbug Ads**, and lists offered by various dealers.

Dealer lists often contain prices at odds with other dealers, so it pays to do some comparative shopping. Also, some dealers are more reliable than others and it might be wise to check with other collectors before dealing with them. Naturally, the more sources you check, the better your chance of zeroing in on an accurate price for the camera you are seeking. With more dealers now more knowledgeable than they were a decade ago, fewer bargains are available. In addition, their asking prices are not always the same as the selling prices—especially for more common models, where some give-and-take may result in a substantial savings in dollars.

In dealing with any of the above sources, the condition of the camera is important.

Mint condition cameras do exist—occasionally they are offered still in their boxes and with the original instruction sheets included. They may have been used once or twice or a few times, but have spent a number of years in protected storage. Their original finish is intact, with no marks to detract from their wood, leather, brass or metal parts.

Most cameras are in less impressive condition, which is understandable since cameras were frequently taken on travels and treated with less respect than should be accorded an optical instrument. Any camera with slight scuffs or scratches, worn metal, or other minor marring or aging would qualify for the good condition or very good condition categories, depending on the degree of wear. So long as there is no substantial damage, no missing parts, no rust or corrision or pitmarks or cracks other than what might be considered reasonable, then the camera can still be admitted to this category. Cameras in good or very good condition are worth anywhere from 15 to 25 percent less than if they were in excellent (just about mint) condition.

If a camera does not need parts, is unusually well worn, has disfiguring cracks, corrosion, marks, rust, or a shutter that is inoperable, consider it in fair condition and subtract about 50 to 75 percent. Just because it's beat up a bit? Yes. Most cameras were produced in sufficient quantities that condition can make that big a difference—presuming there are other examples on the market. When it comes to those rarities of which only a handful are known to exist, it's a somewhat different ballgame (usually the seller can just about name his price and, with a bit of patience, get it).

Buyers of cameras in need of repairs should consider the cost of those repairs before buying. For some cameras, it may not be worth it. Some cameras can be repaired with reproduction parts. Exact replicas of winding keys and brass string pull knobs for old string-set Kodaks are available.

# USING THE PRICE GUIDE

The list of cameras presented here is not exhaustive. We have listed all pre-1950 cameras for which we were able to get solid price information; although the list is fairly thorough, there **are** collectible pre-1950 cameras which are not listed. Hopefully, later editions will include some of those models omitted here.

Prices or price ranges are drawn from a variety of sources, mostly ads in trade publications such as **Shutterbug Ads** or photographic magazines but also from prices asked at trade fairs, publicized dealer transactions, collectors' evaluations, dealer auction and sales lists, and discussions with collectors and experts in specialized areas of the camera collecting hobby. Naturally, the figures have been evaluated for accuracy, especially where a number of prices showed a significant variance. For the most part, these are retail prices; dealers are likely to offer to pay lower figures for the cameras listed, since they must buy at the wholesale level. And due to the fluctuations in the popularity of various kinds of cameras, as well as regional preferences, certain cameras may be offered for prices somewhat higher or lower than the priced listed here. Since our sources in many cases provided a variety of values for single cameras (Zeiss specialists, for example, tend to value Zeiss equipment higher than other collectors) we have had to list a price range showing a divergence of prices, although we have narrowed the range as much as possible.

Cameras are listed by manufacturer, alphabetically. Where only one camera by a given manufacturer is listed, the manufacturer's name simply preceeds the camera listing. The date tells the approximate year or the decade in which the camera was first marketed, or the span of years during which it was produced.

● Adams & Co. (London, England)
Minex SLR, Leather covered, c. 1900 . . . . . . .          200.00
Minex folding tropical camera . . . . . . . . . . . . 2,500.00-3,000.00
Yale No. 2 detective magazine camera, c.
 1895 . . . . . . . . . . . . . . . . . . . . . . . . . . . . . .   200.00-250.00

●Adams & Westlake Co. (Chicago, Ill.)
Adlake 4x5″ plate camera, c. 1897.......... **75.00-80.00**
Adlake Repeater 4x5″ plate camera........ **60.00-75.00**
Adina 6x9cm camera, f6.3/105mm Roden-
stock Trinar........................ **15.00-20.00**
●Adox Kamerawerk (Wiesbaden, Germany)
Adox 35mm, 1930s.................... **20.00-25.00**
Adrette 35mm, f2.9/50mm Schneider
Radionar........................... **25.00-30.00**
Blitz bakelite box camera for 120 film,
f6.3/75mm ......................... **10.00-15.00**
Sport camera for 120 film, f4.5 Radionar.... **10.00-15.00**
●Agfa Kamerawerke (Munich, Germany,
merged with Ansco in 1928)
Agfa folding camera for 116 or 120 film..... **5.00-10.00**
Agfa plate camera, f4.5 anast., dial Com-
pur Shutter........................ **45.00-50.00**
Cadet metal box camera.................. **5.00**
Captain box camera..................... **5.00**
Clack box camera...................... **5.00-10.00**
Clipper PD-16 metal camera, for 116
film meniscus lens.................... **5.00**
Clipper Special, f6.3 anastigmat lens........ **10.00**
Isolar folding plate camera, 9x12cm,
f4.5/135mm ........................ **60.00**
Isolette camera, f4.5/85mm Apotar or
Agnar lens, Compur shutter............ **20.00**
Isolette Super for 120 film, f3.5/75mm
Solinar............................ **80.00**
Karat Model 12 folding camera for 35mm
film, c. 1938....................... **30.00**
Major folding bed camera for 120 film...... **10.00**
Memo viewfinder for 35mm film, f3.5/50mm
anast.............................. **45.00-60.00**
Memo "half-frame" model (18x36mm), 1940 **50.00**
Nitor rollfilm camera, f4.5/105mm......... **20.00-25.00**
Optima 35mm rangefinder, f2.8/45mm,
Compur ........................... **30.00-40.00**
Plenax PD-16 folding camera for 116 firm,
f6.3, c. 1940....................... **10.00**
Solinette II camera for 35mm film, f3.5/50
mm Apotar......................... **15.00-20.00**
Speedex folding rollfilm camera, f4.5, c. 1940 **20.00-30.00**

Standard folding camera for 616 film,
f6.3/135mm, 1932.................... 15.00
Standard folding sheet film camera, 9x12,
f4.5 anast........................... 45.00-50.00
Ventura folding camera for 120 film, f4.5
Apotar.............................. 10.00
View camera, 4x5", wooden body, Bausch
& Lomb portrait lens, Packard-type shutter 100.00-120.00
Viking folding camera for 116 or 120 film,
f6.3................................. 5.00-10.00
●Altissa Kamerawerk (Dresden, Germany)
Altiflex TLR, 6x6cm, f4.5/75mm Roden-
stock Trinar, 1930s.................. 30.00-40.00
Altissa box camera for rollfilm............ 15.00-20.00
●Al-Vista—see Multiscope & Film Co.
●Amerex 16mm subminiature (produced in
Occupied Japan)...................... 15.00-20.00
●American Camera Mfg. Co. Inc. (Northboro,
Mass., merged with Kodak in 1899)
Folding plate camera, 4x5", red bellows..... 125.00
No. 1 Tourist Buckeye folding rollfilm
camera, wooden lens plate, maroon bel
lows, c. 1895........................ 75.00-85.00
No. 2 Buckeye rollfilm box camera, 4x5",
c. 1899............................. 30.00-35.00
No. 3 Buckeye folding rollfilm camera,
c. 1895............................. 25.00

Right: No. 1 Folding Pocket Ansco, c.
1915, $15. Below: 4x5 Adlake camera,
by Adams & Westlake, c. 1897,
$50-$60.

●American Minute Photo Co. (Chicago, Ill.)
American Sleeve Machine street camera
for tintypes........................... 140.00-160.00
American Optical Co. (New York, N.Y.,
merged with Scovill in 1865)
Henry Clay folding plate camera, 5x7",
c. 1895............................. 275.00-325.00
Horizontal Format plate camera, 5x8"...... 200.00
View camera, 11x4"...................... 250.00
●American Safety Razor Corp. (New
York, N.Y.)
ASR Foto-Disc, 1950 version of Stirn's
Vest camera using disc of film for eight
22x24mm exposures.................... 400.00

Ansco No. 3 folding camera, $15.

Ansco No. 3A folding Ansco for 18A
or 18B film, $20.

●Ansco (Binghamton, N.Y., merged with Agfa
in 1928)
Ansco Automatic Reflex TLR for 120 film,
f3.5/83mm lens, 1947.................. 90.00-130.00
Anscoset 35mm rangefinder, f2.8/45mm
Rokkor lens.......................... 25.00-30.00
Automatic folding camera for rollfilm, f6.3
anast., c. 1925....................... 150.00
Buster Brown box cameras............... 5.00-15.00
Buster Brown folding camera No. 1......... 15.00

No. 3A folding pocket Ansco, c. 1915, $25.

Ansco Memo, 1926, by Ansco, Binghampton, N.Y., $50-$65.

| | |
|---|---:|
| Buster Brown folding camera No. 2A....... | **15.00** |
| Buster Brown folding camera No. 3......... | **10.00** |
| Buster Brown folding camera No. 3A (Actus shutter)....................... | **15.00-20.00** |
| Buster Brown Junior folding camera for 116 film............................. ...... | **15.00** |
| Cadet Model B2 box camera.............. | **5.00** |
| Clipper..................................... | **5.00** |
| Commander, f6.3/105mm Agnar, with case.. | **10.00-15.00** |
| Dollar box camera, c. 1910............... | **15.00-25.00** |
| Goodwin No. 1 Junior, folding camera, c. 1920s............................. | **20.00** |
| Goodwin No. 2 box camera.............. | **5.00** |
| Goodwin No. 3 box camera.............. | **5.00** |
| Lancer ................................... | **5.00** |
| Memo half-frame 35mm camera, f6.3/40mm Wollensak, alte 1920s (in the 1930s, it became the Agfa Memo)............... | **50.00-65.00** |
| Memo Boy Scout Model, wooden box camera painted olive green.................... | **90.00-110.00** |
| No. 1 Ansco Deluxe folding camera, rapid rectilinear lens....................... | **25.00-30.00** |
| No. 1 Ansco Special folding camera, f7.5 anast., c. 1924........................ | **15.00** |

No. 1A Ansco Junior folding camera...... **15.00**
No. 3 Ansco folding camera for 118 film.... **15.00**
No. 3A Ansco folding camera, Wollensak
  lens.................................... **20.00**
No. 4 Ansco folding camera, models C & D
  with Wollensak lens, c. 1905............ **25.00**
No. 5 Ansco folding pocket camera, Wollen-
  sak lens, c. 1905...................... **25.00**
No. 6 Ansco folding camera, f4 Wollensak
  lens, red bellows, c. 1907.............. **25.00-30.00**
No. 7 Ansco folding camera, red bellows,
  brass Wollensak lens................... **25.00**
No. 9 Ansco folding camera, Model B, red
  bellows................................ **25.00**
No. 10 Ansco folding camera, 1980......... **35.00**
View camera, 11x14".................... **200.00-225.00**

No. 1 Readyset Royal, c. 1915, by Agfa Ansco Corp., Binghampton, N.Y., $15.

No. 2 Vest Pocket Ansco, c. 1916, $25.

●E. & H.T. Anthony (Binghamton, N.Y.,
  merged with Scovill in 1902)
  Ascot box camera for rollfilm, c. 1905...... **30.00**
  Ascot box camera for 4x5" plates, c. 1903.... **70.00**
  Ascot Cycle No. 1 folding camera for 4x5"
    plates, c. 1900....................... **60.00-75.00**
  Ascot No. 25 folding camera for plates, 1900. **75.00**
  Ascot No. 30 folding camera for 5x7" plates. **80.00-90.00**
  Buckeye box camera for rollfilm, c. 1896.... **50.00-75.00**

Buckeye Special........................   **70.00-90.00**
Climax Detective Camera................   **1,200.00**
Climax Enlarging Camera, c. 1898.........   **100.00-150.00**
Klondike box camera for plates, c. 1898.....   **70.00-80.00**
Normandie camera for 5x7″ or 8x10″
  plates, 1891..........................   **200.00-250.00**
Novelette view camera for plates, c. 1885....   **100.00-150.00**
PDQ detective plate box camera for 4x5″
  plates or film (Letters PDQ stand for
  ''Photography Done Quickly,'' not to be
  confused with PDQ made by Mandel Bro-
  thers, Chicago Ferrotype Co.), c. 1890....   **700.00-750.00**
Satchel Detective Camera................**6,000.00-7,000.00**
Stereo camera for 5x8″ plates, with lens.....   **330.00-440.00**
Studio Camera for 8x10″ plates, 1890s......   **350.00-450.00**
View Camera, 4x5″, c. 1890..............   **60.00-75.00**
View Camera, 5x7″......................   **80.00**
View Camera, 5x8″, c. 1888..............   **100.00-125.00**
View Camera, 6½x8½″.................   **65.00-75.00**
View Camera, 8x10″.....................   **100.00-125.00**
View Camera, 11x14″...................   **150.00-250.00**
●Apparate & Kamerabau (Friedrichshafen,
  Germany)
  Akarette I & II, c. 1950..................   **20.00-25.00**

Left: Anthony Studio camera, c. 1899,
$350-$450. Above: Argus AF, 1937,
$12-$18.

Above left: Argus AZF, 1939, $15-$20.
Above right: Argus c-3, 1939, $20.
Opposite: Argus CC, 1941, $35.

●Argus Inc. (Ann Arbor, Mich., and, later, Chicago, Ill.)

| | |
|---|---:|
| Argoflex TLR (including Models E, Em, EF, 40, 75, Super 75), 1948-58 . . . . . . . . . . . . . . | **12.00** |
| Argus A cartridge camera for 35mm film, f4.5/50mm anast., gold colored, c. 1936-41 | **15.00-25.00** |
| Argus AF for 35mm film, 1937-38 . . . . . . . . . . | **15.00** |
| Argus AA for 35mm film, 1940-42 (called Argoflash) . . . . . . . . . . . . . . . . . . . . . . . . . . . . | **15.00-20.00** |
| Argus A2 for 35mm film, with extinction meter, 1b39-50 . . . . . . . . . . . . . . . . . . . . . . | **10.00** |
| Argus A2B for 35mm film, f4.5/50mm, 1939-50 . . . . . . . . . . . . . . . . . . . . . . . . . . . . | **10.00-30.00** |
| Argus A2F for 35mm film, with extinction meter, 1939-41 . . . . . . . . . . . . . . . . . . . . . . | **15.00-20.00** |
| Argus A3 for 35mm film, f4/60mm anast., 1940-42 . . . . . . . . . . . . . . . . . . . . . . . . . . | **20.00-35.00** |
| Argus B for 35mm film . . . . . . . . . . . . . . . . . . | **75.00** |
| Argus C3 ''Brick'' camera, 1939 . . . . . . . . . . | **12.00-35.00** |
| Argus K, with coupled extinction meter, f4.5/50mm anast., 1939-40 . . . . . . . . . . . . . | **150.00** |
| Markfinder 21, f3.5/50mm Cintar, 1947-52 . . | **18.00** |

●Arnold, Karl (Marienburg, Germany)

| | |
|---|---:|
| Karma box camera for 120 film, trapezoid-shaped, f3.5/75mm . . . . . . . . . . . . . . . . . . | **195.00-200.00** |

Karmaflex SLR for 127 film, c. 1937 . . . . . . .     **150.00**
● Autographiccameras—seeEastman-KodakCo.
● Autographic cameras—see Eastman-Kodak Co.
    Tom Thumb camera radio, c. 1948 . . . . . . . .     **85.00**
● Balda-Werk (Dresden, Germany)
    Balda, f4.5/100mm Radionar . . . . . . . . . . . . . .     **15.00-20.00**
    Baldarette folding camera for 127 film, f4.5/
      85mm Rodenstock Trinar . . . . . . . . . . . . . . .     **20.00**
    Baldax folding camera for 120 film, f3.5/
      73mm, Compur shutter, 1930s . . . . . . . . . .     **25.00-35.00**
    Baldaxette Model I rangefinder for 120 film,
      f2.8/80mm Zeiss Tessar . . . . . . . . . . . . . . . .     **40.00-50.00**
    Baldi camera for 127 film, f3.5/50mm
      Trioplan, 1930s . . . . . . . . . . . . . . . . . . . . . . .     **30.00-40.00**
    Baldina folding camera for 35mm film,
      f2/45mm Xenon lens, 1930s . . . . . . . . . . . .     **25.00**
    Baldinette camera for 35mm film, late 1930s.     **20.00**
    Jubilette folding camera for 35mm film,
      f2.9/50mm Baltar, 1938 . . . . . . . . . . . . . . . .     **25.00**
    Rigona folding camera for 127 film, f2.9
      Schneider Radionar lens, c. 1937 . . . . . . . . .     **20.00**
    Super Baldina, f2.8 Tessar, late 1930s . . . . . . .     **40.00**
    Super Baldina, f2.9/50mm Gorlitz, with case.     **45.00-50.00**
● Batam—see Eastman-Kodak Co.
● Bausch & Lomb
    Camera obscura, oak body . . . . . . . . . . . . . . .     **200.00-225.00**
● Bazin & Leroy (Paris, France)
    Le Stereocycle stereo camera for 6x13cm
      plates, guillotine shutter, c. 1898 . . . . . . . . .     **700.00-900.00**
● Beck, R. & J., Ltd. (London, England)
    Frena detective box camers 4x5 ", late 1890s . .     **150.00**
    Frena Deluxe (metal parts gold plated),
      c. 1897 . . . . . . . . . . . . . . . . . . . . . . . . . . . . .     **325.00-350.00**
● Beier, Woldemar (Freital, Germany)
    Beiera camera for 35mm film, f2.7/50mm
      lens, 1930s . . . . . . . . . . . . . . . . . . . . . . . . . . .     **40.00**
    Beierax folding camera for 6x9cm rollfilm,
      f4.5/105mm Victar lens, 1930s . . . . . . . . . .     **10.00**
    Beierette folding camera for 35mm film, f2.9
      Rodenstock Trinar . . . . . . . . . . . . . . . . . . . .     **20.00-30.00**
    Precisa folding camera for 120 film, f4.5/
      75mm . . . . . . . . . . . . . . . . . . . . . . . . . . . . . . .     **25.00**
● Beil & Freund (Berlin, Germany)
    Plate camera, 9x12cm, f8 anast., c. 1890 . . . . .     **90.00-100.00**

● Belcawerke (Dresden, Germany)
Belfoca folding camera for 120 film, f4.5,
1940s ................................. **25.00-35.00**
Beltica folding camera for 35mm film,
f2.8/50mm Zeiss Tessar, 1940s .......... **30.00-35.00**
● Bell Camera Co. (Grinnel, Iowa)
"Straight Working" Panorama camera, fixed
lens, c. 1908 ......................... **300.00-350.00**
● Bell & Howell (Chicago, Ill.)
Foton spring-motor-driven camera for 35mm
film, f2/50mm with case, c. 1948 ........ **500.00-600.00**
TDC Stereo Colorist stereo camera for 35mm
film, f3.5 Rodenstock Trinar ............ **50.00-75.00**
TDC Stereo Vivid, f3.5 Trinar ............ **80.00-90.00**
● Bellieni, H. et fils (Nancy, France)
Jumelle camera for 9x12cm plates, f8/136mm
Zeiss Protar ......................... **200.00-225.00**
Stereo Jumelle camera for 9x18cm plates,
f6.9/110 lenses, c. 1896 ................ **200.00-250.00**
● Benetfink (London, England)
Lightning Detective Camera for plates,
c. 1895 .............................. **175.00-190.00**
● Benson Dry Plate & Camera Co.
Street camera set-up, including tank and
tripod ............................... **120.00**
● Bentzin, Curt (Gorlitz, Germany)
Planovista twin-lens non-reflex camera for
127 film, c. 1930 (Marketed under name of
Planovista Seein-Camera Co. Ltd. of
London) ............................. **500.00-550.00**
Primar folding camera for 120 film, f4.5
Zeiss Tessar ......................... **15.00**
Primar folding reflex plate camera, f3.5/
210mm Tessar ........................ **160.00**
Primarflex SLR, f3.5/105 Tessar, c. 1930s ... **70.00**
Stereo Reflex ............................ **400.00**
● Berning, Otto & Co. (Dusseldorf, Germany)
Robot I spring-motor-driven camera for
35mm film, f2.8/32mm Zeiss Tessar ...... **85.00-90.00**
Robot II, f1.9/40mm lens, c. 1938 .......... **80.00-90.00**
Robot Junior, f3.5/38mm Schneider Radio-
nar, 1940s ........................... **60.00-65.00**
Robot Luftwaffe Model, f2/40mm or 75mm. **225.00-250.00**
Robot Star, f1.9 Xenon .................. **80.00-100.00**

Robot Star II........................ 200.00
Robot Royal 36....................... 200.00
●Bessa—see Voigtlander
●Bettax folding 6x9cm rollfilm camera, f4.5/
  100mm Radionar..................... 20.00
●Bischoff, V. (Munich, Germany)
  Detective camera, 9x12cm plates, c. 1890.... 500.00-550.00
●Blair Camera Co. (Boston, Mass., merged
  with Eastman Kodak in 1907)
  Baby Hawkeye miniature box camera, c. 1897 150.00-165.00
  Combination Hawkeye for 103 film or 4x5"
    plates, Bausch & Lomb Lens........... 425.00-450.00
  Detective Hawkeye box camera for 4x5"
    plates, c. 1890s..................... 130.00-140.00
  Detective Hawkeye for 4x5" plates,
    all wooden body..................... 190.00-200.00
  Folding Hawkeye 5x7", c. 1890s........... 200.00-225.00
  Hawkeye Junior box camera for rollfilm or
    4x5" plates 1895-1900................. 80.00-90.00
  Hawkeye folding camera for 4x5" plates,
    1895-98 ............................ 160.00-170.00
  Kamaret box camera for 100 exposures on
    4x5" plates or rollfilm, 1891........... 400.00
  Lucidograph folding plate camera, all wood,
    c. 1885-1886........................ 650.00-750.00
  No. 2 Weno Hawkeye rollfilm box camera... 55.00
  No. 3 Combination Hawkeye, c. 1904....... 250.00-275.00
  No. 3 Folding Hawkeye, model 3 for roll-
    film, Bausch & Lomb lens, maroon bel-
    lows, c. 1902........................ 35.00
  No. 3 Weno Hawkeye box camera.......... 65.00-70.00
  No. 4 Folding Hawkeye, c. 1903........... 50.00-70.00
  No. 4 Weno Hawkeye box camera, 4x5"..... 35.00-50.00
  No. 6 Weno Hawkeye box camera, c. 1891... 60.00-75.00
  No. 7 Weno Hawkeye box camera for
    rollfilm, c. 1897..................... 30.00-35.00
  Premier box camera for 4x5" plates,
    c. 1890............................. 125.00-130.00
  Stereo Hawkeye camera for rollfilm, maroon
    bellows............................. 175.00-200.00
  Tourist Hawkeye folding camera for roll-
    film................................ 100.00-150.00
  View camera, 5x7" field type with lens...... 150.00
  View camera, 11x14" with lens........... 200.00

Bolsey Model B2, 1949 by Bolsey Corp., USA. $20.

Weno stereo camera for rollfilm, maroon
    bellows................................. **175.00-200.00**
●Bolsey Corp. of America (New York, N.Y.)
    Bolsey Model B Compact camera for 35mm
        film, f3.2/44mm anast., c. 1947.......... **20.00-25.00**
    Bolsey Model B2 (manufactured for U.S. Air
        Force), c. 1949....................... **20.00-25.00**
    Bolsey B22 Set-O-Matic, f3.2 Wollensak
        anast................................. **15.00-20.00**
●Bolta (Nurmberg, Germany)
    Photavit camera for 35mm film............ **90.00-100.00**
●Boots special 5x7″ view camera, f8 Bausch
    lens, walnut box, black bellows........... **160.00**
●Borsum Camera Co. (Newark, N.J.)
    Reflex SLR camera, 5x7″ f7.7 Goerz
        Dagor lens, c. 1898-1900............... **250.00-275.00**
●Boston Camera Co. (Boston, Mass., merged
    with Kodak 1907)
    Bullseye box camera for rollfilm, wood cov-
        ered with leather, c. 1892-1895........... **40.00-50.00**
    Hawk-Eye "detective" box camera for 4x5″
        plates, all wood body, c. 1888-92......... **150.00-160.00**
    No. 4 Bullseye, Model C, box camera....... **60.00-80.00**
●Braun, Carl (Nurmberg, Germany)
    Paxette 1 camera for 35mm film............ **15.00-20.00**
●Brooklyn Camera Co. (Brooklyn, N.Y.)
    Brooklyn view camera for plates, collapsible
        bellows, c. 1885....................... **250.00-300.00**
●Brownell, Frank (Rochester, N.Y.)
    Stereo dry-plate camera, sold under his name
        (he later pioneered cameras for Eastman
        Dry Plate & Film Co.), c. 1885........... **500.00-600.00**
●Brownie—see Eastman-Kodak Co.

●Buckeye—see Eastman-Kodak Co., American Camera Mfg. Co., or Anthony
●Bullard Camera Co. (Springfield, Mass.)
Folding camera for 4x5″ plates, Bausch & Lomb lens, red bellows, c. 1900 . . . . . . .     **60.00-70.00**
Magazine camera for 4x5″ plates, with bellows, c. 1889 . . . . . . . . . . . . . . . . . . . . . .     **175.00-200.00**
●Bulls-Eye—see Boston Camera Co., Eastman Kodak Co.
●Burke & James (Chicago, Ill.)
Ideal view camera, 6½x8½ . . . . . . . . . . . . . . .     **75.00**
Ingento 3A Jr. . . . . . . . . . . . . . . . . . . . . . . . . . .     **20.00-30.00**
Rexo box camera for rollfilm . . . . . . . . . . . . .     **5.00-10.00**
Rexo 1A Jr. for 116 film, anast. lens . . . . . . . ˙.     **10.00**
Rexo 3 camera for rollfilm . . . . . . . . . . . . . . . .     **15.00**
Roxoette box camera, c. 1910 . . . . . . . . . . . . .     **10.00**
Vest Pocket Rexo, Wollensak anast. lens . . . .     **10.00**
View Camera, 5x7″, fd4.5/7″ Wollensak . . . .     **125.00**
Watson-Holmes Fingerprint Camera . . . . . . . .     **150.00-175.00**
●Busch Camera Co. (also Emil Busch Optical Co., London, England)
Pressman 4x5″, f4.7 Ektar lens . . . . . . . . . . . .     **80.00-90.00**
●Buster Brown—see Ansco
●Butcher, W. & Sons (London, England)
Cameo plate camera, 3½x5½″, f6.3, c. 1912.     **40.00**
Carbine No. 2 box camera for rollfilm, 1930s.     **8.00-10.00**
Carbine Reflex SLR for 120 film, 1920s . . . . .     **125.00-150.00**
Klimax 4x5″ folding plate camera, f7.7, 1912.     **45.00**
Klimax 5x7″, f7.7 . . . . . . . . . . . . . . . . . . . . . . .     **80.00-90.00**
Midg box cameras, for film or plates, models 0, 00, 1, 1A, 2, 3, 4, 4A, 4B, c. 1905-1915. .     **40.00**
Watch Pocket Carbine folding camera for rollfilm, f7.7/3″ lens . . . . . . . . . . . . . . . . . .     **40.00-50.00**
●Cadet—see Agfa, Ansco
●Cadot, A. (Paris, France)
Scenographe Panoramique plate camera, 9x18cm, jumelle style, moveable lens . . . . . .     **250.00-300.00**
●Cameo—see Butcher, Houghton-Butcher
●Cameradio—see Universal Radio Mfg. Co.
●Candid Camera Corp. of America
Perfex Fifty-Five, f3.5 with extinction meter, 1940-47 . . . . . . . . . . . . . . . . . . . . . . . . . . . . .     **28.00-35.00**
Perfex Forty-Four, 35mm with couple rangefinder, f3.5/50mm anast., 1939-40 . . . . . . . .     **40.00**

**Perfex One-O-One, f4.5/50mm Wollensak**
  anast., 1948...........................  **35.00**
Perfex One-O-Two, f3.5/50mm, 1948.......  **35.00**
Perfex Speed Candid rangefinder for 35mm
  film, f3.5/50mm anast., 1938............  **75.00**
Perfex Thirty-Three, f3.5/50mm anast, 1940.  **35.00-40.00**
●Canon Camera Co. (Tokyo, Japan)
Demi half-frame camera for 35mm film, f2.8/
  28mm lens............................  **50.00-60.00**
L-I rangefinder, f1.9.....................  **125.00**
●Carbine—see Butcher
●Carmen (France)
Pygmee camera for 828 rollfilm, meniscus
  lens, 1930s...........................  **140.00-150.00**
●Carpentier, Jules (Paris, France)
Photo Jumelle binocular-style box camera
  for 12 6x9cm or 4.5x6cm plates, not a
  stereo camera, 1890s..................  **250.00-300.00**
●Century Camera Co. (merged with Kodak in
1903)
Field camera, 4x5"........................  **45.00-50.00**
Field camera, 5x7"........................  **65.00**
Field camera, 8x10".......................  **100.00**
Field camera, 11x14".....................  **125.00-135.00**
Stereo folding camera for 5x7" plates.......  **350.00**
●Certo Kamerawerk (Dresden, Germany)
Certonet folding camera for 120 film, f4.5/
  120mm Schneider Radionar, c. 1926......  **25.00**
Certosport folding plate camera, f4.5 Schnei-
  der, c. 1930...........................  **40.00-50.00**
Certotrop folding plate camera, 6x9 or 9x12..  **35.00**
Dollina II...............................  **35.00**
Dollina folding camera for 35mm film,
  1930s .................................  **40.00-45.00**
Dolly compact folding camera for 127 film,
  f3.5....................................  **30.00-40.00**
Doppel box camera for 120 film, 1935.......  **40.00-45.00**
Super Dollina rangefinder for 35mm film,
  f2.8/50mm  Tessar....................  **45.00-50.00**
●Chase Magazine Camera Co. (Newburyport,
Mass.)
Chase magazine camera for 4x5" plates,
  c.  1899...............................  **90.00-100.00**

●Chicago Camera Co. (Chicago, Ill.)
Photake cylindrical camera for 2x2" glass
plates, f14/120mm achromat lens, c. 1896. **3,000.00-3,500.00**
●Chicago Ferrotype Co. (Chicago, Ill.)
Mandel No. 2 postcard machine street
camera, 1913-30..................... **150.00-200.00**
Mandelette street camera, 2½x3½, with tank **90.00-110.00**
PDQ street camera, direct positive type...... **125.00-135.00**
Wonder Automatic Cannon Photo Button
Machine, all-metal street camera for 1" dia.
photos., c. 1910..................... **600.00-700.00**
●Ciro Cameras Inc. (Delaware, Ohio)
Ciro 35 rangefinder for 35mm film, f2.8 or
f4.5, 1949........................... **20.00**
Ciroflex TLR, 6x6cm, models A thru F,
1940s .............................. **25.00-30.00**
●Clarus Camera Mfg. Co. (Minneapolis,
Minn.)
MS-35 rangefinder for 35mm film, f2.8/
50mm Wollensak, 1946................ **35.00-45.00**
●Close & Cone (Chicago, Boston & New York,
N.Y.)
Quad box plate camera for 3½" square plate,
1896 ............................... **60.00-75.00**
●Cocarette—see Zeiss, Contessa-Nettel
●Columbia Optical & Camera Co. (London,
England)
Pecto No. 1A camera for 4x5" plates, red
bellows............................. **65.00-75.00**
Pecto No. 5 folding bed plate camera, for
9x12cm plates, Bausch & Lomb lens, c.
1897 ............................... **65.00-75.00**
●Compagnie Francaise de Photographie (Paris
France)
Photosphere plate camera with hemisphere-
shaped shutter, one of the first all-metal
cameras, could also take film, c. 1888..... **1,000.00-1,500.00**
●Compass Cameras Ltd. (London, England)
Compass Camera, made by LeCoultre & Cie,
Switzerland, for Compass Cameras Ltd.,
London. 35mm compact rangefinder,
aluminum body, f3.5/50mm lens, can also
use glass plates...................... **700.00-750.00**

●Conley Camera Co. (Rochester, Minn.)

Conley Jr. folding camera for rollfilm....... **15.00**

Conley magazine camera, leather covered
wooden box for 4x5″ plates, 1903........ **50.00-60.00**

Folding plate camera, postcard size, red
bellows, c. 1900-1910.................. **35.00-40.00**

Folding plate camera, 4x5″, red bellows,
6″ lens, 1900......................... **50.00**

Folding plate camera, 4x5″, red bellows,
10″ lens.............................. **60.00**

Folding plate camera, 5x7″............... **50.00-55.00**

Folding camera for 122 film, postcard size,
f6.3 Vitar anast...................... **20.00**

Kewpie No. 2 box camera for 120 film....... **5.00-10.00**

Kewpie No. 2A box camera............... **10.00-15.00**

Kewpie No. 3........................... **10.00-15.00**

Kewpie No. 3A postcard size............. **20.00**

Stereo box camera for 4¼x6½ ″ plates...... **350.00-400.00**

View camera, 6½x8½ ″ size............. **100.00**

View camera, 8x10″, with lens............ **75.00-100.00**

●Contessa-Nettal (Stuttgart, Germany, merged
with Zeiss in 1926)

Adoro folding camera for 9x12cm plates,
f4.5 Tessar........................... **30.00**

Citoskop stereo camera, f4.5/65mm Tessars,
stereo Compus, c. 1924................ **185.00-200.00**

Clarissa Tropical plate camera, brass struts,
red bellows, f3/75mm Meyer Gorlitz Trio-
plan lens............................. **550.00-600.00**

Cocarette folding bed rollfilm camera for 120
or 116 film, 1930s.................... **40.00-45.00**

Contessa-Nettel folding camera for 9x12cm
plates .............................. **40.00**

Deckrullo-Nettel folding plate camera, f4.5/
150mm Zeiss Tessar, ground glass back... **135.00-145.00**

Deckrullo Tropical folding camera for
98x12cm plates, f4.5/120mm Tessar, 1927. **400.00-500.00**

Deckrullo Nettel Stereo, f4.5/90mm Tessar.. **240.00-250.00**

Deckrullo Stereo tropical model for 9x12cm
plates, f2.7/65mm Tessars, brown bellows. **650.00-750.00**

Donata folding plate camera, f6.3 Tessar,
1920s ............................... **25.00-35.00**

Duchessa folding plate camera, f6.3/75mm
Citonar anast., 1920s.................. **75.00-85.00**

Univex Mercury II, 1943, by Universal Camera Corp., $10.

| | |
|---|---|
| Ergo plate camera, looks like half a binocular, f4.5/55mm Tessar............... | **700.00-725.00** |
| Miroflex SLR for 9x12cm plates, f4.5/150mm Tessar, c. 1924 (Zeiss-Ikon Miroflex dates from later and is more common)......... | **190.00-225.00** |
| Picolette vest pocket folding camera for 127 film, f4.5/75mm Tessar, 1920s........... | **50.00-60.00** |
| Sonnar folding camera for 9x12cm plates, f4.5/135mm Contessa-Nettel Sonnar..... | **35.00-40.00** |
| Sonnet No. 21 folding camera for 6.5x9cm plates, teakwood body, 1920s........... | **300.00-500.00** |
| Sonnet No. 21 folding plate camera, 4.5x6cm plates, 1920s...................... | **500.00-600.00** |
| Stereax stereo camera.................... | **250.00-275.00** |
| Steroco, f6.3 Tessar lens................. | **100.00-120.00** |
| Taxo folding camera for 9x12cm plates, f8/135mm........................... | **25.00** |
| Tessco folding plate camera, f4.5/135mm Contessa-Nettel Sonnar lens............ | **35.00-45.00** |
| ●Cornu Co. (Paris, France) | |
| Ontobloc compact metal-body camera for 35mm film, f3.5/50mm lens, c. 1935...... | **40.00-50.00** |
| Ontoflex TLR, f3.5 berthiot lens, compur shutter............................... | **225.00-250.00** |
| Reyna II camera for 35mm film, telescoping f3.5/50mm lens....................... | **30.00-35.00** |
| ●Coronet Camera Co. (Birmingham, England) | |
| Vogue folding camera for "Vogue 35" film, brown bakelite body.................. | **30.00-35.00** |

●Cyclone—see Western Camera Co. and
   Rochester Optical Co. Daiichi Kogaku
   (Japan)
   Zenobia folding camera for 120 film, 1949. . .          **20.00**
●Dallmeyer, J.H. (London, England)
   Dallmeyer "Speed" camera, f2.9 Pentec lens,
   1920s . . . . . . . . . . . . . . . . . . . . . . . . . . . . . . . .   **225.00-250.00**
●Dan 35 compact camera for 828 film, f4.5
   Dan anast., c. 1950. . . . . . . . . . . . . . . . . . . .          **20.00**
●Dancer, J. B. (Rochester, England)
   Stereo plate camera for twelve 30½x7″
   plates, c. 1956. Holds record for highest
   price paid for an antique camera . . . . . . . .       **37,500.00**
●Daydark Specialty Co. (St. Louis, Mo.)
   Daydark Tintype camera, amateur model . . . .  **100.00-130.00**
   Postcard street camera for tintypes or post-
   cards, with tank, sleeve, etc. . . . . . . . . . . . . .  **160.00-185.00**
●Debrie, Andre (Paris, France)
   Sept spring-motor-driven camera for 35mm
   stillshots or movies, f3.5/50mm Roussel
   Stylor lens, 1920s . . . . . . . . . . . . . . . . . . . . .  **150.00-200.00**
●Deckrullo—see Contessa-Nettel
●Delmar—see Seroco
●Derogy (Paris, France)
   Derogy wooden camera for 9x12cm plates,
   Derogy Aplanat No. 2 brass barrel lens, c.
   1880 . . . . . . . . . . . . . . . . . . . . . . . . . . . . . . .   **175.00-200.00**
●Dick Tracy novelty camera for 127 film,
   plastic body . . . . . . . . . . . . . . . . . . . . . . . . .    **15.00-20.00**
●Doris folding camera for 120 film, f3.5/
   75mm, 1940s . . . . . . . . . . . . . . . . . . . . . . . .     **5.00-10.00**
●Dossert Detective Camera Co. (New York,
   N.Y.)
   Dossert Detective box camera for 4x5″
   plates with reflex viewing, leather cover
   designed to resemble a satchel, c. 1880 . . . .   **600.00-700.00**
●Dubroni, Maison (Paris, France)
   Le Photographe de Poche box camera,
   wooden body with in-camera processing
   system, several models, c. 1960s . . . . . . . . . . **2,000.00-2,500.00**
●Ducati (Milan, Italy)
   Ducati half-frame rangefinder for 35mm film,
   f3.5/35mm Ducato Etar lens, late 1930s . . .    **200.00-225.00**

- Duchess half-plate field camera, British
  made, mahogany body with maroon bellows
  and brass barrel lens, c. 1887 . . . . . . . . . . . . .     **300.00-400.00**
- Durst S.A.
  Duca 35mm camera, f11/50mm Ducan, 1946.     **50.00-60.00**
- Eastman-Kodak Co. (Rochester, N.Y.)
  (Including cameras by Eastman Dry Plate &
  Film Co.)

## THE EARLY KODAK CAMERAS

Eastman Detective Camera, 4x5" box plate
loaded, c. 1887 (of the few made, none is
known to survive). . . . . . . . . . . . . . . . . . . . . . .

The Kodak Camera—the original Frank
Brownell-designed model produced in 1888
thru 1889, factory-loaded with 100 expo-
surs 2½" in diameter, string-set shutter
with f9/57mm rapid rectilinear lens, the
first camera to use rollfilm. . . . . . . . . . . . . . **3,000.00-4,000.00**

The Kodak No. 1 box camera with Sector-
type shutter, otherwise similar to original
model and with same number of exposures,
1889-1895 . . . . . . . . . . . . . . . . . . . . . . . . . . .     **900.00-1,500.00**

The Kodak No. 2, factory-loaded for 60
3½" diameter exposures, 1889-1897. . . . . .     **400.00-500.00**

The Kodak No. 3, factory loaded for 60 or
100 exposures, string-set box camera,
Bausch & Lomb lens, exposures 3¼x4¼".     **350.00-375.00**

The Kodak No. 4, box camera, string-set,
factory-loaded for 48 4x5" exposures, 1890-
1897 . . . . . . . . . . . . . . . . . . . . . . . . . . . . . . .     **300.00-375.00**

Brownie Developing Box, Eastman Kodak Co. c. early 1900s.

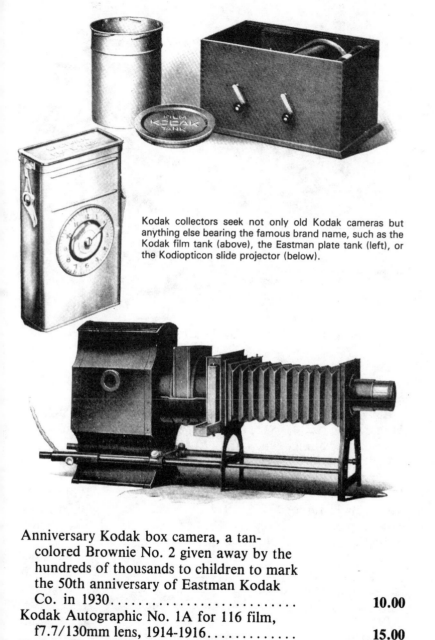

Kodak collectors seek not only old Kodak cameras but anything else bearing the famous brand name, such as the Kodak film tank (above), the Eastman plate tank (left), or the Kodiopticon slide projector (below).

Anniversary Kodak box camera, a tan-colored Brownie No. 2 given away by the hundreds of thousands to children to mark the 50th anniversary of Eastman Kodak Co. in 1930............................. **10.00**

Kodak Autographic No. 1A for 116 film, f7.7/130mm lens, 1914-1916............. **15.00**

Kodak Autographic No. 2, 2¼x3¼......... **8.00-10.00**

Kodak Autographic No. 2C for 130 film, 1916-1924 ........................... **15.00-20.00**

Kodak No. 3A Autographic Model c. 1920, f7.7/170mm, Kodak anast. lens, $15.

No. 1A Autographic Kodak Jr. $15.

| | |
|---|---:|
| Autographic No. 3 for 118 film, f7.7/130mm lens, 1914-26 | **15.00-20.00** |
| Autographic No. 3A postcard-size for 122 film, f7.7/170mm Kodak lens, 1914-24 | **15.00-25.00** |
| Autographic No. 4, 4x5″, red bellows | **30.00-40.00** |
| Autographic Junior No. 1 for 120 film, f7.7/100mm lens, 1914-24 | **10.00-15.00** |
| Autographic Junior No. 2C for 130 film, 1925-27 | **10.00-15.00** |
| Autographic Junior No. 3, 1914-27 | **10.00-15.00** |
| Autographic Special No. 1A, 1914-28 | **25.00-40.00** |
| Autographic Special No. 1, Bausch & Lomb lens | **30.00-40.00** |
| Autographic Special No. 2C, 1923-28 | **40.00-50.00** |
| Autographic Special No. 2, 1914-26 | **30.00** |
| Autographic Special No. 3A, for 122 film, 1914-27 | **50.00** |
| Baby Brownie box camera for 127 film, 1934-41 | **5.00-10.00** |
| Bantam camera for 828 film, f4.5, 1935-41 | **25.00** |
| Bantam camera for 828 film, f5.6/50mm anast., 1938 | **20.00-25.00** |

| | |
|---|---|
| Bantam camera for 828 film, f6.3 anast., 1935 | **10.00-15.00** |
| Bantam camera for 828 film, f/840mm Kodalinear lens, 1938 | **8.00-10.00** |
| Bantam Flash, f4.5/48mm Kodak anast., 1947-53 | **30.00** |
| Bantam Special camera, Supermatic shutter, 1941-48 | **135.00** |
| Beau Brownie box camera for 120 film, two-tone color, 1930-32 | **15.00** |
| Boy Scout camera for 127 film, an olive-green vest pocket camera, 1930-34 | **28.00** |
| Brownie No. 0 box camera for 127 film, 1914-17 | **10.00-15.00** |
| Brownie No. 1 box camera for 117 film, produced for only a few months, faulty back design, 1900 | **250.00-275.00** |
| Brownie No. 1 box camera, improved version for 117 film, 1900-1915 | **25.00-30.00** |
| Brownie No. 2 box camera for 120 film, meniscus lens, 1901-24 | **5.00-10.00** |
| Brownie No. 2A box camera for 116 film, 1907-24 (color models 1929-33) | **5.00-10.00** |
| Brownie No. 2C box camera for 130 film, 1917-34 | **5.00-10.00** |
| Brownie No. 3 box camera for 124 film, 1908-34 | **5.00-10.00** |
| Brownie folding camera No. 2 for 120 film, maroon bellows, c. 1904 | **15.00** |
| Brownie folding camera No. 2A for 116 film. | **20.00** |
| Brownie folding camera No. 3 for 124 film c. 1903 | **15.00-20.00** |
| Brownie folding camera No. 3A, postcard size, maroon bellows, 1909-15 | **20.00** |
| Brownie folding Autographic No. 1A | **10.00** |
| Brownie folding Autographic No. 2 for 120 film, c. 1916 | **10.00** |
| Brownie folding Autographic No. 2A for 116 film, c. 1921 | **5.00-10.00** |
| Brownie folding Autographic No. 3 | **10.00-15.00** |
| Brownie folding Autographic No. 3A, c. 1916-26 | **10.00-15.00** |
| Brownie folding pocket camera No. 2, c. 1907 | **15.00** |

No. 1A Pocket Kodak Autographic, Series II, $10.

No. 3 Kodak Autographic, Series III, $15, 1920s.

Kodak No. 1 Autographic Jr. $10-$15, 1914-1916.

Autographic Kodak Special Nola, $30, 1914-1927.

No.1A Autographic Kodak $15, 1914-1916.

3A Autographic Kodak, $15, 1914-1924.

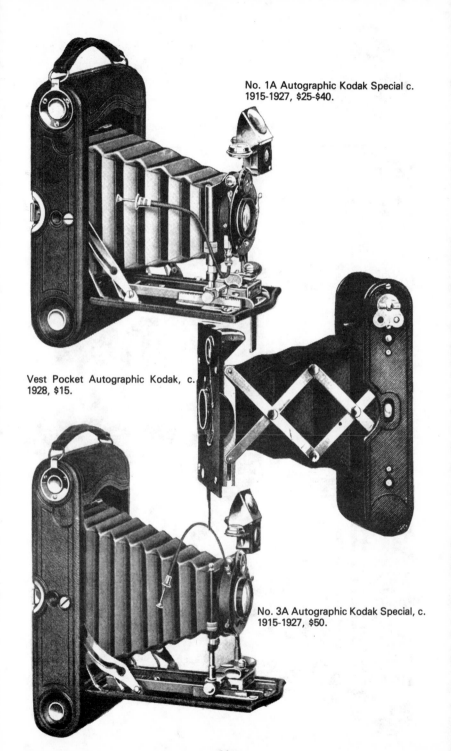

No. 1A Autographic Kodak Special c. 1915-1927, $25-$40.

Vest Pocket Autographic Kodak, c. 1928, $15.

No. 3A Autographic Kodak Special, c. 1915-1927, $50.

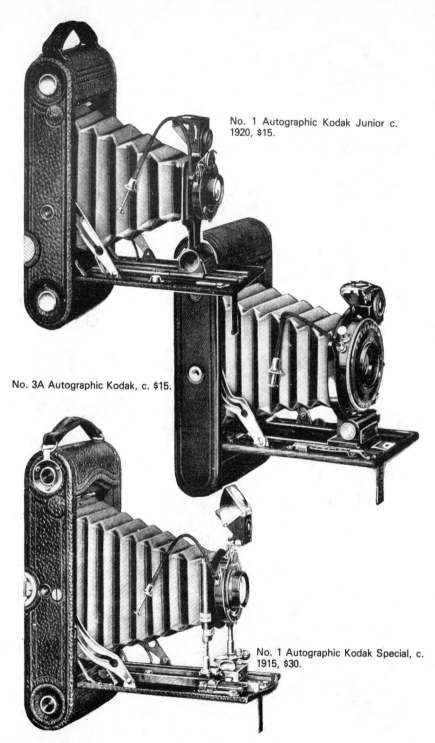

No. 1 Autographic Kodak Junior c. 1920, $15.

No. 3A Autographic Kodak, c. $15.

No. 1 Autographic Kodak Special, c. 1915, $30.

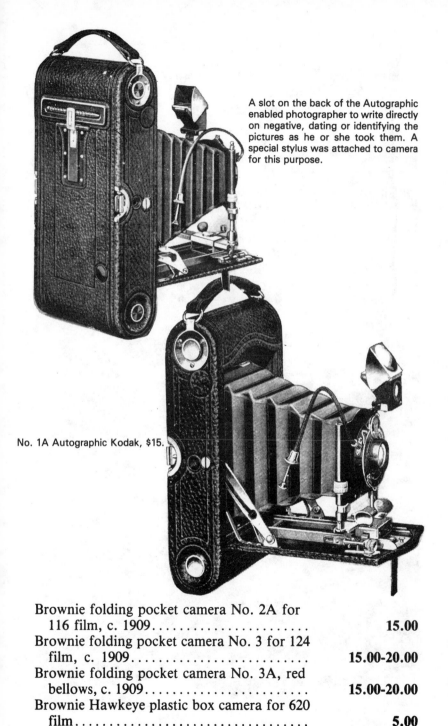

A slot on the back of the Autographic enabled photographer to write directly on negative, dating or identifying the pictures as he or she took them. A special stylus was attached to camera for this purpose.

No. 1A Autographic Kodak, $15.

| | |
|---|---:|
| Brownie folding pocket camera No. 2A for 116 film, c. 1909...................... | **15.00** |
| Brownie folding pocket camera No. 3 for 124 film, c. 1909......................... | **15.00-20.00** |
| Brownie folding pocket camera No. 3A, red bellows, c. 1909....................... | **15.00-20.00** |
| Brownie Hawkeye plastic box camera for 620 film................................ | **5.00** |

Brownie Special folding pocket camera,
trapezoid-shaped ..................... **5.00**
Brownie Stereo camera No. 2 for rollfilm,
red bellows, 1905-10.................. **170.00**
Buckeye folding bed camera for rollfilm,
wood covered with leather, c. 1899....... **85.00-90.00**
Bullet camera for 127 film, 1936-46........ **8.00-10.00**
Bullet No. 2 box camera for 101 rollfilm for
glass plates, 1895-1896................ **30.00-40.00**
Bullet No. 4 for 103 rollfilm or plates, c. 1900 **60.00-70.00**
Bullet Special No. 4, 1898-1904........... **100.00**
Bulls-Eye No. 1 wooden box camera, leather
covered c. 1896...................... **30.00**
Bulls-Eye No. 2, 1896-1913.............. **25.00-30.00**
Bulls-Eye No. 3 for 124 film, 1908-1913..... **35.00-40.00**
Bulls-Eye No. 4 for 103 rollfilm........... **50.00-80.00**
Bulls-Eye folding camera No. 2, c. 1899..... **85.00-90.00**

No. 3 Brownie, c. 1902. $10.

Six 20 brownie Kodak, model C, c.
1935, $5.

No. 1 Brownie, c. 1915, $15.

No. 0 Brownie, c. 1915, $15.

No. 00 Cartridge Premo, by Kodak, c. 1918, $25.

No. 4 Bullseye, Kodak, c. 1897. $60-$80.

Jiffy Kodak Six-$6. $15.

Kodak No. 2 Stringset camera $400-$500. c. 1890-1897.

Two versions of No.2 Brownie (aluminum on left, cardboard on right) $5 aluminum, (1924) $10 cardboard (after 1901).

Baby Brownie Special Kodak, c. 1939, $10-$15.

Brownie Six-20. $5.

Brownie Target Six-16. $5.

Kodak Cirkut 8 c. 1905, $500.

| | |
|---|---|
| Bulls-Eye Special No. 2, c. 1898 . . . . . . . . . . . . | **50.00-65.00** |
| Bulls-Eye Special No. 4 for 103 film, c. 1896-1904 . . . . . . . . . . . . . . . . . . . . . . . . . . . . . . . | **65.00-70.00** |
| Cartridge camera No. 3 for 119 film, c. 1900-1907 . . . . . . . . . . . . . . . . . . . . . . . . . . . . . . . | **70.00** |
| Cartridge camera No. 4 for 104 film, red bellows, Bausch & Lomb lens, c. 1897-1907 | **55.00-70.00** |
| Cartridge camera No. 5 for 155 film, red bellows, Bausch & Lomb lens, c. 1898-1907 . . . | **80.00-95.00** |
| Cirkut No. 5 (with tripod), 1907 . . . . . . . . . . . | **300.00-325.00** |
| Cirkut No. 6 (with tripod), c. 1906 . . . . . . . . . | **350.00-375.00** |
| Cirkut No. 10 . . . . . . . . . . . . . . . . . . . . . . . . . | **900.00** |
| Cirkut No. 16 . . . . . . . . . . . . . . . . . . . . . . . . . | **1,200.00** |
| Daylight A rollfilm box camera, 1891-1895 . . . | **1,000.00-1,200.00** |
| Daylight B rollfilm box camera . . . . . . . . . . . . . | **350.00-400.00** |
| Daylight C rollfilm box camera, 4x5″, 1891-95 | **550.00-650.00** |

Duex camera for 620 film, 1940-46 . . . . . . . . .        **15.00-20.00**
Duo-620 folding camera for 620 film, f3.5/
  70mm Kodak anast. or Zeiss Tessar, 1934-
  37 . . . . . . . . . . . . . . . . . . . . . . . . . . . . . . . . . . . . . . .        **45.00-50.00**
Duo-620 Series II folding camera, f3.5/75mm
  Kodak anast., 1939-40 . . . . . . . . . . . . . . . . .        **45.00-50.00**
Duo-6209 Series II folding camera, f4.6
  Schneider Xenar lens . . . . . . . . . . . . . . . . . .        **150.00**
Eastman plate camera No. 4, Series D,
  4x5" plate camera, c. 1903 . . . . . . . . . . . . . .        **90.00-100.00**
Ektra 35mm rangefinder, f1.9/50mm lens,
  1940s . . . . . . . . . . . . . . . . . . . . . . . . . . . . . . . .        **200.00-225.00**
Eureka No. 2 box camera, for 106 film,
  1898-1899 . . . . . . . . . . . . . . . . . . . . . . . . . . . .        **75.00**
Eureka No. 2 Junior . . . . . . . . . . . . . . . . . . . . . .        **40.00-55.00**
Eureka No. 4 for 109 film, 1899 . . . . . . . . . . .        **80.00-90.00**
Falcon No. 2 box camera for 101 film, 1897-
  1899 . . . . . . . . . . . . . . . . . . . . . . . . . . . . . . . .        **45.00-50.00**
Flat folding camera, Kodak's first folding
  camera, 1895 . . . . . . . . . . . . . . . . . . . . . . . . .        **400.00-425.00**
Flexo No. 2 box camera for 101 film, 1899-
  1913 . . . . . . . . . . . . . . . . . . . . . . . . . . . . . . . . .        **40.00**

No. 2A folding Autographic Brownie
Kodak c. 1921, $10.

No. 2 folding Autographic Brownie
Kodak c. 1916, $10.

Flush Back No. 3 folding camera for 118 film
or plates, Bausch & Lomb lens, c. 1902.... **65.00**

Folding camera No. 1A, f6.3/100mm, c. 1902 **21.00**

Folding camera No. 2..................... **14.00**

Folding camera No. 3 for 118 film, f5.6/
130mm, c. 1902....................... **16.00**

Folding camera No. 4 (satchel-style), for glass
plates or rollfilm, 1890-1892............. **450.00-475.00**

Folding camera No. 4, models A & B for
4x5″ exposures, red or black bellows, 1907-
1914.................................. **50.00**

Folding camera No. 4A for 126 film, red bellows, 1906-15........................ **90.00-95.00**

Folding camera No. 5 for 5x7″ film or plates. **450.00-500.00**

Folding camera No. 6 for 6½x8½″ plates... **1,000.00**

Folding Pocket Camera, first model for 105
rollfilm, 1898-1904, brass struts, red bellows.................................. **125.00**

Folding Pocket Camera, first model for 105
rollfilm, 1898-1904, nickel struts......... **50.00**

Folding Pocket No. 0 for 121 film, 1902-1906 **75.00**

Folding Pocket No. 1 for 105 film, 1898-1904 **25.00-50.00**

Folding Pocket No. 1A for 116 film, red
bellows, 1899-1904.................... **20.00-25.00**

Folding Pocket No. 2 for 101 film.......... **35.00**

Folding Pocket No. 3, models A & B for
118 film, 1900-1915................... **20.00-25.00**

Folding Pocket No. 3A for 122 film, red
bellows, 1903-08...................... **20.00-40.00**

Folding Pocket No. 4 for 123 film, 4x5″ exposures, red bellows, c. 1906-1915........ **40.00-50.00**

Folding Pocket Special No. 1A for 116 film,
red bellows, c. 1900-1912............... **20.00-35.00**

Folding Pocket Special No. 3............. **70.00-85.00**

Folding Pocket Special No. 3A, f6.3 Zeiss-
Kodak anast........................... **40.00**

Folding Cartridge Hawkeye No. 2 for 120
film, 1913-30......................... **12.00**

Folding Cartridge Hawkeye No. 2A for 116
film, 1913............................ **30.00-10.00**

Folding Cartridge Hawkeye No. 3A for 122
film, 1913-33......................... **15.00-25.00**

Folding Film Pack Hawkeye No. 2, c. 1923.. **10.00**

Folding Hawkeye No. 1.................. **20.00**

No. 2A folding pocket Brownie, c. 1909, $15.

No. 3 folding Brownie, c. 1903, $20.

No. 3A folding Brownie, c. 1910-1915, $20.

No. 2 Folding Pocket Brownie, c. 1908, $15.

| | |
|---|---|
| Folding Hawkeye No. 1A, red bellows, 1913-1915 . . . . . . . . . . . . . . . . . . . . . . . . . . . . . . . . . | **15.00-25.00** |
| Folding Hawkeye No. 2 for 120 film, 1930-40 | **10.00-15.00** |
| Folding Hawkeye No. 2A, c. 1917 . . . . . . . . . . | **8.00** |
| Folding Hawkeye No. 3 for 118 film, 1904-1915 . . . . . . . . . . . . . . . . . . . . . . . . . . . . . . . | **20.00-25.00** |

Folding Hawkeye No. 3A for 122 film, 1908-1915 ................................ **25.00**
Folding Hawkeye Six-16, 1933-34 ......... **10.00**
Folding Hawkeye Six-20, 1933-34 ......... **10.00**
Folding Hawkeye Special, f6.3 Kodak anast., 1930 ............................... **15.00-20.00**
Folding Rainbow Hawkeye No. 2 for 120 film **25.00**
Folding Rainbow Hawkeye No. 2A for 116 film .................................. **14.00**
Folding Rainbow Hawkeye No. 2 Special, f6.3 anast ............................ **30.00-40.00**
Gift Camera (a Kodak Pocket No. 1A) for 116 film, special edition covered with brown leather, art deco features, originally priced at $15, 1930-31 ................. **100.00-125.00**

No. 4A Folding Kodak, c. 1906. $100.

No. 4 Folding Kodak, c. 1892, $450-$475.

Kodak Folding Brownie, No. 3A, 1910-1915, $20.

No. 1A Folding Kodak, c. 1902, $20.

No. 1 Folding Pocket Kodak model
C., c. 1905, $25-$35.

Monitor View Camera (without
lens), Rochester, c. 1900, $60-$75.

| | |
|---|---:|
| Girl Scout camera for 127 film, bright green with GSA emblem, 1929-34........ | **50.00** |
| Hawkette No. 2 for 120 film, British-made folding camera with bakelite body, 1930s .............................. | **10.00-15.00** |
| Hawkeye Film Pack No. 2 box camera, all metal, 1899-1916...................... | **10.00** |
| Hawkeye Special No. 2 & 2A box cameras for rollfilm, f6.3, 1928-30................. | **10.00-15.00** |
| Hawkeye Stereo, red bellows, Bausch & Lomb lenses, 1904-14................... | **140.00-150.00** |
| Hawkeye Target box cameras No. 2, 2A, Six-16, Six-20........................ | **5.00** |
| Hawkeye Vest Pocket, 1927-31............ | **15.00-20.00** |
| Hawkeye Weno box camera Nos. 2, 4, 5, 7, various sizes, c. 1910.................. | **20.00-40.00** |
| Jiffy Six-16 for 116 film, 1933-46........... | **10.00** |
| Jiffy Six-20 for 620 film, 1937-39........... | **10.00-15.00** |
| Jiffy Vest Pocket for 127 film, 1935-42...... | **10.00** |
| Junior No. 1 for 120 film, f7.7 anast., c. 1914............................... | **10.00-15.00** |
| Junior No. 1A for 116 film, c. 1914......... | **8.00** |
| Junior No. 2C for 130 film................ | **15.00** |
| Junior No. 3, factory rollfilm, 1890-1897.... | **350.00-400.00** |
| Junior No. 3A for 122 film, c. 1915......... | **10.00** |

No. 2 Folding Cartridge Hawk-Eye Kodak, c. 1929, $5-$10.

No. 2A Folding Cartridge Hawk-Eye Kodak, c. 1929, $5-$10.

Kodak Folding pocket Model 2A, f7.7 Kodak anast. lens. c. 1905, $30.

Kodak No. 2A Folding Hawk-Eye c. 1917, $8.

| | |
|---|---|
| Junior No. 4, 4x5" exposures on rollfilm, 1890-97 | **350.00-400.00** |
| Kodet No. 4 box camera for plates or roll film, 4x5", 1894-97 | **325.00-350.00** |
| Kodet No. 4 folding bed camera for plates or rollfilm, 4x5", 1894 | **500.00** |
| Medalist for 620 film, f3.5 Ektar | **75.00** |
| Medalist I rangefinder, 1940s | **100.00** |
| Medalist II, late 1940s | **150.00** |
| Monitor Six-16 folding camera for 116 film, 1939-46 | **15.00-20.00** |
| Monitor Six-20 folding camera for 620 film, 1939-46 | **15.00-20.00** |
| Nagel Jr. camera for 620 film, f7.7 Kodak lens, made in Germany | **5.00-10.00** |
| Ordinary "A", 1891-1895 | **1,000.00-1,500.00** |
| Ordinary "B", 1891-95 | **750.00-800.00** |
| Ordinary "C", 1891-95 | **600.00-750.00** |
| Panoram No. 1 for 105 film, models, A, B, C, d, 1900-1914 | **125.00-160.00** |
| Panoram No. 3A for 122 film, 1926-28 | **160.00-170.00** |
| Panoram No. 4 for 103 film, 1899-1924 | **150.00-225.00** |
| Petite vest pocket camera for 127 film, colored models, 1929-34 | **25.00-30.00** |
| Pocket Kodak box camera for 102 film, c. 1895-1900 | **65.00-80.00** |
| Pocket Kodak No. 1 for folding camera for 120 film, 1926-31 | **10.00** |
| Pocket No. 1 Autographic, f7.9 Kodar lens | **25.00-30.00** |
| Pocket No. 1, Series II, 1922-24 | **15.00** |
| Pocket No. 1A for 116 film, 1926-31 | **5.00-10.00** |
| Pocket No. 1A Autographic | **10.00** |

Kodak Ektra c. 1941, $200-$225.

Flash Bantam Kodak c. 1948.

Jiffy Kodak Series II
Six-20 c. 1938, $5-$10.

Kodak Pony 828 c.
1950, $10.

Jiffy Kodak Six-20
Series II, c. 1937, $10.

| | |
|---|---|
| Pocket No. 1A, Series II, 1923-31.......... | **10.00** |
| Pocket No. 1A, colored models, 1929-31.... | **20.00** |
| Pocket No. 2C for 130 film, 1925-32........ | **15.00** |
| Pocket No. 3 for 118 film, 1926-34......... | **10.00** |
| Pocket No. 3A for 122 film, 1927-33........ | **22.00** |
| Pocket No. 3A Autographic............... | **25.00** |
| Pocket Junior No. 1 for 120 film, 1929-31... | **15.00** |
| Pocket Junior No. 1, colored models........ | **15.00** |
| Pocket Junior No. 1 Autographic.......... | **15.00** |
| Pocket Junior No. 1A for 166 film, 1929-31 (some in colors)........................ | **15.00** |
| Pocket Special No. 1A for 116 film, 1926-34. | **20.00** |
| Pocket Special No. 3 for 118 film, 1926-34... | **25.00** |
| Pocket Special No. 3 Autographic for 118 film, f4.5............................. | **30.00** |
| Pony 135 camera, first model for 35mm film, 1950-54 ............................... | **10.00** |
| Pony 828 for 828 film, 1949-59............. | **12.00** |
| Premo folding camera for plates, 2¼x3¼", 1916-22 ............................... | **25.00** |
| Premo folding camera for plates, 3¼x5½, red bellows............................. | **30.00** |
| Premo 4x5" size........................ | **25.00-40.00** |
| Premo 5x7" folding camera for plates, red bellows................................. | **50.00** |

Premo Cartridge No. 00 box camera for roll-
film, meniscus lens, c. 1916.............. **25.00**
Premo Cartridge No. 2 for rollfilm, 1918.... **10.00**
Premo Cartridge No. 2A................. **10.00**
Premo No. 1 filmpack folding camera, var-
ious sizes, 1906-16.................... **15.00-25.00**
Premo filmpack box camera, various sizes,
1903-08 ............................. **15.00**

Kodak Junior Six-20, Series II. $12.

No. 1A Kodak Jr. c. 1914, $8.

Junior Six-20 Kodak, c. 1935, $15.

Medalist II by Kodak, c. 1946,
$130-$150.

Premoette Jr. No. 1A Kodak, c. 1912-16, $20.

No. 1A Pocket Kodak Series II, c. 1920s, $10.

| | |
|---|---|
| Premo folding camera for plates or rollfilm, various sizes, c. 1910.................. | **25.00-30.00** |
| Premo Special folding camera for plates or rollfilm, various sizes, 1912-16.......... | **50.00** |
| Premo folding cartridge No. 2 for 120 film... | **10.00** |
| Premo folding cartridge No. 2A for 116 film. | **10.00** |
| Premo folding cartridge No. 2C for 130 film. | **12.00** |
| Premo folding cartridge No. 3 for 124 film... | **15.00** |
| Premo folding cartridge No. 3A for 122 film. | **10.00** |
| Premo Junior No. 0 box camera, 1911-16.... | **15.00** |
| Premo Junior No. 1 box camera, 1909-16.... | **5.00-10.00** |
| Premo Junior No. 3 box camera, 1909-19.... | **15.00** |
| Premo Junior No. 4 box camera, 4x5″ exposures, 1909-14...................... | **10.00-15.00** |

The Panoram Kodak c. 1910, $150.

| | |
|---|---|
| Premo pocket folding camera for filmpacks.. | **15.00** |
| Premo pocket folding camera for plates, model C, 1904-16..................... | **20.00** |
| Premo Pony 4x5″ folding plate camera, red bellows, Bausch & Lomb lens........... | **30.00** |
| Premo Pony 5x7″ folding plate camera, Bausch & Lomb lens................. | **50.00-65.00** |
| Premo Pony folding plate camera, 6½x8½″. | **180.00** |
| Premo Senior, red bellows............... | **75.00** |
| Premo Star, 4x5″, c. 1903-1908........... | **35.00** |
| Premoette No. 1 film pack camera, meniscus lens, 1906-1908...................... | **20.00** |
| Premoette No. 1A filmpack camera, meniscus lens, 1909-12........................ | **30.00** |

Kodak No. 8 Premo, f6/180mm
Ernemann Dopple anast. lens. $30.

No. 2A folding cartridge Premo, $10.

No. 9 Premo, $30.

Kodak Premo early 1900s, $60-$70.

| | |
|---|---|
| Premoette No. 1 Special, f6.3 Kodak anast., 1913-18 | 25.00 |
| Premoette No. 1A, 1912-16 | 25.00 |
| Premoette No. 1A Special, f6.3 Kodak anast. | 25.00 |
| Premoette Senior, c. 1915-22 | 15.00 |
| Pupille for 127 film, made in Germany for Kodak, f2 Schneider Xenon lens, 1932-34 | 175.00-200.00 |
| Quick Focus No. 3B box camera for 125 film, 1906-10 | 90.00-100.00 |
| Rainbow Hawkeye No. 2, 1931-32 | 10.00 |
| Rainbow Hawkeye No. 2A, 2½x4¼" | 10.00 |
| Recomar Model 18, 6x9cm, f4.5/105mm Kodak anast. | 60.00 |
| Recomar Model 33, 9x12cm plate camera, f4.5/135mm Kodak anast. in Compur | 50.00 |
| Reflex TLR 2¼ format camera for 620 film, f3.5/80mm | 30.00 |
| Regent camera for 620 film, f3.5/105mm Schneider Xenar lens, made in Germany for Kodak, c. 1935 | 40.00 |
| Retina, original model, f3.5/.50mm Xenar, 1934-37 | 50.00 |
| Retina Model I, 1936-50 | 45.00 |
| Retina Model 1A | 45.00 |
| Retina Model 1B | 50.00-60.00 |
| Retina Model II, 1937-50 | 50.00 |
| Retina Model IIa rangefinder, f2 Xenon | 50.00-60.00 |
| Retina Model IIc, f2.8 Xenon 50mm | 60.00 |
| Retina Model IIIc, f2/50mm | 85.00 |

Kokak No. 1 Diodeck for 616 film, $5.

No. 1A Kodak Autographic Junior, $10-$15.

| | |
|---|---|
| Retina Model IIIc........................ | **100.00** |
| Retinette folding camera, original model, for 35mm film, f6.3 Kodak anast., 1939...... | **60.00** |
| Retinette II folding camera for 35mm film, f4.5/50mm Schneider anast., 1940s....... | **50.00** |
| Retinette IA non-folding camera.......... | **30.00** |
| Screen Focus No. 4 for 123 film........... | **300.00-325.00** |
| Screen Focus No. 5.................... | **375.00-425.00** |
| Six-16 for 616 film, 1930s................ | **10.00-15.00** |
| Six-16 Special, f4.5/127mm Kodak anast., 1937-39 .............................. | **30.00** |
| Six-20 for 620 film, 1930s................ | **10.00-15.00** |
| Six-20 Special, f4.5/Kodak anast., 1937-39.. | **22.00-25.00** |

Folmer & Schwing/Eastman Kodak, Reversible-back Cycle Graphic, c. 1905. $175.

Senior Six-16 Kodak, c. 1938, $15.

| | |
|---|---|
| Special No. 1A folding camera, f6.3 Zeiss-Kodak, 1912-14....................... | **50.00** |
| Special No. 3 for 118 film, f6.3 Kodak anast., 1911-14....................... | **30.00-40.00** |
| Special No. 3A folding camera, 1910-14..... | **40.00-50.00** |
| Speed Camera No. 1A for 116 film, f6.3 Contessa-Nettar anast..................... | **80.00-140.00** |
| Speed camera No. 4A for 125 film, 1903-13.. | **300.00-350.00** |
| Stereo camera, original model of 1917-25, for 101 film, f7.7/130mm Kodak anast., original model of 1917-25.................. | **185.00-200.00** |

Vigilant Six-20 Kodak, c. 1946. $15.

Vest Pocket Hawk-Eye Kodak, c. 1929, $15-$10.

| | |
|---|---:|
| Stereo No. 2 box camera for 101 film, f14/125mm, 1901-05 | 330.00 |
| Super Six-20 for 620 film, f4.5 Kodak anast., electric eye model, 1938-45 | 800.00-900.00 |
| Tourist folding camera for 620 film, 1948-51. | 10.00 |
| Vanity vest pocket camera for 127 film, 1928-1933 | 25.00-30.00 |
| Vest Pocket camera, Autographic Model B, 1912-34 | 15.00-20.00 |
| Vest Pocket Special Autographic camera, 1912-34 | 35.00-40.00 |
| View camera, 5x7" | 90.00 |
| View camera, 8x10" | 100.00-125.00 |
| Vigilant folding camera for 116 film, 1939-48. | 10.00-15.00 |

The Kodak Box No. 2. c. 1901, $10. (camera only)

Vollenda camera for 127 film, manufactured
by Nagelwerk of Germany for Kodak, f3.5/
40mm Schneider Radionar, 1932-37...... **40.00-50.00**
Vollenda camera for 616 film, f4.5/120mm.. **45.00**
Vollenda 620 Junior...................... **25.00**
Zenith box camera for plates, late 1890s..... **140.00-150.00**

Vest Pocket Autographic Kodak, c. 1920. $15-$20.

The Brownie Enlarging camera (below and right) was used to make prints for existing negatives. Camera collectors often add such equipment to their collections.

Ernemann, H. (Dresden, Germany, merged
with Zeiss in 1926)
Bob I folding camera, f6.8................ **25.00**
Bobette I for 35mm film, 1920s............ **50.00-60.00**
Box camera, wood body covered with leather,
for 120 film, f12.5 meniscus lens........ **30.00**
Box camera, Model K................... **75.00**
Ermanox box camera, all metal, f1.8/85mm,
c. 1924.............................**1,000.00-1,125.00**
Ermanox collapsible bellows-type camera,
f1.8 Ernostar lens..................... **500.00-600.00**
Ernoflex folding reflex camera, f4.5/80mm
Tessar, c. 1925...................... **900.00-1,200.00**
Ernoflex Simplex stereo reflex camera, f3.5/
75mm Ernon lens..................... **600.00-800.00**
Globus folding camera, f4.6 Goerz double
anast. brass lens, early 1900s............ **400.00**
Heag I folding plate camera, f6.8........... **30.00-35.00**

Heag XV folding plate camera, f6.8/80mm double anast.................................. 65.00-80.00

Klapp folding bellows camera, 6.5x9cm, f3.5 Ernon...................................... 225.00-260.00

Klapp folding bellows camera, 9x12cm, f4.5/ 150mm Tessar, c. 1925.................. 175.00-200.00

Klapp miniature, 4.5x6cm, f2.7/75mm, c. 1925...................................... 500.00

Lilliput folding bellows camera, 4.5x6cm, c. 1913...................................... 50.00-60.00

Lilliput stereo folding camera, 1915......... 150.00-160.00

Reflex SLR, f4.5/75mm Ernoplast......... 150.00-175.00

Reporter folding camera for 9x12″ plates, f5.5/120mm Meyer anast., c. 1905........ 75.00-80.00

Rolf vest pocket folding camera for 127 film, f12...................................... 25.00

Simplex stereo camera for plates, c. 1920.... 150.00-170.00

Stereo box camera, meniscus lens, c. 1912... 120.00-130.00

Tropical Heag folding camera, 9x12cm plates, f6.8 Ernemann Vilar lens, c. 1920........ 280.00-300.00

Tropical Klapp folding camera, teakwood with brass fittings, 9x12cm, f4.5/150mm Ernostar, horizontal format............. 450.00-500.00

Tropical Klapp folding camera, vertical format, 9x12cm, f3.5/150mm Ernon, c. 1925................................. 1,000.00-1,250.00

Tropical Reporter folding camera, f4.5/ 165mm Tessar, c. 1915.................. 850.00-900.00

Unette miniature box camera for rollfilm, 1920s ..................................... 100.00-110.00

●Etui—see Guthe & Thorsch

●Exacta—see Ihagee

●Expo Camera Co. (New York)

Easy-Load box camera for cartridge film, meniscus lens, c. 1926................. 75.00-80.00

Police Camera for special film cassettes, c. 1915 ..................................... 190.00-235.00

Watch Camera, shaped like a railroad pocket watch, for special film cartridges, 1905-36. 130.00-150.00

●Fed (Russian copies of Leica cameras in a variety of models)

Fed camera, f3.5 Fed lens, 1930s........... 65.00-75.00

●Ferrania (Milan, Italy)
Ferrania Rondine metal box camera for 127
film, f7.5 meniscus lens................ 25.00
●Folmer & Schwing (New York City and
Rochester, merged with Kodak in 1905)
Cameras by Folmer & Schwing are listed
under Graflex (Graphic) as well as Eastman-
Kodak (Cirkut)
●Foth, B. E. & Co. (Berlin, Germany)
Foth Derby Model I for 127 film, f2.5/
50mm Foth anast., 1930s............... 35.00-40.00
Foth Derby Model II, 1930s.............. 40.00-45.00
Fothflex TLR for 120 film, f3.5/75mm
Foth anast., 1930s.................... 60.00
Foth folding camera for 116 film, f4.9/
120mm anast......................... 20.00-25.00
●Frankawerk (Beyreuth, Germany)
Rolfix folding camera for 120 film, f4.5/
105mm Schneider, 1940s............... 25.00-30.00
Solida folding camera for 120 film, f6.3/
75mm............................... 25.00
Franke & Heidecke (Braunschweig, Germany)
Heidoscop stereo camera, 6x13cm, f4.5/
75mm Zeiss Tessar, 1930s.............. 285.00-300.00
Rollei-16 subminiature camera for 16mm
film, f2.8 Tessar..................... 50.00-60.00
Rollei-35 for 35mm film, f3.5/40mm Tessar.. 75.00-100.00
Rolleicord I TLR, 6x6cm, f4.5 Zeiss Triotar,
1933 ............................... 50.00
Rolleicord II, f3.5 Triotar................. 35.00-40.00
Rolleicord III, f3.5 Triotar or f3.5 Schneider
Xenar............................... 50.00-60.00
Rolleicord IV........................... 75.00
Rolleicord V........................... 80.00-90.00
Rolleidoscop reflex stereo camera for 120
film, f4.5/75mm, c. 1926.............. 600.00-700.00
Rolleiflex I TLR for 117 film, f3.8/75mm
Tessar, rim-set Compur shutter, 1929..... 100.00-140.090
Rolleiflex TLR for 120 film, c. 1932........ 75.00-100.00
Rolleiflex TLR for 127 film, 4x4, f2.8/
60mm Tessar......................... 50.00-100.00
●Fuji Photo Film Co. (Japan)
Lyra folding camera for 120 film, f3.5/75mm,
1940s .............................. 15.00

Rolleiflex Original, c. 1921 by Franke & Heidecke.

Rolleicord II, c. 1938, by Franke & Heidecke, $35-$40.

Baby Roller, c. 1931, by Franke & Heidecke, Braunschweig, Germany.

| | |
|---|---|
| Mini 35mm camera, f2.8/25mm............ | **60.00** |
| ●Gallus, Usines (France) | |
| Gallus Stereo metal jumelle-type camera, 1920s ................................ | **150.00** |
| ●Galter Products | |
| Hopalong Cassidy plastic box camera for 120 film, 1950........................... | **10.00** |

●Garland (London, England)
Wet plate camera, 8x10″, c. 1865 . . . . . . . . . . .      **1,400.00**
●Gaumont, L. & Cie (Paris, France)
Block-Notes 4.5x6cm folding plate camera, c.
1904 . . . . . . . . . . . . . . . . . . . . . . . . . . . . . . .      **130.00**
Block-Notes 6x9cm, f6.3 Tessar . . . . . . . . . . .      **130.00**
Block-Notes stereo folding camera, f6.3 . . . . .    **325.00-350.00**
●Genie Camera Co. (Philadelphia, Pa.)
Genie magazine box camera for 3¼x4x4″
plates, c. 1892 . . . . . . . . . . . . . . . . . . . . . . . .    **650.00-675.00**
●Gennert, G. (New York, N.Y.)
Folding Montauk plate camera, 4x5 or 5x7 . . .    **100.00-150.00**
Montauk detective plate camera, c. 1890 . . . . .    **100.00-125.00**
Penny Picture camera, 5x7″, 1890s . . . . . . . .    **225.00-250.00**
●Gilles-Faller (Paris, France)
Studio camera, 18x24cm, f4.5/270mm Delor
lens . . . . . . . . . . . . . . . . . . . . . . . . . . . . . . . .    **300. 00-350.00**
Glunz, S., Kamerawerk (Hannover,
Germany)
Folding plate camera, 9x12cm, f6.8 Goerz,
1920s . . . . . . . . . . . . . . . . . . . . . . . . . . . . . . .      **50.00**
Glunz folding cameras for rollfilm, f6.3
Tessar . . . . . . . . . . . . . . . . . . . . . . . . . . . . . . .    **20.00-25.00**
●Goerz, C. P. (Berlin, Germany, merged with
Zeiss in 1926)
Ango folding camera, f6.8  Goerz Dagor,
1899-1929 . . . . . . . . . . . . . . . . . . . . . . . . . . .    **100.00-125.00**
Ango stereo camera, c. 1906 . . . . . . . . . . . . . .    **190.00-200.00**
Anschutz folding camera, bedless "strut"
type, various sizes, c. 1890 . . . . . . . . . . . . . .    **125.00-135.00**
Goerz folding reflex SLR for 4x5″ plates,
c. 1912 . . . . . . . . . . . . . . . . . . . . . . . . . . . . .    **150.00-175.00**
Goerz folding camera for 120 or 116 rollfilm.    **25.00-35.00**
Goerz Stereo Photo Binocle detective camera,
disguised as field glasses, c. 1899 . . . . . . . . .**2,000.00-2,250.00**
Stereo Tenax folding camera for plates, f4.5/
60mm Dogmar lens . . . . . . . . . . . . . . . . . . .    **175.00-180.00**
Tenax folding vest pocket camera for plates,
f6.8 Dagor, c. 1909 . . . . . . . . . . . . . . . . . . .      **80.00**
Tenax folding vest pocket camera for 127
film, f6.3/75mm Dogmar, Compur shutter    **20.00-25.00**
Tenax folding camera, 6x9cm size, f6.3,
Compur  shutter . . . . . . . . . . . . . . . . . . . . . . .    **20.00-30.00**

Tenax folding camera for plates, 3¼x4x4¼ ",
   c. 1915-20 . . . . . . . . . . . . . . . . . . . . . . . . . . . .     **65.00**
Tenax folding camera for 9x12cm plates,
   1920s . . . . . . . . . . . . . . . . . . . . . . . . . . . . . . .     **50.00**
Tengor box camera for 120 film, 1920s . . . . . .   **15.00-20.00**
Tengor vest pocket folding camera for 127
   film, f9/45mm . . . . . . . . . . . . . . . . . . . . . . .   **30.00-35.00**
●Goldmann, R. A. (Vienna)
Press folding camera for 9x12cm plates, f6.3
   Tessar, c. 1900 . . . . . . . . . . . . . . . . . . . . . .   **150.00-175.00**
●Goltz & Breutmann (Dresden, and Gorlitz,
Germany)
Mentor Compur Relfex SLR box camera for
   plates, f2.7 Zeiss Tessar, 1928 . . . . . . . . . . .     **175.00**
Mentor folding reflex SLR for plates, 1915-30   **140.00-150.00**
Mentor Reflex box camera with bellows, f4.5
   Tessar . . . . . . . . . . . . . . . . . . . . . . . . . . . . .   **100.00-125.00**
Mentor II folding plate camera, f6/12mm Tri-
   plan, 1907 . . . . . . . . . . . . . . . . . . . . . . . . . .   **90.00-100.00**
Mentorett TLR for 120 film, f3.5 Mentor, c.
   1935 . . . . . . . . . . . . . . . . . . . . . . . . . . . . . .     **150.00**
●Goodwin—see Ansco
●Graflex Inc. (Rochester, N.Y.; including
Folmer-Schwing cameras)
Auto Graflex, 3½x4¼ ", 1907-23 . . . . . . . . . .     **75.00**
Auto Graflex, 4x5 " . . . . . . . . . . . . . . . . . . . . .   **75.00-80.00**
Auto Graflex, 5x7 . . . . . . . . . . . . . . . . . . . . . .     **100.00**
Combat Graphic 4x5 " olive drab camera
   produced for armed forces . . . . . . . . . . . . .   **175.00-180.00**
Compact Graflex . . . . . . . . . . . . . . . . . . . . . .   **100.00-125.00**
Graflex Series B, 4x5 ", 1925-42 . . . . . . . . . . .   **65.00-75.00**
Graflex 22 TLR for 120 film, f3.5/85mm
   Graftar . . . . . . . . . . . . . . . . . . . . . . . . . . . .   **45.00-50.00**
Graflex 3A for 122 film . . . . . . . . . . . . . . . . . .     **75.00**
Graflex Fingerprint 1:1 copying "Inspect-
   ograph" camera . . . . . . . . . . . . . . . . . . . . . .   **175.00-250.00**
Graflex Home Portrait 5x7 SLR camera,
   1912-42 . . . . . . . . . . . . . . . . . . . . . . . . . . .   **125.00-150.00**
Graphic No. 0 for 127 film, f6.3 Zeiss Kodak
   anast., 1909-23) . . . . . . . . . . . . . . . . . . . . .   **175.00-180.00**
Graphic View Camera, 4x5 ", 1941-49 . . . . . . .   **225.00-250.00**
National Graflex SLR for 120 film, f3.5/
   75mm Tessar, 1933-41 . . . . . . . . . . . . . . . . .   **90.00-125.00**

RB Series B Graflex, by Graflex Inc.,
f4.5/127mm Kodak Ektar. $90-$100.

3A Graflex, 1907, by Folmer & Schwing, $75.

| | |
|---|---:|
| Naturalist's Graflex, 26″ focal length max. bellows, 1907-21 | **4,500.00-5,000.00** |
| Pacemaker Crown Grphic 4x5″, c. 1949 | **150.00** |
| Pacemaker Speed Graphic | **150.00-160.00** |
| Press Graflex 5x7″, 1907-23 | **150.00-175.00** |
| RB Auto Graflex, 3¼x4¼″, 1909-1942 | **100.00-120.00** |
| RB Cycle Graphic folding camera, red bellows, wood body, 5x7″, Bausch & Lomb rapid rectilinear lens | **175.00-180.00** |
| RB Graflex Series B, 2¼x3¼″, 1925-50 | **90.00** |
| RB Graflex Series B, 3¼x4¼″, 1932-42 | **90.00-100.00** |
| RB Graflex Series B, 4x5″, 1923-42 | **100.00-140.00** |
| RB Graflex Series C, 1926-35, 3¼x4¼″ | **95.00-100.00** |
| RB Graflex Series D, 3¼x4¼, 1929-41 | **95.00** |
| RB Graflex Series D, 4x5″, 1929-45 | **100.00-125.00** |
| RB Graflex Super D, 3¼x4¼″, 1941-43 | **150.00** |
| Speed Graphic folding camera, pre-1938 models, various sizes | **75.00-80.00** |
| Speed Graphic folding camera, 1940-47 models, various sizes | **90.00-125.00** |
| Stereo Auto Graflex for plates, 5x7″, f4.5/135mm Bausch & Lomb lens, 1907-22 | **1,300.00-1,500.00** |
| Stereo Graphic, 5x7″, 1904-1921 | **700.00-800.00** |
| ●Gray, Robert D. (New York, N.Y.) | |
| View camera, 8x10″, No. 4 lens, c. 1880 | **150.00-160.00** |

●Griffiths, Walter M. & Co. (Birmingham,
England)
Magazine camera for plates, 3¼x4¼ ″, c.
1890 . . . . . . . . . . . . . . . . . . . . . . . . . . . . . . . .     **150.00-160.00**
●Gundlach Optical Co. (Rochester, N.Y.)
Korona folding bed view camera, 4x5 ″ . . . . . .     **45.00**
Korona folding bed view camera, 5x7 ″ . . . . . .     **50.00**
Korona folding plate camera, 3¼x4¼ ″, red
bellows . . . . . . . . . . . . . . . . . . . . . . . . . . . . . .     **50.00-60.00**
Korona Stereo folding plate camera for 5x7 ″
plates . . . . . . . . . . . . . . . . . . . . . . . . . . . . . . . .     **275.00-300.00**
●Guthe & Thorsch Kamera Werkstatten (Dres-
den, Germany)
Kawee folding plate camera, 6x9 and 9x12cm.     **50.00-60.00**
KW Patent Etui folding plate camera, 6x9cm,
f4.5/100mm Tessar, c. 1930 . . . . . . . . . . . .     **50.00-60.00**
KW Patent Etui Deluxe, 6x9cm . . . . . . . . . . .     **180.00-200.00**
KW folding plate camera, 6x9cm, f4.5/
105mm . . . . . . . . . . . . . . . . . . . . . . . . . . . . . . .     **30.00-35.00**
KW Reflex SLR box camera for 120 film,
f4.5/105mm KW anast., c. 1930 . . . . . . . . . .     **70.00-80.00**
Pilot 6 SLR for 120 film, f3.5/75mm, c. 1930s     **45.00**
Pilot Reflex TLR for 127 film, c. 1930s . . . . . .     **60.00**
Pilot Super SLR for 120 film, f4.5 Pilotar
lens . . . . . . . . . . . . . . . . . . . . . . . . . . . . . . . . . .     **50.00**
Praktiflex SLR for 35mm film, f2.9/50mm
Victor, 1938 . . . . . . . . . . . . . . . . . . . . . . . . . .     **30.00-40.00**
Praktiflex II SLR for 35mm film, f2.9/50mm
Victor . . . . . . . . . . . . . . . . . . . . . . . . . . . . . . . .     **40.00**
●Hall Camera Co. (Brooklyn, N.Y.)
Hall Mirror SLR camera, 4x5 ″, f4.5/180mm,
1910 . . . . . . . . . . . . . . . . . . . . . . . . . . . . . . . .     **90.00-100.00**
●Harboe, A. O. (Altona, Germany)
Harboe box camera for glass plates, wooden
body, brass barrel lens, 1870s . . . . . . . . . . . .     **650.00-700.00**
●Hare, George (London, England)
Half-plate tourist camera, Fallowfield Rapid
Doublet lens, c. 1865 . . . . . . . . . . . . . . . . . .     **600.00-800.00**
Stereo camera for plates, Dallmeyer lens, red
bellows . . . . . . . . . . . . . . . . . . . . . . . . . . . . . .     **675.00-700.00**
●Hawkeye—see Eastman-Kodak, Blair, or
Boston

Herco (Herbert George Co.)
Donald Duck camera for 127 film, meniscus
    lens, 1940s........................... **25.00-30.00**
Imperial folding camera for 127 film, f4.5/
    50mm Ludwig, 1930s.................. **10.00-15.00**
Official Boy (or Girl) Scout camera......... **5.00-8.00**
Roy Rogers & Trigger plastic box camera for
    620 film, 1940s....................... **8.00-10.00**
●Hermagis, J. Fleury (Paris, France)
Velocigraphe detective magazine plate
    camera, 1892.......................... **400.00-450.00**
●Hess-Ives Corp. (Philadelphia, Pa.)
Hirco Color box camera (color photos by
    separation process in camera), c. 1915..... **120.00-125.00**
●Hetherington & Hibben (Indianapolis, Ind.)
Heatherington Magazine Camera for 4x5″
    plates, c. 1892....................... **475.00-500.00**
●Hirco—see Hess-Ives Corp.
●Hofert, Emil, Kamera Fabrik (Dresden,
Germany)
Eho Altiflex TLR for 120 film, f4.5/75mm
    Ludwig Victar, 1930s.................. **30.00**
Eho Altiscop for 120 film, f4.5/75mm...... **40.00-45.00**
Eho-Altmann Juwel Altissa TLR for 120
    film, 1938............................ **15.00**
Eho box camera for 127 film, f11 Duplar,
    1930s ................................ **40.00**
Eho Stereo box camera for 120 film, f11/80
    Duplar, 1930s........................ **55.00**
●Hornby
Field camera, quarter-plate size............ **190.00**
●Horsman, E. I. Co. (New York, N.Y.)
No. 3 Eclipse folding camera for plates, brass
    barrel lens, c. 1896................... **175.00**
●Houghton, George & Son Ltd. (London, Eng-
land; merged with Butcher in 1925)
Houghton Autorange 220 Ensign folding
    camera for 120 film, f4.5 Tessar, 1941..... **50.00**
Cupid box camera for 120 film, f11 meniscus
    lens.................................. **20.00-25.00**
Ensign Model I for roll film.............. **15.00**
Ensign box camera...................... **10.00**
Ensign folding camera for 122 film, post-
    card size exposures.................... **25.00-50.00**

Houghton Ensing folding roll film camera. c. 1925, $15.

The Hit a Japanese novelty camera, c. 1950, $10.

Ticka, 1906, by Houghton Ltd., England c. $135-$150.

| | |
|---|---:|
| Ensign Reflex SLR for plates, c. 1915....... | **80.00-90.00** |
| Ensign Reflex SLR for 120 film, 1900s...... | **55.00-65.00** |
| Ensignette folding camera for rollfilm, c. 1910-30 ............................. | **40.00** |
| Houghton-Butcher tropical pocket watch carbine camera, metal body, tropical bellows. | **175.00-185.00** |
| Klito magazine box camera for plates, 1905.. | **45.00-50.00** |
| Klito folding camera for 3¼x4¼ " sheet film. | **35.00-40.00** |
| Midget folding camera for 127 film, c. 1912.. | **45.00-50.00** |
| Sanderson folding plate camera, various sizes | **140.00-150.00** |
| Ticka detective camera shaped like pocket watch (identical to the Expo Watch Camera by the Expo Camera Co.) for special casette film, f16/30mm meniscus lens, c. 1905.... | **135.00-150.00** |
| Hunter Purma Special box camera for 127 film, bakelite and metal body, f6.3 plastic lens, 1930s......................... | **35.00** |

●Hunter, R.F. Ltd.
  Purma Special box camera for 127 film, bakelite and metal body, f6.3 plastic lens,

1930s ................................ **35.00**

●Hurlbut Mfg. Co. (Belvedere, Ill.)
Velox magazine detective camera for plates, c.
1890 ................................. **775.00-800.00**

●Huttig, R., A.G. (Dresden, Germany)
Folding plate camera, red bellows, c. 1906... **25.00**
Helios folding plate camera, 185mm lens.... **55.00-60.00**
Ideal folding plate camera, red bellows,
9x12cm, c. 1908...................... **30.00-35.00**
Ideal Stereo plate camera, c. 1908.......... **100.00-125.00**
Lloyd folding camera, f6.8/135mm Goerz
Dagor................................ **40.00**
Record stereo camera for 9x18cm plates, f6.8
Huge Meyer Aristostigmat.............. **120.00**
Tropical folding plate camera, brown bellows **280.00-290.00**

●ICA, A.G. (Dresden, Germany, merged with
Zeiss in 1926)
Atom folding plate camera, c. 1910-20...... **90.00**
Atom folding plate camera, f4.5/65mm
Tessar, horizontal format, c. 1910-20..... **150.00**
Bebe folding plate camera, f4.5/75mm
Tessar, horizontal format.............. **175.00**
Bebe folding plate camera, f3.5 Tessar,
vertical format...................... **35.00-40.00**
Cameo stereo folding camera for plates, c.
1912................................. **150.00**
Cupido folding camera for 6x9cm plates,
f4.5/12cm Tessar..................... **40.00**
Folding plate camera, 9x12cm or 6x9cm size. **30.00**
Icar folding plate camera, 9x12cm f4.5/
135mm lens, 1920s.................... **25.00**
Icarette folding camera for 120 rollfilm...... **40.00-45.00**
Ideal folding plate camera, 6x9cm, f6.3/
90mm Tessar, 1920s.................... **35.00-40.00**
Ideal folding plate camera, 9x12cm, f4.5/
150mm Tessar, 1920s.................. **50.00**
Ideal folding plate camera, 9x12cm, f6.3/
135mm Doppel-Amatar, 1920s........... **65.00-70.00**
Juwel folding plate camera, 1920s.......... **100.00**
Lloyd folding stereo camera for plates or roll-
film, f6.8/90mm anast. Maximar lenses... **200.00-225.00**
Maximar folding plate camera, 9x12cm, f4.5/
135mm Novar......................... **40.00**
Minimal folding camera for sheet film,
9x12cm, f6.8/120 Goerz Dagor.......... **40.00**

Minimum Palos folding camera for plates,
  f2.7/80mm Tessar, 1930s .............  **100.00**
Nelson 225 folding plate camera, 9x12cm,
  f4.5/150mm Tessar, 1915 .............  **40.00-45.00**
Nero magazine box camera, 9x12cm plates,
  1905 ...............................  **65.00-70.00**
Niklas folding plate camera, f4.5 Litonar or
  Tessar, 1920s .......................  **35.00**
Nixie folding camera for 122 film, or 9x12cm
  plates, 1920s .......................  **50.00-60.00**
Periscop camera for 9x12cm plate .........  **25.00**
Plascop camera for plates or rollfilm, 1920s..  **80.00-100.00**
Polyscop stereo camera, f4.5 Tessar lenses,
  1920s ...............................  **175.00-190.00**
Reflex SLR for plates, f4.5/150mm Tessar,
  1920s ...............................  **100.00-125.00**
Reflex folding SLR camera, f4.5 Tessar .....  **200.00**
Sirene folding plate camera, f6.8 Eurynar lens  **20.00**
Stereo camera for 122 film, f6.3 Zeiss lens...  **200.00-210.00**
Stereo Ideal folding camera for plates, f6.3
  Tessar lenses ........................  **195.00-225.00**
Stereolette compact folding stereo camera for
  plates, 1912-26 ......................  **170.00**
Teddy folding plate camera, 9x12cm ........  **20.00**
Trilby 18 magazine box camera for 9x12cm
  plates for sheet film, c. 1912 .............  **100.00-110.00**
Trix camera for packfilm, c. 1915 ..........  **35.00-45.00**
Tropica 285 folding plate camera, tropical
  model, 9x12cm, teak body with brass trim.  **400.00-500.00**
Victrix folding camera for plates, f4.5/75mm  **80.00-100.00**
●Ihagee Kamerawerk (Dresden, Germany)
Duplex folding plate camera, 6x9 or 9x12cm,
  1920s ...............................  **140.00-150.00**
Duplex folding plate camera, vertical format,
  f3.5 Steinheil lens, 1940s ................  **35.00**
Exa SLR, various models .................  **30.00**
Exakta SLR for 127 film, f3.5 Tessar,
  1935 ...............................  **100.00-110.00**
Exakta B .............................  **110.00-120.00**
Exakta Junior .........................  **200.00**
Exakta 66 SLR for 120 film, 1930s-40s ......  **200.00**
Ihagee folding camera for 6x9 or 9x12cm
  plates, f4.5/105 Tessar ................  **35.00-40.00**

Ihagee folding camera for 120 film, f4.5
anast.................................... **20.00**
Paff SLR box camera for 120 film, 1920s.... **50.00**
Parvola telescoping camera for 127 film,
1930s ................................ **50.00**
Patent Klapp folding SLR for 6x9 or 9x12cm
plates, f4.5 Tessar, 1920s............... **220.00-225.00**
Stereo folding camera for plates, f6.3/80mm
Trioplan lens.......................... **150.00**
Ultrix folding camera for 127 film, 1930s.... **25.00**
●Ikoflex, Ikonta, Ikomat—see Zeiss-Ikon
●Japy & Cie (France)
Le Pascal box camera for rollfilm, late 1890s. **500.00**
●Joux, L. & Cie, (Paris, France)
Joux Alethoscope stereo camera for plates, c.
c. 1912................................ **175.00-200.00**
●Kalart Co. (New York, N.Y.)
Kalart Press camera, f4.5/127mm Wollensak
Raptar lens........................... **100.00-125.00**
●Kameret Jr. No. 2 box camera, ofr 1¼x2"
cut film, Japanese made, 1930s............ **10.00**
●Kemper, Alfred C. (Chicago, Ill.)
Kombi metal box camera for rollfilm (can
also be used as a viewer for transparencies),
1890s ................................ **100.00-125.00**
●Kengott, W. (Stuttgart, Germany)
Kengott folding plate camera, 6x9cm,
f4.8/105mm Leitmeyr Sytar, 1920s....... **30.00**
Kengott tropical plate camera, 10x15cm,
f4.5/150mm .......................... **200.00-225.00**
●Keystone Ferrotype Camera Co. (Philadel-
phia, Pa.)
Keystone box camera, model A............ **15.00-20.00**
Keystone street camera with developing tank
inside ................................ **130.00-135.00**
●Kinn (France)
Kinax folding camera for 120 film, f4.5/105
Berthiot lens.......................... **10.00-15.00**
●Kleffel, L.G. & Sohn, Berlin, Germany)
Kleffel field camera, 5x7", horizontal format
wood with brass trim and brass barrel..... **150.00-175.00**
●Knack Detective Camera—see Scovill

● Kochmann, Franz (Dresden, Germany)
Korelle K 35mm camera, 18x24mm size,
f2.8/35mm Tessar..................... 25.00-30.00
Korelle telescoping camera for 127 film,
f2.9/50mm Schneider Radionar......... 50.00
Korelle P folding camera for 4x6cm plates,
f2.8/75mm Tessar..................... 100.00
Reflex Korelle SLR for 120 film, 1930s...... 80.00-85.00
● Kombi—see Kemper
● Konishiroku Kogaku (Japan)
Pearl folding camera for 127 film, f4.5/50mm
Optor............................... 30.00-35.00
Pearl II folding camera for rollfilm, 6x9cm,
1920s .............................. 15.00-20.00
Pearlette folding camera for 127 film, f6.3/
75mm Rokuohsha Optar, 1920s.......... 25.00-30.00
Semi-Pearl folding camera for 120 rollfilm,
4x6cm, f4.5/75mm, 1930s-40s........... 30.00-40.00
● Krauss, G.A. (Stuttgard, Germany and Paris,
France)
Eka camera for 35mm film, f3.5/50mm Zeiss
Tessar, 1920s....................... 800.00
Peggy I folding camera for 35mm film,
f3.5/50mm Tessar, 1930s.............. 150.00-175.00
Peggy II rangefinder camera for 35mm film,
f2.8 Tessar, 1930s................... 160.00-175.00
Photo Revolver magazine camera for plates
or rollfilm, 1920s.....................1,500.00-1,750.00
Polyscop stereo camera for plates, 1910..... 160.00-175.00
Rollette folding camera for rollfilm, f6.3/
90mm Krauss Rollar, 1920s............. 35.00
● Krugener, Dr. Rudolf (Frankfurt, Germany)
Delta Periscop folding camera for plates,
wood with red bellows, c. 1900.......... 50.00
● Kurbi & Niggeloh (Germany)
Bilora Blitz Box box camera for 120 film.... 5.00
Bilora Radix box camera for 35mm film..... 15.00
● Lancaster, J. (Birmingham, England)
Instantograph half-plate view camera, brass-
barrel lens, c. 1894................... 175.00-180.00
Instantograph quarter-plate view camera,
brass-barrel lens, c. 1891............... 200.00
Kamrex quarter-plate camera, mahogany with
brass trim, red bellows, c. 1900........... 100.00-110.00

Lancaster Ladies' half-plate camera, 1890s.. **225.00**
Le Merveilleux quarter-plate camera, Aplanat
lens, 1890s.......................... **180.00**
●Lehmann, A. (Berlin, Germany)
Cane-handle detective camera, very rare, c.
1903 ................................ **6,000.00-8,000.00**
●Leica—see Leitz
●Leitz, Ernst, GmbH (Wetzlar, Germany)
Leica A 35mm viewfinder, f3.5/50mm
Elmax, 1920s....................... **4,000.00-4,500.00**
Leica A 35mm viewfinder, f3.5/50mm Elmar,
late 1920s........................... **350.00-400.00**
Leica B "Compur" model, 35mm viewfinder,
f3.5/50mm Elmar, dial-set Compur shut-
ter, 1926-29......................... **3,500.00-4,000.00**
Leica B "Compur" model 35mm viewfinder,
f3.5/50mm Elmar, rim-set Compur shutter,
1929-31 ............................ **3,500.00-3,750.00**
Leica C 35mm viewfinder, f3.5/50mm...... **275.00**
Leica D 35mm rangefinder, f3.5/50mm
Elmar, 1930s-40s.................... **175.00-200.00**
Leica E 35mm viewfinder, f3.5/50mm Elmar,
1930s-40s........................... **275.00**
Leica F (III) 35mm rangefinder, f3.5/50mm
Elmar, 1930s........................ **130.00-150.00**
Leica FF (250) (Reporter) rangefinder design-
ed to hold unusually long rolls of 35mm
film, 1930s-40s...................... **2,750.00**
Leica G (IIIa), f3.5/50mm Elmar, 1930s-40s. **125.00**
Leica G (IIIa), f2/50mm Summar.......... **125.00**

Leica III g, c. 1957, $275.

Leica III F, c. 1950, $150.

Leica Motor driven camera, price unknown.

Leica A, 1926-30, dial-set "compur" model, $4,000.

| | |
|---|---|
| Leica "Monte en Sarre" model (IIIa),<br>post World War II model.............. | 3,000.00 |
| Leica G (IIIb) without lens, 1930s-40s....... | 125.00 |
| Leica IIIc, f3.5/50mm Elmar............. | 110.00-115.00 |
| Leica IIIc, f2/50mm Summitar............ | 120.00 |
| Leica IIIc Model K (for "Kugellager,"<br>German for ball-bearing, denoting the type<br>of shutter produced for military use)...... | 500.00 |
| Leica IIIc "Luftwaffe" model............. | 700.00-1,000.00 |
| Leica IIc, late 1940s.................... | 125.00 |
| Leica Ic, c. 1949....................... | 200.00 |
| Leica IIIf rangefinder, f2/50mm Summitar,<br>1950-56 .............................. | 150.00 |
| Leica 72 35mm rangefinder, f3.5/50mm<br>Elmar, only 200 produced, 1954-57....... | 4,000.00-5,000.00 |
| ●Leroy, Lucien (Paris, France) | |
| Leroy Minimus stereo camera............. | 200.00-225.00 |
| Leroy Stereo Panoramique plate camera,<br>f8.5/80mm Goerz Doppel anast., c. 1906.. | 250.00-300.00 |
| ●Levy-Roth (Berlin, Germany) | |
| Levy-Roth Minigraph camera for 35mm film,<br>f3.5, c. 1915........................... | 1,500.00-1,750.00 |
| ●Lilliput detective camera (sold by Anthony),<br>disguised as a satchel, for plates........ | 1,500.00 |
| ●Linhof Parzisions Kamerawerk (Munich,<br>Germany) | |
| Stereo Panorama folding camera for plates,<br>f5.5/150mm Reitzschel Linar, 1920s...... | 275.00-285.00 |
| Technika I, f4.5 Tessar, early 1930s........ | 150.00 |
| ●Lionel Mfg. Co. (New York, N.Y.) | |
| Linex stereo miniature camera for rollfilm,<br>f8/30mm lenses, late 1940s............. | 45.00-50.00 |

●Lizars, J. (Glasgow, Scotland)
Challenge camera for rollfilm or plates, f6
Aldis or f6.8 Goerz, c. 1905. . . . . . . . . . . .     **90.00-100.00**
Challenge Dayspool tropical camera, mahog-
any body with red bellows. . . . . . . . . . . . .     **250.00**
Challenge stereo camera, model B, for plates,
teak with brass trim, Bausch & Lomb Rapid
Rectilinear lenses, c. 1905. . . . . . . . . . . . . .     **350.00**
Challenge stereo camera, model IB, Aldis
anast. lenses, c. 1910. . . . . . . . . . . . . . . . .     **700.00**
●Lloyd, Andrew J. & Co. (Boston, Mass.)
Lloyd box camera for glass plates. . . . . . . . . .     **20.00-25.00**
●Loeber Brothers (New York, N.Y.)
Folding plate camera, brass-barrel lens, 1890s     **200**

Twin Lens Reflex, c. 1910, by London
Stereoscopic Co., $200.

●London Stereoscopic & Photo Co. (London,
England)
Wet-plate stereo camera, sliding box type,
brass barrel lenses, 4x5″, c. 1855. . . . . . . . . **1,500.00-2,000.00**
●Lumiere & Cie (Lyon, France)
Lumiere Eljy 35mm camera, f3.5/50mm
Lypar lens, 1937. . . . . . . . . . . . . . . . . . . . . .     **50.00**
Lumiere Lumix F folding camera for rollfilm.     **5.00-10.00**
Lumiere Sinox folding camera for rollfilm,
f6.3. . . . . . . . . . . . . . . . . . . . . . . . . . . . . . . .     **10.00**
Lumiere Sterelux folding stereo camera for
116 film, f4.5/80mm Spector anast., c.
1920 . . . . . . . . . . . . . . . . . . . . . . . . . . . . . .     **150.00-160.00**
●Lundelius Mfg. Co. (Port Jervis, N.Y.)
Magazine camera for plates, 1890s. . . . . . . . . .     **150.00**

●Luttke, Dr. & Arndt (Wandsbek, Hamburg &
  Berlin, Germany)
  Folding camera for rollfilm, 8x10cm, Luttke
    Periplanat lens........................    50.00
  Folding horizontal format camera for 9x12cm
    plates, Luttke Periscop lens, red bellows...    70.00
●Mackenstein, H. (Paris, France)
  Francia folding stereo camera for plates, red
    bellows, c. 1906.....................    190.00
  Stereo Jumelle magazine camera for 9x18cm
    plates, c. 1893......................    200.00
●Magic Introduction Co. (New York, N.Y.)
  Photoret Watch Camera for sheet film, meni-
    scus lens, c. 1894....................    350.00-375.00
●Mamiya Camera Co. (Tokyo, Japan)
  Mamiyaflex TLR camera, f3.5/75mm, 1940s.    25.00
●Mandel—see Chicago Ferrotype Co.
●Manhattan Optical Co. (New York, N.Y.)
  Bo-Peep 5x7″ plate camera, brass lens.......    65.00
  Bo-Peep, Model B 4x5 folding plate camera,
    red bellows, c. 1890s.................    35.00
  Night-Hawk Detective camera for 4x5″
    plates, Rapid Achromatic lens, c. 1895....    375.00-400.00
  Wizard folding plate camera, 4x5″ or
    5x7″, various models.................    50.00-60.00
  Wizard 5x7″ "Cycle" long-focus camera,
    triple extension bellows................    100.00
●Marion & Co. Ltd. (London, England)
  Perfection 10x12″ folding field camera,
    f8 Dallmeyer Rapid Rectilinear lens, 1890s.    190.00-225.00
  Soho Reflex SLR for rollfilm, f4.5 Tessar....    250.00-260.00
  Soho quarter-plate camera, f3.5 lens........    190.00
  Soho Tropical Reflex, f3.5/150mm Dallmeyer
    lens, red bellows......................1,600.00-1,700.00
●Mason, Perry & Co. (Boston, Mass.)
  Mason Harvard all-metal pinhole camera for
    plates, meniscus lens, c. 1890............    140.00-150.00
●Mazo, E. (Paris, France)
  Mazo field and studio camera for 5x7″
    plates, f8 Mazo & Magenta lens, c. 1900...    200.00
●Memo—see Agfa, Ansco
●Mendel, Georges, (Paris, France)
  Mendel detective camera for plates, rapid
    rectilinear lens........................    140.00

●Mentor Kamerawerk (Dresden, Germany)—
  see Goltz & Breutmann
●Mergett, J.E., Co. (Newark, N.J.)
  Mergett Jem Jr. 120 box camera, 1940s . . . . . .          5.00
●Merit box camera for 127 film, bakelite body,
  f11 Rodenstock lens, c. 1935 . . . . . . . . . . . . .      20.00
●Mick-A-Matic camera for 126 film, shaped
  like Mickey Mouse's head, meniscus lens . . .        15.00-20.00
●Midas hand-crank camera, f2.5 lens . . . . . . . .    75.00-80.00
  Mikut Color Camera for three color separ-
  ation negatives on one plate, f3.5/130mm
  Mikutar, c. 1937 . . . . . . . . . . . . . . . . . . . . . .   280.00-300.00
●Mimosa I 35mm camera, f2.9/50mm Meyer
  Triplan, c. 1947 . . . . . . . . . . . . . . . . . . . . . . .      50.00
●Mimosa II 35mm camera, f2.9 Trioplan . . . . .          20.00
●Minolta (Chiyoda Kogaku Seiko Co. Ltd.,
  Osaka, Japan
  Autocord TLR, 6x6cm . . . . . . . . . . . . . . . . . .      35.00
  Minolta-Six folding camera for 120 film,
  f4.5/80mm Coronar anast. lens, 1930s . . . .        30.00
  Minolta 35 rangefinder, f2.8/45mm Kokkor,
  late 1940s . . . . . . . . . . . . . . . . . . . . . . . . . . .     65.00
  Semi-Minolta folding camera for 120 roll-
  film, f4.5/75mm Coronar anast. . . . . . . . . .       30.00
●Minox—see Valsts Electro-Techniska Fabrika
●Miroflex—see Contessa, Zeiss
●Mitsukoshi (Japan)
  Picny compact camera for 127 film, c. 1935 . .     75.00-80.00
●Monroe Camera Co. (Rochester, N.Y.;
  merged with Eastman-Kodak in 1907)
  Monroe folding plate camera, vest pocket
  size, 2x2½ " . . . . . . . . . . . . . . . . . . . . . . . . . . .   110.00-120.00

Multiscope & Film Co., Al-Vista panoramic camera for 5" film, c. 1898. $170.

Micro 16 by Whittaker Co., Los Angeles, Calif., c. 1950, $20.

Monroe folding plate camera, pocket size,
3½x3½ " ............................ **125.00**

Monroe Pocket Poco A folding plate camera,
3½x4¼ " ............................ **190.00-200.00**

Monroe Model 7 cycle camera for 5x7" plates,
Rapid Rectilinear lens ................. **90.00-100.00**

●Montgomery Ward & Co.
Model B 4x5", Wollensak shutter ........... **50.00**

●Monti, Charles (Paris, France)
Monte Carlo folding camera for 210 film,
f4.5/90mm, 1930s ................... **25.00**

●Moore & Co. (Liverpool, England)
Moore Aptus Ferrotype camera for plates,
meniscus lens, 1890s .................. **350.00-400.00**

●Multiscope & Film Co. (Burlington, Wisc.)
Al-Vista panoramic camera for 4" wide rollfilm, 1891-1900s ...................... **150.00-175.00**

Al-Vista panoramic camera for 5" wide rollfilm, 1891-1900s ..................... **150.00-180.00**

Al-Vista Panoramic camera, model 5f ....... **350.00**

●Murer & Duroni (Milan, Italy)
Express magazine box camera for plates, c.
1900 ............................... **80.00**

Murer reflex camera for 6x9cm plates, f4.5
Murer anast ........................ **90.00**

Murer stereo folding camera, f4.5/60mm
Murer anast ........................ **250.00-300.00**

●Mutschler, Robertson & Co.—see Ray
Camera Co.

●Nagel, Dr. August, Camerawerk (Stuttgart,
Germany)
Nagel 18 folding camera for 6x9cm plates,
f6.3 Nagel anast., c. 1928 .............. **60.00-70.00**

Nagel 18 folding camera for 6x9cm plates,
f4.5 Elmar lens ...................... **200.00**

Nagel 30 folding camera for 9x12cm plates,
f6.3 Nagel anast ...................... **60.00**

Pupille for 127 film, f2 Schneider Xenar,
1930s ............................. **150.00**

Rance camera for 127 film, f4.5/50mm
Nagel, 1930s ....................... **130.00**

Recomar 33 camera for plates, f4.5/135mm
lens ............................... **50.00**

●National Camera (England
 Half-plate folding field camera, f6.3 seven
 inch lens.............................. **120.00**
●Nettel Kamerawerk (Sontheim-Heilbronn
 Germany; mergede with Contessa in 1919
 and Zeiss in 1926)
 Nettel Argus detective camera, monocular
 eyepiece............................... **700.00**
 Nettel Deckrullo camera for 9x12cm plates,
 f6.3 135mm Zeiss Tessar................ **125.00**
 Nettel folding camera for 9x12cm plates,
 f6.3/135mm Tessar.................... **45.00**
 Nettel Sonnet tropical camera, f4.5/75mm
 Tessar................................ **375.00-400.00**
●New Ideas Mfg. Co. (New York, N.Y.)
 Magazine camera detective box, wood body.. **375.00-400.00**
●New York Ferrotype Co. (New York, N.Y.)
 Tintype camera for postcard-size tintypes,
 Wollensak shutter, c. 1906.............. **135.00**
●Newman & Guardia (London, England)
 Baby Sibyl folding camera for 4x6cm plates,
 f4.5/75mm Ross Express lens, c. 1913..... **100.00**
 Folding reflex camera for 6x9cm plates, f2.9. **130.00**
 New Ideal Sibyl folding camera for plates,
 f4.5/135mm Tessar, c. 1913............. **75.00**
 New Special Sibyl folding camera for 120
 film, f4.5 Ross Express lens.............. **75.00**
 Sibyl folding camera for 6x9cm plates, f6.3/
 120mm Tessar, 1907-20................ **120.00-125.00**
●Nodark—see Popular Photograph Co.
●Nomar No. 1 metal box camera for 127 film.. **10.00**
●Norris folding camera for 120 film, f2.9 lens. **30.00**
●Noviflex SLR for 120 film, f2.9 Schneider
 Radionar, c. 1930s..................... **80.00**
●Orion Werk (Hanover, Germany
 Box camera for 6x9cm glass plates, f17 lens.. **50.00**
 Folding camera for 9x12cm plates, f6.3
 Meyer Trioplan....................... **25.00**
●Palmer & Longking
 Half-plate daguerreotype camera, bellows
 type ................................. **4,000.00**
●Panoram—see Eastman-Kodak

●Papigny (Paris, France)
  Jumelle stereo camera for 8x8cm plates,
    1890s .................................    250.00-300.00
●PDQ—see Anthony, Chicago Ferrotype Co.
●Perka Prazisions Kamerawerk (Munich,
  Germany)
  Perka folding camera for plates, f4.5/150mm
    Tessar, 1920s..........................    50.00
●Perken, Son & Rayment (London, England)
  Studio full-plate camera, 1890s.............    125.00-130.00
●Petitax novelty camera for rollfilm.........    15.00
●Petri Camera Co. (Japan)
  Petri 6x6 folding camera for 120 film, f3.5/
    75mm, 1940s...........................    15.00-20.00
●Photak Corp. (Chicago, Ill.)
  Foldex folding camera for 620 film.........    5.00-10.00
●Photo Materials Co. (Rochester, N.Y.)
  Trokonette camera......................    300.00-400.00
●Photavit—see Bolta
●Photoscopic (Brussels, Belgium)
  Photoscopic 35mm camera, f3.5/45mm,
    1930s ...............................    200.00-225.00
●Photo-See box camera, art deco style.......    20.00
●Photosphere—see Compagnie Francaise de
  Photographie Pignons, A.G. (Switzerland)
  Alpha Reflex SLR for 35mm film, designed
    by Jacques Bolsey, 1940s...............    300.00

Pearl II, c. 1954, Japan. $45.

Polaroid Model 95, c. 1950, $25-$30.

Bolsey SLR for 35mm film, f2.8/50mm Bolca anast., late 1930s..................... **500.00**

●Pipon (Paris, France)

Pipon magazine camera for 9x12cm plates, f9, 1900............................. **50.00-60.00**

●Planovista Seeing Camera Ltd.—see Bentzin

●Plaubel Feinmechanik & Optic (Frankfurt, Germany)

Plaubel Makina I folding camera for sheet film, f2.9/100mm Anticomar, Compur dial set shutter. 1920-32.................... **125.00-150.00**

Plaubel Makina II folding viewfinder press camera, f2.9/100mm Anticomar, Compur, 1938................................... **150.00**

Plaubel Makina III folding camera, f2.9/ 100mm Anticomar, Compur, c. 1930..... **150.00**

Plaubel folding cameras for 6x9cm or 9x12cm plates, Compur shutter................ **40.00-50.00**

Rollop folding camera for 120 film, f2.8/ 75mm Anticomar, Compur, 1930s........ **140.00-150.00**

Stereo Makina folding camera for 6x13cm plates, f2.9/90mm Anticomar lenses, black bellows, 1930s...................... **600.00**

●Poco—see Monroe, Rochester Optical Co.

●Pocket Platos folding camera for 6x9cm plates, f6.2/90mm Splendor lens.......... **75.00**

●Popular Photograph Co. (New York, N.Y.)

No-Dark box camera for ferrotype plates, all wood body, c. 1899.................... **600.00-700.00**

●Premier Instrument Co. (New York, N.Y.)

Kardon 35mm SLR Leica copy, f2 Ektar lens, 1940s............................ **140.00-150.00**

●Premium box camera for plates, 1890s...... **200.00**

●Premo—see Eastman-Kodak, Rochester Optical Co.

●Puck—see Thornton-Picard

●Putnam, E. (New York, N.Y.)

Marvel folding view camera, 5x8″ horizontal format, Scovil Waterbury lens, 1890s..... **125.00-150.00**

●QRS DeVry Corp. (Chicago, Ill.)

QRS Kamra, bakelite box camera for 35mm film, f7.7 Graf anast., late 1920s......... **25.00-35.00**

●Rajar No. 6 folding camera for 120 film, 1920s ................................ **20.00-25.00**

Reflecta Stelo, by Welta Kamera Werke, Germany, $20.

Imperial Reflex for 620 film, Herco (Herbert George Co.), Chicago, Ill., 1940s, $8.

●Ray Camera Co. (Rochester, N.Y.)
   Ray box camera for 301/2x301/2" plates....    **50.00-60.00**
   Ray Junior box camera for 2½" plates, 1890s    **75.00**
   Ray No. 1 wooden folding camera for plates,
     red bellows, 1890s.....................    **35.00**
   Ray No. 2 folding camera for 5x7" plates, red
     bellows..............................    **40.00-45.00**
●Recomar—see Eastman-Kodak, Nagel Camerawerk
●Reflex Camera Co. (Yonkers, N.Y.)
   Junior Reflex box camera for plates, c. 1905.    **150.00**
   Patent Reflex Hand Camera with red focusing
     hood.................................    **400.00**
   Reflex folding focal camera for plates, post-
     card size, c. 1912.....................    **130.00**
   Reflex camera for plates, 4x5..............    **250.00-300.00**
   Reflex camera for plates, 5x7", f16/210
     mm anast., 1898......................    **300.00-350.00**
●Reichenbach, Morey & Will Co. (Rochester, N.Y.)
   Alta D folding camera for 5x7" plates.......    **75.00**
●Reitzschel, A. Heinrich, GmbH (Munich, Germany)

Clack folding camera for 9x12cm plates, red
bellows, f6.3 ....................... 55.00-60.00

Heli-Clack folding camera for 9x12cm plates,
f6.8 double anast ..................... 80.00

Cosmo Clack stereo folding camera, f4.5
Reitzschel c. 1914 .................... 175.00-200.00

Reitzschel folding camera for 6x9 plates,
f6.8/105mm Dailyt lens ............... 35.00

Special Wiphot folding camera for 9x12cm
plates, f515 anast .................... 60.00

Le Reve folding camera for plates or rollfilm, made in France, f6.3 Becker lens, red
bellows, c. 1908 ...................... 150.00

●Rex Magazine Camera Co. (Chicago, Ill.)
Rex magazine camera for 4x5″ plates, 1899.. 100.00
Rex magazine camera, 2x2″ format ........ 65.00-70.00

●Richard, Jules (Paris, France)
Glyphoscope metal stereo camera, meniscus
lens, 45x107mm size, c. 1905 ............ 125.00-150.00

Homeos stereo camera for 35mm film,
f4.5/28mm Zeiss Krauss lens, c. 1914 ..... 2,000.00

Verascope stereo box camera, metal body,
fixed focus lenses, c. 1898 ............. 125.00-150.00

●Rochester Optical Co. (Rochester, N.Y.;
merged with Kodak 1907)
Cyclone cameras—pre-1901 Cyclone cameras
are listed under Western Camera Mfg. Co.

Richoflex Model VII, by Ricoh, c.
1950s, $25.

No. 2 Buckeye, American Camera Mfg. Co., Rochester, N.Y. C. 1900, $30.

5x7 Reversible Back Premo Rochester Optical & Camera Co., c. 1898, $100-$120.

Premo, 1902, by Rochester Optical Co., Rochester, N.Y. $50.

| | |
|---|---|
| Cycle Poco folding camera for 4x5″ plates, Bausch & Lomb lens, red bellows, various models, 1890s | 50.00-60.00 |
| Cycle Poco folding camera for 5x7″ plates, red bellows, various models, early 1900s | 50.00-60.00 |
| Cyclone Junior box camera for 3½x3½″ plates | 25.00-30.00 |
| Cyclone Senior box camera for 4x5″ plates | 25.00 |
| Favorite box camera for 8x10″ plates, Emile No. 5 lens, 1890s | 175.00-200.00 |
| Gem Poco box camera for 4x5″ plates | 50.00 |
| Gem Poco folding camera for 4x5″ plates, red bellows, 1890s | 70.00-80.00 |
| Handy detective box camera for 4x5″ plates, 1892 | 110.00-120.00 |
| Ideal folding view camera, 4x5″ | 75.00-100.00 |
| Ideal folding view camera, 8x10″ | 100.00-125.00 |
| King Poco folding view camera for 5x7″ plates | 75.00-100.00 |

| | |
|---|---:|
| Magazine Cyclone No. 2 box camera for 4x5" plates, 1890s.......................... | **50.00** |
| Magazine Cyclone No. 3 box camera for 4x5" plates................................. | **40.00** |
| Magazine Cyclone No. 4 box camera for 3¼ x4¼" plates, 1890s..................... | **30.00-45.00** |
| Magazine Cyclone No. 5 box camera for 4x5" plates, 1890s.......................... | **40.00-45.00** |
| Monitor View Camera for 8x10" plates, damaged bellows..................... | **75.00-100.00** |
| Pocket Poco folding camera for 3¼x4¼" plates, red bellows, 1890s............... | **30.00-40.00** |
| Poco Telephoto folding camera for 4x5" plates, red bellows, early 1890s........... | **50.00** |
| Poco Telephoto folding camera for 5x7" plates, red bellows, Bausch & Lomb lens, early 1900s............................ | **75.00** |
| Premier detective box camera for 4x5" or 5x7" plates, 1890s...................... | **125.00-150.00** |
| Premo folding camera for 4x5" plates, models A-E, red bellows, Bausch & Lomb lens, c. 1900.......................... | **50.00-75.00** |
| Premo folding camera for 5x7" plates, red bellows, c. 1900....................... | **50.00-60.00** |
| Premo Long Focus folding camera for plates, red bellows........................... | **80.00-90.00** |
| Rochester Stereo folding camera for plates, red bellows, Bausch & Lomb lenses....... | **400.00** |
| Rochester folding view camera for 4x5" plates, maroon bellows................. | **100.00** |

Moniter View Camera (without lens), Rochester c. 1900, $60-$75.

Samoca 35, San Ei, Japan, c. 1956. $15-$25.

●Rodenstock Optische Werke (Munich, Germany)
Clarovid folding camera for rollfilm, f4.5 Trinar anast., c. 1932 . . . . . . . . . . . . . . . . . . **50.00**
Rodenstock folding camera for 120 film, f2.9 Rodenstock Trinar lens . . . . . . . . . . . . . . . **25.00**
●Rollei—see Franke & Heidecke
●Ross, Thomas & Son (London, England)
Sutton Panoramic Camera (made for Thomas Sutton by Ross); only known sales are two in 1972 for $25,000 & $28,000 respectively. **30,000**
●Scenex plastic novelty camera for 828 film, meniscus lens . . . . . . . . . . . . . . . . . . . . . . . . **10.00**
●Schmitz & Thienemann (Dresden, Germany)
Uniflex Reflex Meteor SLR box camera for 6.5x9cm plates, f4.5/105mm Meyer Trioplan, c. 1931 . . . . . . . . . . . . . . . . . . . . . . . **175.00**
●Scovill Manufacturing Co. (New York, N.Y.; merged with Anthony in 1902)
Detective box camera for 4x5″ plates, oak body, string set, c. 1890 . . . . . . . . . . . . . . . . **750.00-800.00**
Detective camera for 4x5″ plates, red bellows, top-loading, leather exterior, 1886 . . . . . . . . **800.00-900.00**
Knack detective box camera for 4x5″ plates, early 1890s . . . . . . . . . . . . . . . . . . . . . . . . . . **650.00**
Mascot box camera for 4x5″ plates, string-set, early 1890s . . . . . . . . . . . . . . . . . . . . . . . . . . **500.00-600.00**
Triad detective box camera for 4x5″ plates or rollfilm, string-set, 1892 . . . . . . . . . . . . . . . **450.00-475.00**
Scovill folding view camera for 4x5″ plates, Waterbury lens, c. 1888 . . . . . . . . . . . . . . . . **150.00**
Scovill folding view camera for 5x8″ plates, Waterbury lens, c. 1888 . . . . . . . . . . . . . . . . **125.00**
Scovill folding view camera for 8x10″ plates, Waterbury lens, c. 1888 . . . . . . . . . . . . . . . . **165.00-180.00**
Scovill stereo folding camera for 5x8″ plates, Waterbury lenses, c. 1885 . . . . . . . . . . . . . . **400.00**
Stereo Solograph folding camera for plates, 1899 . . . . . . . . . . . . . . . . . . . . . . . . . . . . . . **300.00-400.00**
Waterbury detective box camera, all wood, side-loading plates, 4x5″ . . . . . . . . . . . . . . . **500.00-600.00**
●Secam (Paris, France)
Stylophot pen-shaped camera for 16mm film, standard and colored models, f6.3 lens . . . . **100.00-150.00**

111

Stylophot pen-shaped camera for 16mm film,
    deluxe model, f3.5/27mm Roussel anast...    **150.00-200.00**

●Seneca Camera Co. (Rochester, N.Y.)

    Busy-Bee box camera for 4x5″ plates, 1903...    **75.00-90.00**

    Chautauqua folding camera for 4x5″ plates,
    Wollensak lens......................    **30.00**

    Chief camera for rollfilm.................    **10.00**

    Competitor folding field camera for 5x7″ or
    8x10″ plates...........................    **90.00**

    Filmet folding camera for filmpacks, c. 1916.    **20.00**

    Seneca box camera for 4x5″ plates..........    **20.00**

    Seneca folding camera for 3¼x4¼″ plates,
    f16 Wollensak.........................    **25.00**

    Seneca folding camera for 4x5″ plates.......    **35.00-40.00**

    Seneca folding camera for 5x7″ plates,
    Seneca anast...........................    **50.00**

    Seneca Pocket Jr. No. 1 folding camera for
    rollfilm...............................    **20.00**

    Seneca Pocket Jr. No. 3A folding camera for
    rollfilm...............................    **40.00-50.00**

    Seneca Scout No. 2A folding camera, Wollen-
    sak lens, c. 1916.....................    **15.00**

    Seneca Scout No. 3 folding camera, c. 1916..    **10.00-15.00**

    Seneca Scout No. 3A folding camera, for 122
    film, c. 1916..........................    **10.00**

    Seneca stereo folding view camera for 5x7″
    plates, Wollensak lenses, c. 1910........    **225.00**

    Seneca vest pocket folding camera for 127
    film, f7.7 Seneca anast.................    **25.00**

    Seneca 5x7″ view camera, f6.8 Goerz Syntor
    lens..................................    **75.00**

    Seneca 5x7″ Improved view camera, Wollen-
    sak, lens..............................    **75.00**

    Trio No. 1A folding camera for 120 film.....    **15.00-20.00**

    Uno folding camera for filmpacks, Wollensak
    brass lens, black bellows, c. 1910.........    **15.00-20.00**

●Sears, Roebuck & Co. (Chicago, Ill.)

    (Cameras made for Sears by various com-
    panies were sold under the Seroco name,
    Seroco being an abbreviation for Sears,
    Roebuck & Co.

    Seroco Delmar box camera for 4x5″ plates...    **20.00-30.00**

    Seroco folding camera for 4x5″ plates,
    Seroco lens, red bellows, c. 1901.........    **50.00**

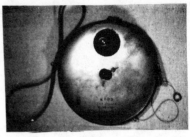

Stirn's Vest Camera, 1888, by R. Stirn, Berlin, $1,000.

4x5 Seneca folding camera for plates, $35-$40. It was manufactured by Seneca Camera Co., of Rochester, N.Y.

| | |
|---|---:|
| Seroco folding camera for 5x7″ plates....... | **60.00** |
| Seroco folding camera for 6½x8½″ plates, red bellows.......................... | **90.00** |
| Seroco stereo folding camera for 5x7″ plates, red bellows.......................... | **230.00-240.00** |
| ●Shew J.F. & Co. (London, England) | |
| Eclipse camera for 3¼x4¼″ plates, f8 Wray brass-barrel lens, 1890s........... | **200.00-225.00** |
| Xit camera for plates, brown bellows, c. 1900 | **200.00** |
| ●Signal Corps (USA) | |
| Press camera, 2¼x3¼″, olive drab, only 300 made ............................... | **225.00** |
| ●Sinclair, James A. & Co. (London, England) | |
| Una half-plate folding camera, f6.8/7″ Goerz lens, wood body, 1890s................ | **200.00-225.00** |
| ●Six-16; Six-20—see Eastman-Kodak | |
| ●Smith, John M. (Chicago, Ill.) | |
| View camera, 5x7″, Wollensak lens......... | **35.00** |
| ●Sonnar—see Contessa-Nettel | |
| ●Steineck Kamerawerk (Tutzing, Germany) | |
| Steineck ABC Wristwatch camera for eight exposures on circular film disc, f2.5/12mm Steinheil lens, 1949..................... | **300.00** |
| ●Steinheil, G.A. Sons (Munich, Germany) | |
| Casca I SLR Leica copy, f2.8/50mm Cilminar lens, c. 1940s........................ | **100.00-125.00** |
| Detective camera for 9x12cm plates, Steinheil lens, 1890s........................ | **500.00** |
| Tropical camera for 9x12cm plates, brown bellows............................... | **200.00-250.00** |

●Stirn, C.P. (Stirn & Lyon, N.Y.; Rudoph
  Stirn, Berlin, Germany)
  Stirn's concealed vest camera for six expo-
  sures on circular glass plates............ **1,250.00-1,500.00**
  Stirn's Wonder Panoramic, c. 1889......... **1,200.00**
●Stockig, Huge (Dresden, Germany)
  Union folding camera for 9x12cm plates, f6.8
  Union Aplanat...................... **70.00**
●Sumner, J. Chase (Foxcroft, Me.)
  Stereo box camera for rollfilm............ **350.00**
●Sunart Photo Co. (Rochester, N.Y.)
  Sunart folding view camera for 4x5″ or 5x7″
  plates, Bausch & Lomb lens, 1890s....... **50.00-65.00**
  Sunart Junior box camera for 4x5″ plates.... **25.00**
●Suter, E. (Basel, Switzerland)
  Detective magazine camera for 9x12cm plates,
  f8 Suter lens, c. 1893.................. **250.00-300.00**
●Taisei Kokii (Japan)
  Welmy Six folding camera for 120 film, f4.5
  Trionar ............................. **25.00-30.00**
●Takahashi Kogaku (Japan)
  Gelto DIII camera for 127 film, f3.5/50mm
  Grimmel, 1930s...................... **25.00**
●Talbot, Romain (Berlin, Germany)
  Errtee button tintype cylindrical "cannon"
  camera for 100 tintypes, with processing
  tank below, f4.5/60mm lens............ **550.00-600.00**
  Errtee folding camera for 9x12cm plates,
  f4.5/135mm Laack Pololyt............. **50.00-60.00**
  Errtee folding camera for 9x12cm exposurers
  on rollfilm, f4.5/105 Talbotar lens........ **30.00-40.00**
●Tauber folding camera for 9x12cm plates,
  German-made, f8 Aplanat lens, 1920s..... **25.00**
●Tenax—see Goerz, Zeiss
●Thornton-Picard Mfg. Co. (Altringham,
  England)
  Puck Special box camera for 4x5″ plates..... **50.00**
  Ruby Deluxe SLR quarter-plate camera, f4.5
  Goerz Dogmar lens................... **90.00**
  Ruby Duplex SLR quarter-plate tropical
  camera, f6.3 Cooke anast.............. **650.00-700.00**
  Ruby folding camera for 3¼x4¼″ plates,
  f6.5 Cooke anast..................... **100.00-125.00**

Ruby folding camera for 5x7″ plates, f5 Zeiss Unar lens, c. 1890................ **150.00**

Ruby Special Reflex camera, 2¼x3¼″, f4.5 Cooke anast......................... **100.00**

Stereo Puck box camera for 120 rollfilm, meniscus lens, 1920s................... **65.00**

Thornton-Picard SLR, 2¼x3¼″, Dallmeyer lens................................... **80.00**

Thornton-Picard SLR, 4x5″, f4.5 six-inch Wray Lustrar lens..................... **80.00-90.00**

●Thowe Camerawerk (Berlin, Germany) Thowe folding camera for 9x21cm plates, f6/ 135mm Doxanar lens, c. 1910............ **35.00-45.00**

●Ticka—see Houghton

●Tisdell Camera & Mfg. Co. (New York, N.Y.) T&W detective box camera for 3¼x4¼″ plates, all wood, c. 1888................ **1,300.00**

Tisdell hand camera, leather covered box, 1893 ................................... **600.00**

●Tivoli (London, England) Mahogany half-plate camera, rectilinear lens, c. 1895............................... **200.00**

●Turret Camera Co. (Brooklyn, N.Y.) Panoramic view camera for 4x10″ plates, c. 1905.............................. **350.00-400.00**

●Underwood, E. T. (Birmingham, England) Underwood field camera for 8x11cm plates, f11 brass barrel lens.................... **125.00**

●United States Camera Corp. (Chicago, Ill.) Reflex TLR camera..................... **10.00**
Vagabond camera....................... **5.00**

Univex Mercury, 1938, Universal Camera Corp., Lockport, N.Y.

Univex Mercury II, 1943, Universal Camera Corp., $25.

●Universal Camera Corp. (New York, N.Y.)
  Buccaneer rangefinder camera for 35mm
    film, f3.5/50mm Tricor lens, 1940s . . . . . . .    10.00-15.00
  Corsair camera for 35mm film, f4.5/50mm
    Univex lens . . . . . . . . . . . . . . . . . . . . . . . . . . . . .    15.00
  Iris camera for No. 00 Universal film, f7.9/
    50mm Vitar lens, c. 1940 . . . . . . . . . . . . . . .    15.00
  Mercury Model CC (first Mercury model) for
    No. 200 Universal 35mm film, f3.5/35mm
    Tricor lens, 1938 . . . . . . . . . . . . . . . . . . . . . .    25.00
  Mercury II for 35mm film, f2.7/35mm Tricor
    lens, 1940 . . . . . . . . . . . . . . . . . . . . . . . . . . . .    25.00
  Meteor camera for 620 film . . . . . . . . . . . . . .    10.00-15.00
  Roamer I folding camera for 620 film, f11
    lens . . . . . . . . . . . . . . . . . . . . . . . . . . . . . . . . .    5.00-10.00
  Roamer 63 folding camera for 620 film, f6.3/
    100mm lens . . . . . . . . . . . . . . . . . . . . . . . . . .    15.00
  Twinflex TLR for No. 00 rollfilm, plastic
    body, meniscus lens . . . . . . . . . . . . . . . . . . .    10.00-15.00
  Uniflex TLR for 120 or 620 film, models I
    and II, f4.5/75mm Universal lens, 1948 . . .    10.00
  Univex plastic box camera for No. 00 film,
    model A, 1936 . . . . . . . . . . . . . . . . . . . . . . . .    10.00
●Universal Radio Mfg. Co.
  Cameradio TLR box camera built into a small
    rectangular tube radio, late 1940s . . . . . . . . .    100.00
●Valsts Electro-Techniska Fabrika (Riga,
  Latvia)
  Minox I 8x11cm subminiature viewfinder
    camera, original model made by Walter
    Zapp, steel body, f3.5/15mm Minostigmat
    lens, 1937 . . . . . . . . . . . . . . . . . . . . . . . . . . .    300.00-400.00
  Minox II, made in Wetzlar, Germany, alum-
    inum body . . . . . . . . . . . . . . . . . . . . . . . . . . .    60.00
  Minox III . . . . . . . . . . . . . . . . . . . . . . . . . . . . . .    70.00
  Minox IIIS, gold-plated model . . . . . . . . . . . . .    500.00-600.00
  Minox "USSR" model, 1940 . . . . . . . . . . . . . .    480.00-500.00
  Minox A, made in Wetzlar, f3.5 Complan
    lens . . . . . . . . . . . . . . . . . . . . . . . . . . . . . . . . .    60.00
●Vega (Geneva, Switzerland)
  Vega folding camera for plates, looks like
    a book hinged at one side with lens in
    the "binding", c. 1900 . . . . . . . . . . . . . . . . .    350.00-400.00

Minox B, a subminiature, 1958, Germany, $350.

Voigtlander Bessa, c. 1939. $50.

● Victo (London, England)

| | |
|---|---|
| Folding field camera, full-plate, brass-barrel lens, c. 1900 | **150.00-160.00** |
| Folding field camera, half-plate, brass-barrel lens, c. 1890 | **86.00-90.00** |

● Viflex SLR box camera for 4x5" plates, c. 1905 .............................. **150.00**

● Vita-Flex TLR for 120 film, German-made, f4.5 lens, 1940s .......................... **10.00-15.00**

● Vive Camera Co. (Chicago, Ill.)

| | |
|---|---|
| M.P.C. (Mechanical Plate Changing) magazine box camera for 4x5" plates, c. 1900 | **50.00** |
| Vive No. 1 box camera for plates, c. 1897 | **75.00** |
| Vive No. 2 box camera for plates, 1897 | **50.00** |
| Vive No. 4 box camera, focusing model, c. 1899 | **50.00** |
| Vive Tourist box camera for 4x5" plates, c. 1897 | **60.00** |
| Vive Stereo box camera for plates | **475.00-500.00** |

● Voigtlander & Son (Braunschweig, Germany)

| | |
|---|---|
| Alpin folding camera for 9x12cm plates, horizontal format, f4.5/135mm Heliar lens | **135.00** |
| Avus folding camera for 9x12cm plates, f4.5/135mm Skopar, 1920s | **35.00** |
| Bergheil folding camera for 6x9cm plates, f4.5/105mm Heliar lens, c. 1930 | **50.00** |

Bergheil Deluxe folding camera for 6x9cm
plates, f4.5/105mm Heliar lens, green
leather covering and green bellows, nickel
trim . . . . . . . . . . . . . . . . . . . . . . . . . . . . . .     **175.00**
Bergheil folding camera for 9x12cm plates,
f4.5/135mm Heliar lens, c. 1920s . . . . . . . .     **50.00**
Bergheil Deluxe folding camera for 9x12cm
plates, green leather covering and green
bellows . . . . . . . . . . . . . . . . . . . . . . . . . . . . . .     **235.00**
Bessa folding camera for rollfilm, f3.5
Skopar, 1930s . . . . . . . . . . . . . . . . . . . . . . . .     **50.00**
Bessa I folding camera for rollfilm, f3.5/
105mm Skopar . . . . . . . . . . . . . . . . . . . . . . .     **60.00**
Bessa 6x6 ''Baby Bessa'' for 120 film, f3.5/
75mm Voigtar, 1930s . . . . . . . . . . . . . . . . ...     **45.00**
Bessa 46 folding camera for 120 rollfilm,
f3.5/75mm Voightar lens . . . . . . . . . . . . . .     **50.00-60.00**
Bessa folding rangefinder camera, f3.5/
105mm Heiliar, C. 1936 . . . . . . . . . . . . . . . .     **100.00**
Brilliant TLR, f7.7 Voigtar . . . . . . . . . . . . . . .     **10.00-15.00**
Inos II folding bed camera for 120 film, f4.5/
105mm Skopar, 1930s . . . . . . . . . . . . . . . . .     **35.00-40.00**
Jubilar folding camera for 120 film, f9
Voigtar . . . . . . . . . . . . . . . . . . . . . . . . . . . . . .     **10.00-15.00**
Perkeo folding camera for 3x4cm exposures
on 127 film, f4.5/55mm Heliar, late 1930s.     **75.00-85.00**
Prominent folding camera for 120 film, f4.5/
105mm Heliar, early 1930s . . . . . . . . . . . . .     **300.00-400.00**
Stereflektoskop stereo camera for plates, f4.5
Heliar . . . . . . . . . . . . . . . . . . . . . . . . . . . . . . .     **175.00-200.00**
Superb TLR for 120 film, f3.5/75mm
Skopar, 1930s . . . . . . . . . . . . . . . . . . . . . . .     **125.00**
Vag folding camera for 6x9cm and 9x12cm
plates, f6.3 Voigtar, 1920s . . . . . . . . . . . . .     **20.00-25.00**
Virtus folding camera for 120 film, f3.5/
75mm Heliar c. 1930s . . . . . . . . . . . . . . . . .     **125.00-150.00**
●Vokar Corp. (USA)
Vokar I rangefinder camera for 35mm film,
f2.8 Vokar anast., 1940s . . . . . . . . . . . . . . .     **85.00**
Vokar II rangefinder camera for 35mm film. .     **75.00**
●Voss, W. (Ulm, Germany)
Diax II rangefinder camera for 35mm film,
f2 Xenon, 1940s . . . . . . . . . . . . . . . . . . . . . .     **25.00-30.00**

●Walker Mfg. Co. (Palmyra, N.Y.)
Takiv cardboard and leatherette magazine
camera for dry plates, c. 1892 . . . . . . . . . . .            **1,000.00**
●Wanaus, Josef & Co. (Vienna, Austria)
Full-plate view camera for 5x7″ plates,
c. 1900 . . . . . . . . . . . . . . . . . . . . . . . . . . . . .       **150.00-200.00**
●Watson, W. & Sons (London, England)
Half-plate field camera, f8 Watson brass-
barel lens, late 1880s . . . . . . . . . . . . . . . . . .     **200.00-250.00**
●Welta Kamerawerke (Waurich & Weber, Frei-
tal, Germany)
Welta folding camera for 6x9cm plates, f4.5/
105mm Xenar lens . . . . . . . . . . . . . . . . . . . .          **35.00**
Welta folding camera for 9x12cm plates f3.5
Rodenstock Eurynar lens . . . . . . . . . . . . . .       **15.00-200.00**
Welta Perfekta folding TLR for 120 film,
f3.8/75mm Tessar, 1930s . . . . . . . . . . . . . .          **150.00**
Welta Perle folding camera for 120 film, f2.8
Xenar lens . . . . . . . . . . . . . . . . . . . . . . . . . .         **25.00-30.00**
Welta Reflekta TLR for 120 film, f3.5 Pololyt
lens . . . . . . . . . . . . . . . . . . . . . . . . . . . . . . . .          **35.00**
Welta Superfekta folding TLR for 120 film,
f3.8/105mm Tessar lens, 1930s . . . . . . . . . .      **150.00-160.00**
Weltaflex TLR for 120 film, f3.5/75mm Lud-
wig Meritar, c. 1950 . . . . . . . . . . . . . . . . . .          **35.00**
Weltax for 120 film, f2.8/75mm Tessar, late
1930s . . . . . . . . . . . . . . . . . . . . . . . . . . . . . .        **20.00-25.00**
Welta folding camera for 35mm film, f2.8/
50mm Tessar, 1930s . . . . . . . . . . . . . . . . . .          **25.00**
Weltini folding camera for 35mm film, f2
Xenon lens, coupled rangefinder, c. 1937 . .        **25.00**
Weltur folding camera for 120 film, f2.8/
75mm Tessar, 1930s . . . . . . . . . . . . . . . . . .          **125.00**
●Western Camera Mfg. Co. (Chicago, Ill.)
(These Cyclone cameras were made before
Western became part of the Rochester Op-
tical and Camera Co. in 1899)
Cyclone Senior box camera for 4x5″ plates . . .        **25.00**
Cyclone Junior box camera for 3½″ square
plates . . . . . . . . . . . . . . . . . . . . . . . . . . . . . .          **35.00**
Magazine Cyclone No. 2 . . . . . . . . . . . . . . . . . .           **60.00**
Magazine Cyclone No. 3, 4x5″35.00
Magazine Cyclone No. 4, 3¼x4¼″ . . . . . . . . .       **35.00-45.00**

Magazine Cyclone No. 5 box camera for 4x5″
plates, 1890s......................... 40.00-45.00
●White, David Co. (Milwaukee, Wisc.)
Realist camera for 35mm film, German-
made, f2.8 Cassar..................... 30.00-35.00
Realist 45 camera for 35mm film, German-
made, f3.5 Cassar..................... 45.00
Stereo Realist for 35mm film, f3.5 lens, c.
1950s ................................ 70.00
Stereo Realist Macro................... 300.00-350.00
●Wing, Simon (Charlestown, Mass.)
New Gem camera for 5x7″ plates, 1901...... 800.00-900.00
Wing Multiplying View Camera for 4x5″
plates, 1860s........................ 600.00-700.00
●Wirgin, Gerb. (Wiesbaden, Germany)
Edinex compact camera for 35mm film, tele-
scoping front, film loads from bottom,
1930s ............................... 35.00
Gewirette camera for 127 film, top loading,
late 1930s........................... 45.00
Klein-Edinex compact camera for 127 film,
f2.9/50mm Steinheil Cassar lens, late 1930s 45.00
Wirgin Stereo for 35mm film, f3.5/35mm
Steinheil Cassar lenses................ 50.00
●Witt Iloca (Hamburg, Germany)
Iloca I, II, IIa cameras for 35mm film, some
with coupled rangefinder, f3.5/45mm Ilitar
lens, 1930s.......................... 20.00-25.00
●Wittnauer
Scout camera for 35mm film, f2.8 Shronex
lens................................. 50.00-60.00
●Wonder magazine box camera for plates..... 65.00-70.00

Contax I, 1932, by Carl Zeiss.
$180-$225.

Stereo Realist ST41, 1951, by David
White Co., Milwaukee, Wisc. $70.

Wunsche, Emil (Dresden, Germany)
Field camera for 5x7" plates, f8 brass-
barrel lens, c. 1900.................... 135.00-150.00
Reicka folding camera for 9x12cm plates,
f5.4/120mm Rodenstock Heligonal lens, c.
1912................................. 50.00-60.00
Zeh, Paul, Kamerawerk (Dresden, Germany)
Zeca folding camera for 9x12cm sheet film,
f6.3/135mm Schneider Radionar lens..... 25.00-30.00
Zeca folding camera for 6x9cm sheet film,
f6.8 Sheinheil lens...................... 15.00-20.00
Zeca-Flex folding TLR for 120 film, f3.5/
75mm Tessar, 1930s................... 300.00-350.00
Zeiss, Carl, Optical Co. (Dresden, Germany;
merged wilth Contessa-Nettel, Ernemann,
Goerz, Ica to form Zeiss-Ikon in 1926)
Adoro folding camera for plates, f4.5/105mm
Tessar............................... 30.00-50.00
Adoro folding tropical camera for 9x12cm
plates, teak body, brown bellows, f4.5/
135mm double anast. lens.............. 175.00-200.00
Bebe folding camera, 6x9cm, f4.5 Xenar.... 50.00
Bob folding camera, 6x9cm, f7.7/105 Nettar. 25.00
Bobette II folding camera for 35mm film,
f2/42mm Ernostar lens, late 1920s........ 250.00-300.00
Baby Box Tengor for 127 film, f11 Goerz
Frontar, 1930s........................ 50.00-60.00
Box Tengor for 127 film, all metal body, f11
Goerz Frontar lens.................... 25.00-35.00
Box Tengor for 120 film, f11 Goerz Frontar
Achromat, c. 1940.................... 35.00-40.00
Box Tengor for 116 film, f11 Goerz Frontar,
1928 ............................... 40.00-45.00
Cocarette folding camera for 120 film, f4.5
Tessar............................... 20.00-25.00
Contaflex TLR for 35mm film, f1.5 or f2
Sonnar, 1930s (not to be confused with post
1950 Contaflex models)................ 700.00-900.00
Contax I "brick" camera for 35mm film, f1.5
or f2 Sonnar of f3.5 Tessar lens, c. 1932... 250.00-300.00
Contax II, f3.5 Tessar, 1930s............. 100.00
Contax IIa, f1.5 Sonnar.................. 125.00-150.00
Contax III, f2.8 Tessar, 1930s............. 125.00-140.00

Contax S SLR for 35mm film, made in East Germany, f2 Biotar lens, c. 1950 . . . . . . . .    **75.00**

Contessa folding camera for 35mm film, f2.8/45mm Tessar, early 1950s . . . . . . . . . .    **75.00**

Donata double extension plate camera for 9x12cm plates, f4.5/135mm Tessar . . . . . .    **25.00-30.00**

Ergo camera, shaped like half a binocular, right-angle viewing, f4.5/55mm Tessar, 1920s . . . . . . . . . . . . . . . . . . . . . . . . . . . . .    **700.00-750.00**

Icarette folding bed camera for rollfilm, various sizes . . . . . . . . . . . . . . . . . . . . . . . .    **40.00-50.00**

Idea folding bed camera for 6x9cm plates . . . .    **40.00**

Ideal folding bed camera for 9x12cm plates . .    **65.00**

Ikoflex I TLR for 120 film, f4.5 Novar, 1930s . . . . . . . . . . . . . . . . . . . . . . . . . . . . .    **125.00**

Ikoflex II, f3.5 Tessar, late4 1930s . . . . . . . . .    **65.00**

Ikoflex III, f2.8/75mm Tessar, late 1930s . . . .    **125.00-135.00**

(Ikomat cameras were re-named Ikonta after 1936 Ikomat folding camera for 120 film, f4.5 Tessar, c. 1935 . . . . . . . . . . . . . . . . . . .    **30.00-35.00**

Ikomat folding camera for 120 film, 2¼x3½ " format, 105mm lens . . . . . . . . . . . . . . . . . .    **35.00**

Super Ikomat A folding camera for 120 film, f2.8 Tessar (re-named Super Ikonta A after 1936), c. 1935 . . . . . . . . . . . . . . . . . . . . . .    **75.00-85.00**

Ikonette folding cameras for 127 film, 1928 . .    **25.00-35.00**

Ikonette plastic camera for 35mm film, f3.5/ 45mm Novar anast. lens . . . . . . . . . . . . . . .    **10.00-15.00**

Ikonta folding camera for 127 film, 3x4cm format, f4.5/50mm Novar, 1930s . . . . . . . .    **50.00-60.00**

Ikonta folding camera for 120 film, f5x6cm format (half-frame), f4.5 Tessar lens . . . . . .    **35.00-40.00**

Ikonta folding camera for 120 film, 6x6cm format, f3.5 Novar lens . . . . . . . . . . . . . . . .    **40.00-50.00**

Ikonta folding camera for 120 film, 6x9cm format, f3.5 Tessar . . . . . . . . . . . . . . . . . . . .    **40.00-45.00**

Ikonta folding camera for 35mm film, Xenar lens . . . . . . . . . . . . . . . . . . . . . . . . . . . . . . .    **40.00**

Super Ikonta A for 120 film, 4.5x6cm format, f3.5/75mm Novar lens, 1950s . . . . . . . . . . .    **90.00-100.00**

Super Ikonta B for 120 film, 6x6cm format, f2.8/80mm Tessar . . . . . . . . . . . . . . . . . . .    **100.00-125.00**

Super Ikonta C for 120 film, 2¼x3¼ " format, f3.5/105mm Tessar . . . . . . . . . . . .    **90.00-100.00**

Ciroflex, by Ciro Cameras, Delaware, Ohio. 1940s, $25.

Ikoflex IIa, 1950, Zeiss Ikon. $65.

| | |
|---|---:|
| Super Ikonta D for 616 film, 2½x4¼″ format, f4.5/120mm Triotar lens......... | **135.00-150.00** |
| Kolibri for 127 film, 3x4cm format (half-frame), telescoping front, f3.5/50mm Tessar.............................. | **175.00** |
| Maximar A folding camera for 6.5x9cm plates, f4.5/105mm Tessar, 1940s........ | **60.00-70.00** |
| Maximar B folding camera for 9x12cm plates, f4.5/135mm Tessar, 1940s............. | **50.00-60.00** |
| Miroflex focal plane SLR camera, 6x9cm format, f3.5 Tessar, 1930s.............. | **135.00-150.00** |
| Miroflex focal plane SLR camera, 9x12cm format, f4.5/165mm Tessar............. | **180.00-190.00** |
| Nettar folding camera for 120 film, f4.5/75mm Novar........................ | **50.00** |
| Nettax folding camera for 35mm film, f4.5 Novar, late 1930s..................... | **150.00-175.00** |
| Nettel Tropical folding camera, brown bellows, 6.5x9cm format, f4.5 Tessar........ | **300.00-350.00** |

Nixe folding camera for rollfilm or plates,
various sizes........................... **70.00-75.00**
Orix folding camera for 10x15cm plates, f6.8
Goerz lens in Compur shutter........... **125.00-135.00**
Picolette camera for 127 film, f4.5/75mm
Tessar, late 1920s.................... **60.00**
Sirene folding camera for sheet film, f4.5/
135mm lens......................... **25.00-30.00**
Super Nettel folding bed camera for 35mm
film, horizontal format, f3.5/50mm Tessar **150.00-175.00**
Taxo folding camera for sheet film, 6.5x9cm. **20.00**
Tenax I for 35mm film, f3.5 Novar, late
1930s ............................... **65.00-75.00**
Tenax II for 35mm film, f2 Sonnar lens..... **150.00-200.00**
Trona folding camera for 9x12cm plates,
f4.5/135mm Dominar lens............. **30.00**
Volta folding camera for 6.5x9cm plates,
f4.5/105mm Tessar................... **20.00-25.00**
Volta folding camera for 9x12cm plates, f6.3
Novar.............................. **20.00-25.00**
● Zenith Edelweiss folding camera for 620 film. **5.00-10.00**
● Zion, Ed. (Paris, France)
Pocket Z folding camera for 6.5x9cm plates,
Rex Luxia lens....................... **65.00-75.00**

ICA Nike (w/f4.5 Zeiss Jena Tessar lens), 1920s, $50.

Zeiss Ikonta by Zeiss Ikon, c. 1935, $30-$50.

Agfa Shur-Shot Special, by Agfa-Ansco, c. 1945, $5.

Ansco VP No. 2, $10.

No. 2A Buster Brown, by Ansco, c. 1910, $15.

Le Physiographe, by Leon Bloch, Paris, 1896 (deceptive angle stereo camera), $1,000-$1,5000.

Century No. 1, $150.

No. 2 Kewpie, by Conley Camera Co., c. 1915, $5-$10.

125

Foth Derby, by Foth & Co., Germany, c. 1940, $40.

Detective Dryplate Camera, 4x5, $100.

Dick Tracy novelty camera. $15-$20.

Graflex fingerprint camera. $225.

Expo Watch camera, Expo Watch Co., c. 1910. $130-$150.

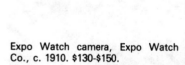

Folmer Graflex Combat Graphic Camera, olive green, $175.

Graflex 4x5 Speedgraphic f/4.5 Ilex
5½" lens, $100.

Herco Imperial 620, $15.

Magazine Cyclone No. 4, c. 1900, $50.

Mick-A-Matic Novelty Camera.
$15-$20.

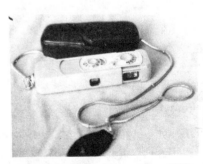

Minox III, Wetzler, Germany, c. 1950,
$50.

Murer's Express, French Stereo
Camera, 1920s, $350.

Roy Rogers Novelty Camera, $10.

Stereo box camera, by P. Andrews, San Francisco. No price data.

No. 8 Verascope Stereo camera for glass plates, $275-$300.

Midget 16, by Utility Mfg. Co., $5.

Zeiss Nettar, by Zeiss Ikon, c. 1939. $25.

Falcon, by Utility Mfg. Co., c. 1935, $10.

# PART II: IMAGES

The photographic image may be the most "collectible" object ever produced by man. It is the perfect souvenir, at once a human creation and a reflection of the human condition.

But old images also constitute one of the most confusing—even treacherous—areas of the collecting hobby.

These "slices of life," as Susan Sontag so aptly calls them in her insightful essay "On Photography," have a subtle way of forcing us to collect them. One has only to consider how difficult it is to wrinkle up an old photograph and throw it away in order to understand that "frozen moments" make demands on eternity. They beg to be saved, and save them we do, by the millions. The family photo album is a tradition with a history as long as that of photography itself, and archives filled with historical photos are as jealously guarded as art museums.

From the moment a photograph emerges from the bath of developing chemicals, it is an instant heirloom—an object to be saved for the future because of what is says about the present. No antique piece of furniture or glass or silver can ever show "the way we were" as eloquently as an old photograph can. While old paintings interpret reality, a photograph is reality. It is a piece of history, a privileged moment to be treasured.

No wonder collectors are busy scouring the nation's attics, basements, desk drawers and old albums for significant pictures to add to their collections. What is cause for wonder is that it took more than a century for the general public to realize the fascination and enjoyment inherent in collecting photographs other then those family snapshots.

Aside from their historical or aesthetic value, photographs attract collectors because of their sheer number, variety, series, and the ease with which they can be acquired and stored. Like seashells, wildflowers, butterflies and rock specimens, vintage photographic images are found in dazzling numbers, thanks to the labors of thousands of photographers during the 150 years since Niepce slowly "snapped'' that first picture of his garden. Today, nearly every inch of our planet has been photographed, and satelites send us daily shots of the entire planet in a single picture.

For many of us, our first collections were accumulations of photographs—in the form of baseball cards. It seems only natural for us to save pictures of things we like or admire.

Still, the boom in collecting old photographic images is just beginning. There are plenty of stories about collectors who bought fine daguerreotypes, ambrotypes or whatever for a mere song and sold them for a fortune. Indeed, this is one of the few areas in which the private collector is on an even footing with the professional dealer. There are plenty of finds to be made, and bargains still exist.

Today's collector tends to specialize. He may seek only a single kind of photograph—daguerreotypes, perhaps, or only full-plate daguerreotypes. Others collect the work of a single photographer, perhaps Alfred Stieglitz or Edward Weston, or a group of photographers such as the Surrealists, or Civil War photographers. Yet other collectors go by subject—they collect images of Civil War soldiers, or wonders of the world, or architectural shots.

# DAGUERREOTYPES

Probably the most highly prized photographic type is the full-plate daguerreotype, which measures 6½x8½ inches. Daguerreotypes by such recognized masters as Jeremiah Gurney, Boston photographers Southworth and Hawes, Anson of New York, or San Francisco's Robert Vance are eagerly sought. Matthew Brady, perhaps the most famous early American photographer, is avidly collected too, but his works are often priced below rarer works by more obscure daguerreotypists.

Other daguerreotypes prized by collectors are those showing military subjects—especially officers and battle scenes—or occupational scenes, portraits of well-known politicians or celebrities, town views, Gold Rush scenes, old buildings and landscapes.

Daguerreotypes are prized not only because they were products of the first commercially successful photographic process, but also because they are the sharpest images ever made, with the kind of quality a connoisseur can relish, regardless or vintage. Technical excellence always appeals to collectors. The daguerreotype's positive image produced directly on a silvered copper plate sensitized with iodine or bromine vapor had exemplary brilliance and incredible sharpness of detail. But more important, the image was unique. There was no negative from which further copies of the same print could be made.

Considering the prices being paid for daguerreotypes today, their singularity seems to outshine their one big drawback—the mirror-like surface which makes it so difficult ot view them. Daguerreotype images can be viewed properly only from certain angles. To the collector, that drawback fades by comparison with the daguerreotype's historical value and the shrinking supply which insures their continued value.

Daguerreotypes are measured in "plate size" rather then inches. The designations for size are derived from the size of the plate originally used by Daguerre himself (6½ by 8½ inches). Sizes of smaller daguerreotypes are not entirely uniform, but the trimmed image usually comes close to the following dimensions:

| | |
|---|---|
| Full-plate | 6½ x 8½ " |
| Half-plate | 4¼ x 5½ " |
| Quarter-plate | 3¼ x 4¼ " |
| Sixth-plate | 2¾ x 3¼ " |
| Ninth-plate | 2 x 2½ " |
| Sixteenth-plate | 1-3/8 x 1-5/8 " |

A handful of photographers used plates larger than "whole" size, some as large as 15 by 17 inches. These, naturally, have added value to collectors.

In America, where the daguerreotype reached its pinnacle of achievement, inventor and artist Samuel F. G. Morse was among the first to attempt to make his own daguerreotypes, and he instructed others in the new process. The first American daguerreotype portrait was probably made by Professor John W. Draper of New York, a friend of Morse's. Alexander S. Wolcott and John Johnson opened the first daguerreotype studio in New York City in March 1840 and by 1844 Mathew Brady was also busy in that city, turning out daguerreotypes as Americans discovered the wonders of the "mirror with a memory."

By the mid-1850s, however, the ambrotype (on glass) and the ferrotype (on metal) appeared, and the fact that these processes produced a negative—and could therefore be produced in multiples—spelled the end of the end of the daguerreo-types's supremacy.

# AMBROTYPES, TINTYPES

Ambrotypes, whose greatest popularity spanned the years 1854-1870, are often found in daguerreotype cases—and the case is often worth more than the image!

Produced by an early wet-plate process, they were made in all sizes of the daguerrean era's cameras. Their faint negative image on glass is viewed as positive when placed against a dark background. A creamy grey color contrasted to jet black makes the image extraordinarily soft yet rich. The process was patented by James A. Cutting of Boston in 1854.

The ambrotype had two advantages over the daguerreotype: it could be viewed from any angle, and the required exposure time was shorter. But the ambrotype lacked the crispness of detail found in daguerreotypes, and it often seemed a bit flat. Today the black backgrounds inserted behind them or painted on them are often shabby. This makes ambrotypes somewhat unattractive, especially to connoisseurs, and they therefore tend to sell for considerably less than daguerreotypes. The subjects usually determine the value, with military subjects easily ranking as the most valuable. Most ambrotypes are portraits (they were popular at a time when family portraits were becoming **de rigeur**). Landscapes, consequently less common, are more valuable.

Popular during the same era, the tintype was a particularly American phenomenon which eventually evolved into the political campaign button. "Tintypes" (also known as ferrotypes) contain no tin. These portraits (which is what almost all of them are) were produced by the collodion process directly on japanned iron. While ambrotypes are easily damaged by attempts to clean their surfaces, the tintype is a sturdy little keepsake which has been used in jewelry, sent through the mail, carried in one's pocket, or even set into a tombstone. Not many of the latter have escaped the hands of vandals, however.

Some tintypes are found today with scratches, or bent out of shape a bit, but they are delightfully inexpensive collectibles— as durable as they were cheap to produce. Most are about as thick as a playing card (some rare thicker versions predated these). Colored tintypes with a "chocolate" brown tone date from the early 1870s.

Tintypes were made in the usual plate sizes in daguerrean cameras, and when multiple-image plates came into use, postage-stamp-size tintypes became the rage—produced at the rate of as many as 32 portraits on a single plate. The images were simply cut apart with shears, mounted in paper holders, and sold for a dime.

While a half-plate ambrotype usually commands anywhere from $25 to $100, a half-plate tintype, by comparison, sells for only $5 to $20—one fifth as much—even though it dates from the same era and shows the same type of subject! The difference in price is a reflection of the difference in rarity of the two processes.

# CARTES DE VISITE

CDVs, as collectors call them, were also produced in such quantity that their value is lower than other types of images from the same era. Why were these on-paper portraits so numerous? Millions were printed because CDVs were one of the great fads of the 1800s. Soon after they reached the United States—around 1859—presenting a portrait to friends became a social nicety so widely practiced that within a year the word "cartomania" was coined to describe the craze for collecting and exchanging cartes de visite. The CDV was the first form of photography (along with the stereograph) to take advantage of the fact that many copies could be produced from a single collodion negative on glass. The prints—usually albumen prints— were mounted on cardboard 2½ by 4¼ inches. Actors and actresses and other prominent persons, eager to bask in the public eye, posed for cards made specifically for wide distribution. The cards became known as "publics." J. M. More, who gave them that name, boasted that he'd sold 35,000 copies of one subject alone—a portrait of actress Maud Branscombe!

Today, a CDV of an unidentified man, woman or child might sell for 50 cents or a dollar, but a Civil War military figure CDV could bring $20 to $40 or even more, as will a portrait of Jenny Lind or some other famous theatrical personality. CDVs also did much to publicize such "celebrities" as Tom Thumb, Admiral Dot, "The Siamese Twins" and other circus attractions—precursors, in their way, of today's grisly Diane Arbus photographs.

When the popularity of the CDV began to wane, a larger version of the same thing swept into vogue. It was the cabinet card, so called because it was large enough for display in the china or curio cabinet. These photographs, mounted on a piece of polished cardboard measuring 4½ by 6½ inches, usually featured an advertisement for the photographer's studio on the reverse—indicative of the greater competition between photographers. The cabinet card might be a portrait of a beloved relative or of one's self, but the biggest trade by far was in the sale of portraits of the admired public personalities of the day. Thousands of images of actors and actresses, statesmen, kings and assorted freaks were produced, and the market seemed insatiable. Albums produced to hold cabinet cards often held more than 100 of them—one or two for the china cabinet was not sufficient, it seems. The method of production allowed manufacturers to turn out a glut of these hard-to-throw-away images. Amassing collections seemed the only way to cope with them. The task for today's collector of cabinet cards is to find examples which are truly interesting, avoiding the trite poses, the over-elaborate backdrops, the stiff and formal settings.

Faced with the plethora of stangers pictured on CDVs and cabinet cards, it is only natural that collectors should place the highest value on "name" items—pictures by famous photographers or pictures of famous subjects. Cabinet cards showing unidentified subjects sell in the same price range as CDVs of unidentified subjects. But theatrical portraits taken in New York by such photographers as Napoleon Sarony or Jose Mora in the late 1890s sell for $3, $5, even $10 each. Other albumen prints which are eagerly sought are those showing western scenes, especially images of American Indians, by William Henry Jackson, Charles R. Savage, or Laton Alton Huffman. These sell for prices ranging from $25 to many hundreds of dollars. When they come up at auction, cabinet cards and CDVs are usually offered in hugh lots. An album containing about 40 portraits of American authors and statesmen sold for $200 at one recent auction—with many of the cards signed. A single cabinet card—a picture of author George Sand by Nadar—also sold for $200, but such prices are the exception rather than the rule. For the most part, cabinet cards are in the 50 cents to $1 range, and their investment prospects pale by comparison with unique images, such as daguerreotypes. Still, rare or especially interesting images remain tucked away in many family photo albums, attics and other repositories of old photographs. Interesting finds will be turning up for years to come.

# STEREO CARDS

The stereograph or stereogram is one of a pair of photographs intended to be viewed in tandem, side by side, through a stereoscope to produce a three-dimensional view with an intriguing effect of depth. For years collectors found them boring; today a renaissance of interest is pushing prices up to levels that would have been unthinkable a mere decade ago. But again, the views which command high prices are those which are rare or unusual. Common scenes sell for about a dollar—up considerably from the average price of 25 cents which prevailed 10 years ago, but still low enough to make collecting stereo views an inexpensive hobby.

Stereo views are an outgrowth of experiments in binocular sight dating back to the 1830s, when Sir Charles Wheatstone began developing the first practical stereoscope. The word "stereograph" was coined by none other than Oliver Wendell Holmes, who developed the stereoscopic viewer most familiar today.

The two views found on stereo cards are not exactly the same, although they appear to be. Each image was taken through a separate lens in the "two-eyed" stereo camera whose lenses are separated by only a couple of inches, corresponding to the space between the human eyes. Early experimental work in stereo employed daguerreotypes and calotypes, but neither was acceptable. Later, after the introduction of the collodion print on paper and on glass, the stereograph came into its own.

What the early stereographs lacked in clarity of image was made up for by their illusion of depth, simulating human vision. Thus, just before the Civil War erupted, another photographic fad was born. In the following decades, millions of stereographs would depict everything from bawdy house scenes to war horrors to tourist attractions.

Rarity is the key factor in collecting stereo cards. It is determined by the process, subject or photographer. Glass stereo plates of the mid-19th century are more highly prized than common albumen stereo images on cardboard dating from the same era. Photo prints produced in the darkroom are considerably more valuable than lithographed cards made for the mass market in the late 1890s.

Cheap to produce in large quanities, stereo cards did much to change photography from a provincial craft to a commercial industry. Studios often purchased negatives from "professional" photographers who roamed the world in search of marketable subjects, sometimes on assignment from the studio. In the U.S., the craze for stereopticon viewing was introduced by the Langenheim Brothers of Philadelphia, who marketed albumen negatives printed on glass, the same method used to produce early lantern slides. Stereo views brought to the Victorian parlor all the delights of distant natural wonders, and today's collectors can easily find views of historical monuments, foreign places, nature and archaeological subjects and famous works of art, by far the most common subjects. Among the major makers and vendors of early views were E. and H. T. Anthony, George Stacy, and D. Appleton, all of New York. Later publishers included Underwood and Underwood, the Langenheim brothers, and the London Stereoscopic Co.

Their size helps date stereographs. The smaller cards, three by seven inches, popular in Europe since 1854, appeared in America around 1860. A slightly larger size, four by seven inches, also known earlier in Europe, was introduced in the U.S. about 1870. In general, earlier cards are more valuable than later cards, since they are rarer, and theme stereo cards showing a series of views of Civil War battlefields, the Gold Rush, or slavery in the South are more valuable than tourist souvenir cards with common scenes of Niagara Falls, Plymouth Rock, the Holy Land or European cathedrals. Stereo views by great photographers such as England's Francis Frith are naturally top price getters.

While the stereo views are cheap, the stereoscopic viewers are not, except for the Holmes-Bates wooden viewer, worth about $20 or $30 (more ornate models of the Holmes-Bates can bring $75 and up). A simple Brewster-type viewer (a sort of binocular you look into rather than through) costs anywhere from $100 to $250, and a John Stull Daguerrean viewer of 1855 has sold for as much as $1,500 to $2,000. Table model viewers for 20 or more glass slides or stereo cards were also produced, some with a knob or sliding switch to change views. The cheapest is the 1859-patent A. Becker's Viewer, selling for $100 to $150.

Ives Kromskop for viewing stereo color plates is worth more than $1,000, and Le Taxiphot, a stereo viewer for 25 cards made by J. Richard of Paris, sells for $275 to $350 or more.

The condition of stereo views can be critical in pricing. Literally millions of them can be found in good to excellent condition, since owners tended to save series in boxes. Yet a rare view in less desirable condition might still command a premium price. One example is a set of three views of Niagara Falls by S. Mason on glass, dating from 1858. It sold for $37.50 at auction, despite the fact that the image was spotted and the glass had some fine cracks.

# THE OTHER "TYPES"

While dauerreotypes, ambrotypes, tintypes, and albumen prints dominated the market for photographic images in the 1800s, there were many other processes, some of which never got much past the experimental stage. Since these processes often produced images of high quality, and since the images were turned out in comparatively small numbers, these photographs are of special interest to collectors who prize historical value and rarity.

The many processes are usually variations on the main "types" of printmaking. Among them are the collotype (also known as Artotype, heliotype, Albertype—basically a photo-gelatin method for reproducing photographs which was an early form of book illustration), aristotype (printed on gelatin chloride paper), bromide print (on paper coated with silver bromide in gelatin), calotype (soft reddish-brown images printed on sensitized writing paper in a method developed by Henry Fox Talbot), collodion print (a "wet plate" photograph producing a negative on glass, which was then used to produce an ambrotype or tintype), gravure or photogravure (a printed copy of an original photograph, ink on paper, produced by an intaglio process), gum print (a "photo-acquatint" or type of highly controlled print, either gum-bichromate or gum-platinotype), mahoganytype (are you paying attention? This was the photographer's joking term for an all-black image resulting from forgetting to put the plate in the camera), melainotype (an early name for tintype), mezzotint (a softened image resulting from tissue paper interposed between negative and printing paper), platinotype (a favorite for art prints, it is an image printed on uncoated paper rendered sensitive with salts of platinum), rayograph (an image of the kind Man Ray began making in 1922 by placing an object directly on sensitized paper to photograph its "shadow"), Talbotype (another name for calotype), and Woodburytype (the earliest form of photo-mechanical print, a sort of halftone but lacking the grain).

These are just a few of the many names collectors encounter, and they often cause confusion. Knowing the difference between one type and another can be important—with the importance often measured in dollars.

# PHOTO ALBUMS

Like an ornate Bible, the family photograph album was found in most homes during the late 19th and early 20th centuries, bound in elaborate velvet, calf or morocco, possibly with brass clasps, and lovingly cared for. Some of the albums even contained music boxes.

The photo album was the family's treasure, its history. Some albums featuring portraits of celebrities or heroes served another purpose—they provided evening entertainment.

Before they became a social nicety, albums were a protective necessity—they held fragile daguerreotypes and ambrotypes, sometimes under glass sheets inserted in the album pages.

The albums themselves, especially the lavish versions, have value even when they contain no photographs. Typical albums from the turn of the century or before are worth $10, $20, sometimes $30.

The old photographs of family, relatives and celebrities are seldom worth much. At best, they're tintypes, ambrotypes or CDVs; at worst, they're snapshots. It is safe to say that the vast majority of images found in old family photo albums are worth nothing at all! Their value to the family, as a record of its evolution, is of course a different matter. There are simply far too many images of unidentified or unknown people on this planet for there to be a market for them. As rising prices bring more publicity to the vintage photograph market, many people come across their family albums of old photos and feel they've found a treasure trove. The odds are greatly against that "trove" amounting to much more than a few dollars at best. Collectors shun snapshots, even when they are offered free.

Albums offered at auction, usually in groups, sell for a variety of prices—they're literally worth what someone is willing to pay for them. One lot of two albums containing a total of nearly 400 photographs, c. 1875 views from around the world, sold for $180 recently. In the same sale a bid of $15 took three somewhat shabby family albums containing studio portraits from about 1910.

The value of albums filled with pictures is determined mostly by the pictures themselves—the earlier, rarer, or "big name" works commanding the most. The top collector albums are often thematic in one way or another. An album containing more than 400 pre-1883 photographs of gravestones was recently priced at $125; an album of 50 photographs of 1860s Minnesota scenes published by Witney's Gallery of St. Paul was valued at $425; an album of 46 mounted photochrome views of the Rocky Mountains, c. 1903, was tagged at $200; and a recent Sotheby Parke Bernet auction sold for $500 an entire 1861 collection of 50 portrait cartes de visite showing various notables of the day. A single family album containing 188 round photographs taken in the early 1890s with the historic Kodak No. 2 camera recently sold for $160.

Such prices are the exception, however. Auction catalogs offer countless albums with prices typically in the $10 to $30 range, rarely more. Perhaps as more family photograph albums come on the market, monetary values will become more standardized. Until then, buy cautiously.

Not to be overlooked is another type of album—not a family album but the photographer's **own** album. Early photographers were often avid collectors of their own material, and they assembled deluxe books or personal albums, sometimes even having them printed in limited editions. Probably the most famous is William Henry Fox Talbot's "The Pencil of Nature," which contained calotypes he pasted in himself by hand. Julia Margaret Cameron, the "grande dame" of early photography, also assembled albums of her work, which she proudly presented to friends. Also notable is Peter Henry Emerson's "Life and Landscape on the Norfolk Broads," containing platinum prints accompanied by a text by famous naturalist Thomas Goodal.

As Francis Wey noted in 1851, "Our albums are our salons." Today, these old albums are often extremely valuable. And even albums by lesser known photographers can be of interest to the collector. Though less costly, they too may turn out to be fine investments.

When it comes to albums assembled by the photographers themselves, the name of the game is names. Famous names, that is. An album of 859 snapshots by Cecil Beaton, for example, sold to a collector in late 1978 for $21,500.

# OLD CASES

The fragile silver-coated copper daguerreotype and the delicate glass ambrotype required protection from fingerprints, oxidization, or contact with objects which might scratch the image. That, in addition to the fact that the photograph is inherently a "treasured object", led to the development of an entire industry geared to the production of suitable display cases.

Early cases were made of leather, wood, or embossed paper. But by the mid-1850s thermoplastic was introduced and patented by samuel Peck. Thermoplastic, the first plastic to be mass-produced in the United States, resembles gutta percha but consists of mostly sawdust and shellac and is surprisingly durable.

The thermoplastic Union Case patented by Peck in 1854 quickly dominated the market. The material could be molded into hundreds of different designs, and manufacturers were soon turning out cases with a variety of scrollwork, geometric or historical motifs. The decorative cases, usually hinged, were originally intended to hold one, maybe two, daguerreotypes or ambrotypes, but they are sometimes found today with more recent images inserted.

The first type of daguerreotype case to be patented (1850) was one designed by Ann F. Stiles of Southbury, Conn. It is a cone-shaped case with a hinged bottom to hold the image. The top contained a magnifying lens for viewing. These rare cases are worth as much as $1,200 to the many collectors who specialize in collecting old daguerrean cases. J. F. Mascher's 1853-patent thermoplastic case, which doubled as a stereo viewer, is worth $500 or more, and probably the most valuable of the old cases in John Stull's stereo daguerreotype case patented in 1953, worth $1,500 to $2,000. Most old cases, however, are worth $10 to $50, with fine examples of the thermoplastic "art" commanding more. A full-plate thermoplastic case depicting Washington crossing the Delaware River is worth $400 to $600. A half-plate case with a rustic country scene was recently priced at $150 at a photographica show—a high price justified, in this case, by the quality of the decoration. A sixth-plate case by Littlefield, Parson and Co., c. 1862, featuring a "scroll, with Constitution and the Laws" in its design, is worth about $50.

Scovill Mfg. Co. of Waterbury, Conn., one of the big suppliers of daguerreotype plates in the U.S. marketed a number of "fancy styles" of the Union cases. These—and any thermoplastic cases—are worthwhile collectibles, often worth considerably more than the images they contain.

# PHOTOGRAPHY AS ART

Ever since his first glimpse of a daguerreotype inspired French artist Paul Delaroche to say "From this day forward painting is dead," the great debate has raged as to whether photography is an art. With the introduction of dry plates, which enabled the photographer to develop negatives at his convenience rather than only while the emulsion was still wet, new aesthetic possibilities became evident, including a wider tonal range. Still, many images were blurred for effect by pictorialists who sought to make "impressionistic" pictures. (Llewellen Morgan went so far as to report in "The Amateur Photographer" that "little details are interesting to the scientist, but of no value to the artist.")

By the turn of the century, photographers such as Stieglitz (1864-1946) had convinced many critics that, yes, a machine **could** produce a work of art. Subsequently, scores of photographers set out not to gather evidence or reproduce Nature, but to create photographs of enduring artistic value. That they succeeded is evident in the number of collectors who today seek not historical photographs—primitive daguerreotypes, charming tintypes portraits, or corny CDV celebrity shots—but art photographs by such "artists" as Alfred Stieglitz, Edward Steichen, Paul Strand, Man Ray, Edward Weston, Julia Margaret Cameron, Eugene Atget, Lewis Hine, Ansel Adams and hundreds of other photographers whose work is now recognized as valuable art. Many of these works are by well-known painters—Lazlo Moholy-Nagy, Alphonse Mucha, Thomas Eakins among others. Some of the pictures were produced as studies for paintings.

Today, the question of whether photography is art is irrelevant. The fact is that collectors and connoisseurs of the medium seek out certain works by certain photographers, and some are simply worth more than others on the photography market. Susan Sontag has noted that "Time eventually positions most photographs, even the most amateurish, at the level of art," and indeed, works by photographers such as Edward Curtis, William Henry Jackson, Francis Frith, Nadar and even works by anonymous photographers are viewed as art if they have those mysterious qualities that qualify them as "artistic."

When bidders gathered at Sotheby Parke Bernet's gallery in Los Angeles in February 1978—a typical sale of 19th-and 20th-century photographs—the division of today's photography market was made abundantly clear. While historical old photographs by Curtis, Frith and others (some of them looking like tourist snapshots) were being auctioned, half the audience looked bored, and a few dozed or read newspapers. When it came time to bid on works by Edward Weston or Ansel Adams, the sleepers came awake and began to bid on the "art photographs" they had come for, while the historic-minded collectors took their daguerreotypes and ambrotypes and went home. Some of them probably wondered why anybody would want to stick around to bid for such strange photographs as Philippe Halsman's portrait of Marilyn Monroe lifting barbells, or Edward Weston's 1930s study of a nude female's buttocks.

Such is the nature of the photographica collecting scene.

The two camps of collectors often fail to understand each other but nonetheless frequently overlap. They share a common goal—the urge to acquire the highest quality images they can get, regardless of the subjects they seek. Thus, the premium prices are paid for images which are in top condition, or which are an important part of the photographer's ouvre, or which have that highly-valued quality of rarity.

If Sontag is right about age turning photographs into works of art (and collectors present persuasive evidence that she is), then someday even family snapshots will be sought by collectors (some, in fact, already are). But again, the "collectible" images are only the best—the cream of the crop—with lesser images worth quite a bit less or nothing at all. The price rules are derived largely from the ancient market for paintings, and like the art market in general, photography collecting is swept by periodic fads which drive prices up one year and downward the next. Photographs as recent as those by Edward Weston are already careening up and down in value, depending on the aesthetic whims of collectors, curators, and historians. These fluctuations—together with the fact that one collector might pay high prices for images that seem unattractive to other collectors—explain the need for a price guide such as we present here.

But whether viewed as art or artifacts, photographic images are valued according to a variety of factors besides aesthetic merit.

# THE PRICING GAME

The Weston print of a nude's buttock in the sale mentioned above sold for $750. The same sale contained 35 lots of "important" Mathew Brady daguerreotypes and ambrotypes, and the catalog even noted that the **Photographic Art Journal** had in 1851 dubbed Brady "an excellent artist." Yet not one of Brady's images brought as much as Weston's detail of the nude. The highest price for a Brady, in fact, was $425. Most sold for considerably less.

The difference is all the more astounding when you consider that the daguerreotype is a unique image, while many prints could be turned out from Weston's negative.

The same sale offered an Edward S. Curtis image of an Indian scout which sold for $1,300, yet for a considerably lower $800 you could have bought a similar but even larger portrait by Curtis—not of a single scout but of *three* Indian chiefs.

Such "irrational" differences in prices for photographs tell much about the market for old images.

In the first place, it's a relatively new market. Besides being "worth a thousand words," pictures are worth whatever someone is willing to pay for them, and nobody, not even the experts, are always sure what that figure will be. Consider, for example, the Thomas Eakins photograph of two male models in classical Greek dress, one holding a scroll. It's a typical Eakins study, but it's unique—the only known print of this particular glass plate negative was offered at Sotheby Parke Bernet's New York gallery Nov. 8, 1977 sale of the Olympia Galleries collection of Eakins pictures. In that sale, Sotheby Parke Bernet's experts estimated the picture's worth at $5,000 to $8,000, obviously expecting the best from those who flocked to the all-Eakins sale. The picture failed to sell.

The same photo—it had to be, since only one print exists—turned up in Sotheby Parke Bernet's Los Angeles sale of Feb. 13-16, 1978. This time it had a pre-sale estimate of only $2,500 to $3,500. The picture sold in that sale for $1,150.

The difference of the estimates (about 50 percent lower

second time around) reflects not so much the variances in the market for Eakins material as it does the lack of accuracy in valuations assigned to photographs. Parke Bernet itself calls its pre-sale estimates little more than "educated guesses."

But auction buyers also account for different prices being paid for the same image. I was amused to note at a Sotheby Parke Bernet auction in Los Angeles that bidders were paying high prices for Ansel Adams silver prints ($950 for a view of Yosemite National Park's Half Dome, $1,700 for "Clearing Winterstorm") which, had they been willing to spend five hours driving time, could have been picked up for considerably less at Ansel Adam's gallery in Yosemite Valley (and the buyer could have had a Yosemite holiday thrown in too, instead of spending a couple hours waiting for his lot to come up at auction.)

It is not unusual, of course, for auction prices to be higher than prices in some retail shop. Nor is it unusual for them to be lower, since dealers often buy their stock at auction, then mark up the price. But it is obviously critical for the collector to know the going retail price to avoid overbidding at auction.

What determines the value of a photographic image? A wide mixture of factors must be considered: the quality of the print, the subject, the photographer, the printer, the rarity, the process, the supply, the demand, the number of other collectors of the same type of work, the provenance, and so forth. In some cases, there's really no explaining why an image sells for what it does—one can only shrug one's shoulders and say once again that a picture is worth whatever someone is willing to pay for it.

Any rules that might exist are consistently broken. Even a badly overexposed picture—so overexposed it's aggravating—can still have condiserable value. An Alphonse Mucha study of a female nude model, quite overexposed in the lower left hand quadrant, is still worth $800 to $1,000, thanks to the Mucha name. Indeed, many of Mucha's photographs tell of incorrect exposure settings and erratic development.

What about the price of $4,500 paid for Stieglitz's "The

Steerage" in New York in 1975. The work is, of course, a vastly popular image. But wait. That price wasn't for a photograph—it was for a *photogravure* of the work. It simply happened that this highly popular image, by a recognized master of the medium, was considered worth that price even though it was really a mechanical "print" of the image (gravures are by far the finest possible reproductions of photographs, but they **are** reproductions, prints of prints, as it were). A bidding battle happened to push the price upwards at that particular sale; the same gravure might bring considerably less at another sale. It is interesting to note that a single photo-mechanical print or gravure of a Picasso masterpiece would probably incite considerably less—if any—interest among bidders. But them, that's just the point: the market for images is irrational, and it probably always will be. Images, like other works of art, have a way of eliciting highly subjecting responses, and when rich bidders become highly excited by a work of art, there may be no telling what they're secretly willing to pay to own the thing.

Which brings us to the central issue: just how **do** you determine the value of a photographic image?

In the long run, one can't determine "value." One can only determine in some measures the "going price" being paid for certain works or kinds of images. An examination of the market yields data in the form of asking prices, prices paid, bid prices, appraisals, even bargain prices and rip-offs. With some knowledge of the market, one can evaluate this data and, by looking at what collectors are actually willing to pay, arrive at some idea of the "value to collectors," the price at which an item will find a buyer rather than go begging.

Even then it is a highly inexact science.

In 1977 a dentist named Roland Bill plunked down $3 at a flea market for a small photograph of a Confederate soldier. In April 1978, the Smithsonian Institution paid him $30,000 for the 5x7-inch picture—it turned out to be an early photograph of Confederate President Jefferson Davis. To the dealer, ignorant of the portrait's identity, the picture was worth exactly $3. To the more knowledgeable Smithsonian, it was worth $30,000. There's no way you can simply average the two prices for an "average value to the average collector." Nor can one really say that the image is automatically "worth $30,000" just because that's what the Smithsonian paid to get it. Maybe it could have been acquired for $10,000. Maybe another collector would have demanded $50,000. Maybe an old trunk in a Southern city will be found to contain a dozen more daguerreotypes of Davis, thereby making this one, even though it is unique, less attractive from the standpoint of rarity. You never know.

Auction prices are not entirely reliable; dealer prices are not entirely reliable; museum prices aren't either, not even when the museum is the Smithsonian.

The prices reported in this guide are listed with this in mind: they are "guide" prices, indications of the price range in which certain works—whether of historical or artistic value, or both—are usually priced by knowledgeable sellers and buyers, as far as we have been able to determine. The price information is drawn from a variety of sources— dealer lists, auction prices considered in relation to experts' pre-sale estimates of value, advertised sale prices in newspapers and magazines aimed at photography buyers, discussions with private collectors, museum experts and appraisers. The price or price ranges are the result, whenever possible, of an informed weighing of many factors—the direction of the market for a certain photographer's work or a certain type of image, the reliability of the source, the human foibles that can greatly affect prices for certain images such as Stieglitz's "The Steerage" mentioned above, the fact that asking prices are often considerably out of line with actual sale prices, and that auction sale prices are often considerably out of line with generally accepted valuations.

Obviously, no author can be an expert on each photographer or each image. In some cases, the prices are simply reported sale prices. In most cases, many dealer or auction prices have been consulted, checked against other advertised prices in such publications as **Shutterbug Ads**, **The Antique Trader**, **Popular Photography** and other publications. Earlier price lists or price guides to images (there have been a small number of these, most of them extremely limited in the number on entries) have also been consulted in some instances. The rapid changes in the erractic market for images, however, have outdated most of the early material (even some prices which were "current" a mere year or two ago), so more recent prices have been given the greatest emphasis. Every attempt has been made to make the information up-to-date, comprehensive and, above all, useful to the collector eager to value an image, compare prices being asked for one photographer as against another, or to simply keep abreast of the photography market.

We realize that the prices for certain old or artistic images are subject to debate among collectors, but we feel the prices we have listed are useful guides for both buyers and sellers.

# WHAT IS COLLECTED

It should be clear by now that collectors have widely divergent tastes—and the market reflects those tastes. Just as anything in the world is a potential subject for the camera, so any image is a potential collectible. But obviously, collectors favor some types of images more than others—and some images, such as family snapshots of the routine sort—are ignored totally.

I feel it is safe to say that the three main categories of collectible photos are daguerreotypes (because of their historical nature and uniqueness), ambrotypes (because of their historical nature and rarity), and art prints (because of their aesthetic values and rarity). Less valuable, in general, but still collectible, are stereographs, CDVs, cabinet photos, color prints, gravures (especially in books or albums), and billions of black and white prints made by photographers ranging from rank amateurs armed with early Kodak box cameras to the Nikon-or Leica-toting masters of our own time. Even the "instant photographs" of the Polaroid SX-70 are being bought and sold by collectors who recognize that the Polaroid is the first popular camera since the daguerrean era to turn out unique images that can't be used to produce endless reprints.

Contemporary auction catalogs and dealer lists are the best indications of what is being collected. These show what is available, not necessarily what is most valuable. Daguerreotypes, for example, face a diminishing supply, and fewer are being offered (some dealers can't even offer them any more, the supply has become so tight). But obviously, the asking prices are getting higher and higher. As the daguerreotype market tightens, more collectors try to buy what they can.

Most other images are plentiful, and some collectors, such as Sam Wagstaff of New York, collect on an incredibly grand scale. Wagstaff's collection contains thousands of prints, as do collections of many other photographica buffs. Yet a collection of a few hundred—or even a dozen—can also be interesting or valuable, depending on what is in it.

Most collectors end up specializing in one way or another. One might seek disaster scenes, another might have a taste for Cecil Beaton or Diane Arbus prints, a third might collect only Civil War battlefield scenes. Some specialities are rigourously narrow—say, only gum bichromate prints, or only panorama shots, or only microphotographs of bontanical subjects.

# GETTING THE PICTURE

How do collectors go about acquiring the images they want? There are many sources, but mail-order and auction-buying dominate the market. Dealer galleries, exhibits by the photographers themselves, antique shops and flea markets, rummaging through attics—these, too, yeild old or artistic images. Not to be overlooked is the network of collectors who buy, sell and trade among themselves, often at swap meets. Usually they are selling one part of their collection in order to upgrade another. All of these buyers and sellers need to know the going price for the image and whether that price is rising or falling.

Auction houses—even those which build worldwide reputations around their art sales—tended to ignore photography altogether until recent years. Sotheby Parke Bernet in New York didn't form a separate photography department until July 1976, and regular sales began only a year earlier. The 1970 Strober sale at New York's PB-84 gallery was the first important U.S. photography sale—a full 136 years after Talbot made his first print on paper. In London, specialist photography sales have been held at Sotheby's Belgravia since May 1973. According to Landt and Lisl Dennis, authors of "Collecting Photography: A Guide to the New Art Boom," 1976 was the "Year of the Photograph," since that's when the media began focusing on the rising prices in articles with such blaring headlines as "Photo Print Boom!" or "Blow Up—The Story of Photography in Today's Art Market."

With the boom came more auctions—at Sotheby Parke Bernet in Los Angeles, at Christie's and Phillip's in New York, at San Francisco's California Book Auction Co., New York's Swann Galleries and Martin Gordon Gallery Inc., and, of course, numerous mail-order auctions held by dealers such as Americana Mail Auction Co. of Allentown, Pa.; John S. Craig of Norfolk, Conn.; Frank D. Guarino of DeBary, Fla.; Maillet of Cliffside Park, N.J.; and others. There is usually a charge for auction catalogs—the best are illustrated and are fine references for the collector even after the sales. Bidding in person or by mail (or by telephone) accounts for many of the transactions on the collector market—especially for many of the most important sales.

Dealer galleries account for a large share of the trade in art prints, but little of the trade in old daguerreotypes and other early images. The specialized images sought by most collectors almost have to be offered in a nationwide marketplace, via advertising or auction, since that is the nature of the game. One could open a daguerreotype gallery in, say, Houston and promptly starve to death, since few of the nation's daguerreotype buffs are going to travel that far to buy. Some photography dealers are beginning to appear at antique shows, and some antiques dealers deal in images as well as other merchandise, so they must be counted as part-time image dealers (not always with the best feel for prices.)

Some dealers in art photographs (a category which often includes early images) do business in most major cities, sometimes doubling as book dealers or poster dealers.

As for antique shops, flea markets, or grandma's attic— these offer the best change for valuable finds (since a photograph dealer or an auction house is likely to know the value of what they have). And finds do exist. But most of the really valuable images have already been ferreted out by collectors.

Still, there's always hope. As the dentist who found that Jefferson Davis daguerreotype noted: "You know, it was every bit as possible that someone—not realizing what it was—might have bought it and put it in a trunk for another 100 years." Indeed they might have.

# BUYING WISELY

More important than where the purchase is made is **how** it is made. The rules for bidding at auction are fairly clearly spelled out, but sometimes you can get a bargain without bidding at all by buying from a dealer who is eager to move his stock or who has underpriced a particular image. Other times, it's better to buy at auction. At the very least, it's wise to find out if the work you want is available elsewhere at a better price. The same day that Steiglitz's "The Steerage" gravure sold for $4,500 at Sotheby Parke Bernet, a gravure of the same subject and of equivalent quality by the same printer was available for more than $1,000 less at nearby Helios Gallery in New York. The bidder didn't need to pay as much as he did to own the Steiglitz gravure.

If you **do** buy at auction, be sure to examine the work during the preview before the sale. This is important at any auction, but especially so at a photography sale, since condition can greatly effect the value of a photo—old or recent. Scratches, stains, and fading cut the value of the print today and the value when resale time comes in future years.

Look not only for condition, but other factors which might affect value, such as signatures, printers' identifying marks, or details overlooked by the firm's catalogers.

The audience at a 1976 auction in New York was horrified when collector Sam Wagstaff and another bidder began "bidding up" the price of a seemingly undistinguished lot containing an 1869 image of women's rights activist Lucretia Coffin Mott and two 1935 copies of photographic portraits by the famous Langenheim brothers. The lot was expected to bring $200 at most, but after furious bidding Wagstaff finally acquired the lot for $1,900! Wagstaff didn't even **want** the Mott portrait. What he and the other shrewd buyer had discovered—by simply turning over the other two images—was that they were not copies but original Langenheim calotypes, dating from about 1849 and signed by both brothers. Even the cataloger had missed the boat.

On the other hand, the lot you buy may turn out to be a fake, or to have been misattributed. So it's wise to get some sort of guarantee—in writing—about who made the image, who printed it, how many other prints exist, and so forth. It isn't alway possible to get all the details in writing, but the more that is known about an old image, the better. Most dealers guarantee authenticity, and any reputable auction house or dealer will take back anything which has been unknowingly misrepresented.

If you forego bidding, you can still bargain. Prices in the photography market are so unstable that even dealers' prices are sometime negotiable, especially if the buyer can demonstrate that the asking price is too high. The shrewd collector keeps tabs on trends in the market and tries to buy and sell at the best price, but for most, the hobby is more than just an exercise in investing—it's in the aesthetics and the history that the real value lies.

The ultimate challenge is to develop the ability to separate the images that are really worthwhile from the millions that aren't, which means studying the medium and the photographers who have used it for the past 150 years.

"I indulge my prejudices," says collector Sam Wagstaff. "That is all I have to say about collecting." But prejudices **alone cannot build a great collection. It takes knowledge,** taste and a dash of intuition to do that, regardless of whether you aim to build a huge Wagstaffian collection or a narrow, specialized collection.

The images that count most on today's market are those which were printed by the photographer himself, especially if they are signed. A photo signed and printed by the late Edward Weston, for example, might be worth $3,000, while a print made by his son Cole—even though it is from the same Edward Weston negative—would bring only $150 to $200.

In a 1975 **New York Times** article, titled "Advice from a Photography Collector," Arnold Crane advised collectors to seek only vintage prints made by the photographer himself, ideally at the time when he took the image. He advised avoiding "anything but vintage work, for the vintage work has the unexplained magic of presence . . . avoid at any cost those posthumous 'limited editions', those Edward Weston prints made by his sons under his direction. And those Walker Evans portfolios printed by one of his students and Frederick H. Evans portfolios printed by one of his disciples."

Collectors are just beginning to realize the value of the artist-made print as opposed to the later print-from-the-negative, and the importance of this to future collectors will probably be even greater. Portfolios — printed, signed, and numbered by photographers — are likely to be good investments because of their careful authentication, while the works of similar aesthetic merit may command far less because they lack those attributes of authenticated rarity which connoisseurs love so much.

But above all, the way to collect is carefully. The photograph is a reproducable item — possibly the most readily faked collectible there is. All one needs is a negative and he can make yet another print. This may be the most disturbing question in the market for artistic images, and in the future it may have far-reaching effects on the desirability of images such as daguerreotypes which can be proven to be unique.

Faced with the problem of reproducability, most photographers will say that they control the number of prints made from their negatives, and they almost always do keep the negatives to themselves. That's fine . . . for now. But what about years from now. What's to keep Ansel Adams from printing up more copies of one of his famous views of Yosemite? What's to keep an archivist in the Library of Congress from taking an old glass-plate negative of Abraham Lincoln and making "new" albumen prints from it and selling them to unwary collectors?

The fact is, those old glass plate negatives in the collection of the Library of Congress are being reprinted every day — and at least one collector nearly got burned when he bought a recent print made from and old negative showing Abe Lincoln. It was offered as a historic print, and it did indeed look old and authentic despite the "scratch" which the would-be seller duly noted. But that "scratch" turned out to be something else — it was there because the glass plate negative had broken, and the print of Honest Abe was one of many which the Library of Congress sells for $2 each. They all have the same flaw. To a collector who knew enough to check, that telltale flaw proved that the photo was not "old" as the seller claimed. Fortunately, he was able to get his money back. But many buyers would never suspect such an image, and might never learn the truth.

As we said, the way to collect is carefully!

# PRESERVING THE OLD IMAGE

What do collectors do with all the old photographs they accumulate? That can be a problem, especially when the collection numbers hundreds of thousands of images — more than can possibly be displayed around the house.

We heard of one collector who kept his historic and valuable prints in a stack under his bed. Other collectors toss the prints in a large drawer, and yet others keep matted prints lined up like books on a shelf, to be viewed only when pulled out.

None of these methods is advisable. For one thing, an old photograph is a fairly fragile artifact — even those old tintypes printed on sheets of japanned iron (despite the name, tintypes contain no tin). According to Eugene Ostroff, the Smithsonian Institution's photography curator and author of an article called "Conserving and Restoring Photographic Collections (*Museum News*, May 1974), "Photographic collections are extremely vulnerable to the effects of residual chemicals. If the chemicals used in processing are not completely removed from the photograph, the image gradually will deteriorate and eventually will be destroyed," usually by fading or acquiring stains in future years. So the first thing to do is check to make sure the image has no residual chemicals left on it (an even fairly recent work, such as a print by Stieglitz, can have this problem). Some photographers were careful to produce clean prints; others, such as Lewis Hine and Walker Evans, were less fastidious, and their prints often need attention before storage or display.

Chemicals used in mounting can also damage prints. Many old Talbot calotypes were mounted with animal adhesives, which may eventually cause fading of the image. Some photographers have used rubber cement, which will eventually cause bleaching.

Protecting the photograph from fingerprints is also a good idea, since fingers leave salt deposits which can eventually leave blotches on the images. Hence, the prevalence of matting, which also serves the aesthetic function of setting the photograph off from its surroundings.

Matting and mounting must be done properly, however, since many materials that might be used are not chemically inert and the acid in some cardboards can eventually damage an image printed on paper. Experts advise against using anything but 100 percent rag board for dry-mounted photographs, and in afixing any image to cardboard one should not use Scotch tape, rubber cement, masking tape, or spray adhesives (despite the fact that the latter are advertised for use in mounting photographs). The best is to consult a local museum expert or reliable frame shop to insure proper mounting and matting of any image that is considered collectible.

Some collectors display their prints behind glass, plexiglass, or non-reflective plastic. In such cases, the print should never touch the surface of the glass. Matting is usually used to keep the two separate. Whether to frame the image or not is entirely up to the collector, of course, and antique images are often best preserved in cases.

Paper images such as art prints which are to be stored away should be mounted (to keep them from being folded crinkled, touched or damaged) and matted (to keep them from coming in contact with each other) and, ideally, stored in a solander box (a type of wooden box lined with acid-free paper which has long been popular with poster and print collectors and others who save paper ephemera and want to avoid the threat posed by various woods and cardboards). Photographic images should be stored in a cool, dry place (humidity, especially, can foster fungus growth) free of termites, silverfish and other little print-loving creatures.

As to restoring old images, especially early daguerreotypes, tintypes and ambrotypes, experts hold a variety of conflicting opinions. The big problem is finding a qualified restorer to begin with, since they are few in number. Photography has been viewed as a restorable medium for only a few years.

Daguerreotypes were usually protected in cases and displayed under glass. But in many cases, the glass has been removed, exposing the daguerreotype to air and, sometimes, oxidization. This defect can be rectified. A $2 oxidized daguerreotype bought at a flea market was recently restored to reveal an image of President Franklin Pierce. It was resold for more than $1,000.

WET PLATE LENS, Dall-
meyer #3A, London, 16",
brass, Petzuall type F4 for portraits.
Ca. 1867          C/$175.00
Courtesy of John Groomes,
Nashville, TN.

Eastman Kodak, GRAFLEX, series B,
3¼ x 4¼".
Ca. 1925-1942          C/$71.00
Courtesy of John Groomes, Nashville,
TN.

MAGIC LANTERN, REFLECTS images
on a wall by kerosene wick which burns inside of the lantern.
Ca. 1880-1890's          C/$75.00
Courtesy of John Groomes, Nashville, TN.

CONLEY (Junior), folding plate camera, polished cherry interior, 4 x 5" exposure.
Ca. 1900-1910        C/$45.00
Courtesy of John Groomes, Nashville, TN.

THORNTON-PICARD, 5 x 7" folding plate view camera, English made.
Ca. 1890        C/$300.00
Courtesy of John Groomes, Nashville, TN.

Rodchester Optical Co., folding plate view camera, 5 x 7".
Ca. 1890        C/$200.00
Courtesy of John Groomes, Nashville, TN.

REGNO, 4 x 5″ Cycle camera, black mahogany, make unknown.

C/$60.00

Courtesy of John Groomes, Nashville, TN.

Eastman Kodak, No.4, 4 x 5″ exposure, black bellows, wood trim on bed, auto shutter.
Ca. 1907-1914          C/$47.00
Courtesy of John Groomes, Nashville, TN.

Burke and James, No.3 REXO JR., 3½ x 4½ single achromatic, Ilex lens.

C/$9.00

Courtesy of John Groomes, Nashville, TN.

AL-VISTA PANORAMIC CAMERA, revolving lens, takes a 180° exposure, 5 x 12″ long.
Ca. 1896-1901                    C/$154.00
Courtesy of John Groomes, Nashville, TN.

Left: Kodak, No.2A BROWNIE
Right: Kodak, No.2A CARTRIDGE HAWKEYE

Kodak, HAWKEYE No.5 WENO, box camera.
Ca. 1904-1914                    C/$58.00
Courtesy of John Groomes, Nashville, TN.

Kodak STEREO, 3½ x 6″ exposures on No.101 rolls.
Ca. 1901-1905                    C/$325.00
Courtesy of John Groomes, Nashville, TN.

REVERSIBLE BACK PREMO, 5 x 7".

Rodchester Optical Co., LONG FOCUS PREMO, made of polished mahogany, covered in leather, red bellows.
Ca. 1895                    C/$70.00
Courtesy of John Groomes, Nashville, TN.

Eastman Kodak, CENTURY-Model 47, folding plate.
Ca. 1907-1926              C/$46.00
Courtesy of John Groomes, Nashville, TN.

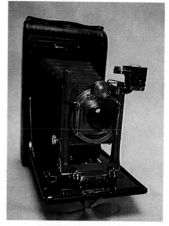

FOLDING KODAK No.4A

Kodak, JIFFY, common rollfilm, pop out front, Twindar lens, and zone focus.
Ca. 1935-1945          C/$10.00
Courtesy of John Groomes, Nashville, TN.

Eastman Kodak, POCKET CAMERA.
Ca. 1920's          C/$20.00
Courtesy of John Groomes, Nashville, TN.

Eastman Kodak, VEST POCKET CAMERA, auto shutter.
Ca. 1912-1934          C/$33.00
Courtesy of John Groomes, Nashville, TN.

Eastman Kodak, No.1A POCKET SERIES II, auto shutter.
Ca. 1910          C/$20.00
Courtesy of John Groomes, Nashville, TN.

Eastman Kodak, No.2A, FOLDING
CARTRIDGE PREMO, rollfilm.
Ca. 1910-1913          C/$8.00
Courtesy of John Groomes, Nashville,
TN.

Ansco, No.1 READYSET ROYAL

KODAK PETITE

Eastman Kodak, folding No.2A.
Ca.1910-1915          C/$23.00-32.00
Courtesy of John Groomes, Nashville,
TN.

Kodak No.2 STEREO BROWNIE, carrying case, 10
stereo pictures.
Ca. 1909                               C/$12.00
Courtesy of John Groomes, Nashville, TN.

ARGUS A2 with extinction
meter, focus 6' to infinity.
Ca. 1936-1950      C/$12.00
Courtesy of John Groomes,
Nashville, TN.

Mercury II, MODEL CX,
takes 18 x 24mm vertical 65 exposures, standard 35mm film,
f2.7/35mm, rotary shutter.
Ca.1940-1950        C/$23.00
Courtesy of John Groomes,
Nashville, TN.

# SOME FURTHER CAUTIONS

It should be obvious by now that collecting old photographs is a hobby which requires the knowledge of a specialist, if not an expert. Only though years of experience can one learn the fine points that separate the serious collector from the amateur.

There are countless pitfalls awaiting the collector who hasn't done his or her homework. Here are a few of them:

Beware of any old image offered for sale at a suspiciously low price. It is a simple matter for someone with an old camera and a bit of familiarity with pioneer photography techniques to make, say, an ambrotype copy of an old image. With a little fake aging, the image will look suitably old itself, and can easily be passed off as a genuine "antique" when it is really a contemporary product. Few cases of this have been reported, but the potential is certainly there, especially as prices for old images soar.

**Popular Photography** magazine surveyed more than two dozen dealers and collectors and found that most of them "had had some kind of direct experience with fakes being presented to them for purchase, or sold to people they knew."

There are practicing tintypists even today, and at Greenfield Village and Henry Ford Museum in Dearborn, Mich., museum tintypist Richard Wolfe has been at work on and off since 1939. One recent summer weekend, he made 166 plates of which 80 percent had four images to the plate, for a total of more than 550 pictures. When he devilishly offered one four-image whole-plate showing **himself** to buyers at a collector and dealers' trade fair, nearly all accepted it as genuine. Finally, after hours of showing it, someone finally noticed that it was a tintype of Wolfe himself and deduced that it couldn't possibly be old! Fortunately, Wolfe was honest.

A quarter-plate tintype of "Honest Abe" Lincoln, copied from an 1863 Alexander Gardner print, sold as a novelty for a couple of dollars at Greenfield Village. One later appeared in an antique shop, priced at $25.

"When it became obvious to the enterprising person that he can get this kind of money for a piece of glass with an image on it, which he can make right in his darkroom, then we've got a real problem," says Jose Oracca, a teacher of old-process photography and a noted image restorer at the University of Delaware.

Tintypes currently being made at the George Eastman House are all embossed with a star in the corner of the plate, and Greenfield Village has decided to emboss the village's name on the back of tintype plates made from now on. That's little consolation, however, since such marks can be cut off or otherwise removed.

The collector must be cautious—and knowledgeable—to reap the rewards that come from building a fine collection of interesting old images.

# IMAGES
# Price Listings

Images are listed in four categories—groups (i.e., lots containing more than one image, as in collections of stereo views), interior views, outdoor views, and portraits (whether of a single person or a number of people). When a generally accepted title for the print exists, that title is used; otherwise, a general description of the image is listed. Measurement of the images are given height before width in inches. Significant defects in condition are listed in cases where such information was available.

# DAGUERREOTYPES

(Most of these images are by anonymous or little known photographers. Images by well known daguerreotypists such as Mathew Brady are listed under the photographers's name in the "Artist-Name Photographs" section.)

Left: John Plumbe, Jr. Right: Half-plate daguerreotype of the Capitol circa 1846. by John Plumbe, Jr. who opened one of the first daguerreian galleries, in Washington, D.C.

Group, two portraits, one showing woman with child, the other a man, in double case, both ¼ plate, c. 1855 . . . . .   **45.00-50.00**

Group, two portraits, one showing a young woman and a young boy (possibly an Indian) holding hands, the other showing a man and woman in their early 30s, both 1/6 plates in case, c. 1860 . . . . .   **35.00-40.00**

Outdoor, 11 people in front of large clapboard cottage with horse and buggy

Anonymous half-plate daguerreotype portrait of man and woman holding hands.
$500-$600.

Sixth-plate daguerreotype, unidentified subject, plain mat, case in fair condition. $15-$20.

Half-plate daguerreotype of Daniel Webster, by Albert Sands Southworth and Josiah Johnson Hawes, c. April 1851. $10,000.

in front, ¼ plate in full case (image slightly solarized)..................... **275.00**

Outdoor, family bidding farewell to visitors about to drive away in buggy, ¼ plate in full case..................... **200.00**

Outdoor, "W. T. Hall and little Will, with Lucy Parker, the mare, going to see mother at Francestown" (handwritten on slip of paper inside case), 1/6 plate in case, hinge split..................... **265.00**

Outdoor, large group of children posed in front of school with teacher, ½ plate in full case......................... **350.00**

Outdoor, four-story columned building identified on back of plate as School Building, Mexico, Oswego Co., N.Y., ½ plate in "Washington Monument" case, hinge split......................... **375.00-400.00**

Outdoor, hotel view, "H. Bell" painted on portico, 1/6 plate in full case, c. 1850 **175.00-185.00**

Outdoor, gold mining scene showing several buildings, identified as "panorama of Grizzly Flat" in California, ½ plate, 1849.................. **2,500.00**

Outdoor, commercial street scene, ½ plate............................. **600.00**

Outdoor, New England factory, 1/6 plate, c. 1850...................... **750.00-800.00**

Outdoor, facades of building, 1/6 plate in "Grecian Urn" case, New York, c. 1841............................. **60.00-75.00**

Portrait, Edgar Allen Poe, c. 1848..... **35,000.-40,000.**

Portrait, Jefferson Davis, ½ plate, mint **30,000.00**

Portrait, man and woman holding hands, ½ plate anonymous, glass and gilt-wood frame, (several scratches).... **500.00-600.00**

Portrait, young woman, three-quarter figure, 1/6 plate tinted, Root's Gallery legend embossed on lining............ **75.00-100.00**

Portrait, old woman in black dress and white lace bonnet, 1/6 plate in "Delicate Roses" case....................... **25.00-30.00**

Portrait, man holding book, 1/9 plate set in brooch-style gilt mat in ¼ plate leather case, c. 1845 . . . . . . . . . . . . . . . . .  **40.0-45.00**

Portrait, sitting boy wearing three-piece suit with hands folded in lap, 1/6 plate in Union Case, New York, c. 1860 . . . . . . .  **30.00-40.00**

Portrait, little girl standing on chair beside Roman Doric column, 1/6 plate in "Flower Medallion" case, c. 1854 . . . .  **30.00-35.00**

Portrait, Cyrus Fields, full plate by anonymous photographer, plush-lined leather case (some scratches) . . . . . . . . . .  **400.00-500.00**

Portrait, mother, father and two daughters, ¼ plate in "Capture of Major Andre" Union case by Samuel Peck, c. 1856 . . . . . . . . . . . . . . . . . . . . . . . . . . . .  **100.00-120.00**

Portrait, man in his mid-20s wearing neck scarf, ¼ plate in "Spray of Roses" case with double mat and glass, c. 1851 .  **50.00-60.00**

Portrait, seated woman wearing gold earrings and brooch, 1/6 plate in Union case by Sameul Peck, New Haven, c. 1857 . . . . . . . . . . . . . . . . . . . . . . . . . . .  **40.00-50.00**

Portrait, middle-aged man, 1/16 plate in circular gilt locket with scroll design, c. 1851 . . . . . . . . . . . . . . . . . . . . . . . . . . .  **20.00-30.00**

Portrait, woman in black dress with lace collar, seated at a table, ¼ plate in "The Memorial" Union case with oval mat and glass, by Samuel Peck & Co., c. 1853 . . . . . . . . . . . . . . . . . . . . . . . . . . .  **90.00-110.00**

Portrait, young woman with her hair in a bun and wearing a high-bodiced dress with lace cuffs and cameo brooch, 1/16 plate in "Love Birds" leather case, c. 1851 . . . . . . . . . . . . . . . . . . . . . . . . . . .  **40.00-45.00**

Portrait, elderly woman in bonnet and robe, 1/6 plate in green velvet case with satin lining (image discolored) . . . . . . . .  **20.00-30.00**

Portrait, two men sitting, 1/6 plate in "Nesting Birds" Union case by Littlefield, Parsons, c. 1860 . . . . . . . . . . . . . .  **40.00**

Portrait, two women wearing bonnets and shawls, 1/6 plate in case, c. 1844...  **40.00-50.00**

Portrait, two young men in black suits, both seated, 1/6 plate tinted, in "Grape Medallion" case, c. 1857.............  **35.00**

Portrait, (self-portrait) of daguerreotypist in a mirror, 1/9 plate in case with floral motif (slight scratches on image)..  **70.00-80.00**

Portrait, man wearing coat and bow tie, ¼ plate in "Delicate Roses" variant case, tinted, matted.................  **20.00-30.00**

Portrait, young woman wearing gold earrings, necklace, 1/6 plate tinted, in "Carved Oval Motif" case, octagonal mat ...............................  **15.00-20.00**

Portrait, two young women, 1/6 plate in case, c. 1855......................  **20.00-30.00**

Portrait, man with a woman in a loose calico dress, 1/6 plate, cased, c. 1860 (some discoloration)................  **20.00-25.00**

Portrait, man, woman and infant, 1/6 plate uncased, c. 1856...............  **35.00**

Portrait, two women in their early 30s, 1/9 plate in union case with variation of "accented oval" motif, mat marked "Anson," c. 1855..................  **20.00-25.00**

Portrait, woman wearing shawl and bonnet with flowers, 1/6 plate in "Flower Medallion" case, c. 1855.............  **20.00-30.00**

Portrait, middle-aged man and woman wearing scarf tied at neck, in "Lily and Rose" case, 1/6 plate, c. 1850.........  **20.00-25.00**

Portrait, middle-aged couple and three children, ¼ plate in "Delicate Roses" variation case, c. 1845...............  **30.00**

Portrait, 12-year-old boy seated at table, 1/6 plate in embossed case, c. 1850.....  **20.00**

Portrait, boy in black suit and vest, 1/9 plate in case with geometric and leaf design, c. 1850......................  **20.00**

Portrait of Daniel Webster, A.S. Southworth and Josiah J. Hawes ½ plate,

| | |
|---|---|
| 1851 (some oxidization at edges)....... | **8,000.-10,000.** |

Portrait, nine-year-old girl in black party dress with lace trim, 1/6 plate cased, New York, c. 1850................... **25.00**

Portrait, man in black suit and vest, 1/6 plate in "Mixed Flowers" variant case, c. 1850............................. **25.00-30.00**

Portrait, man with chin whiskers wearing fancy vest, 1/6 plate in "Spray of Roses" case, c. 1851................ **20.00-30.00**

Portrait, man with mutton-chop sideburns, 1/6 plate in "Thistle Motif" case, c. 1858........................... **25.00**

Portrait, married couple in early 40s, woman wearing plain Quaker-style dress, ¼ plate in "Delicate Roses" variant case, c. 1847................ **25.00-30.00**

Portrait, middle-aged couple, man with gray beard holding pince-nez glasses in his hand, ¼ plate in case, c. 1857...... **30.00**

Portrait, middle-aged man with mutton-chop sideburns and vest, 1/6 plate in Union case......................... **25.00**

Portrait, middle-aged woman in dark dress and white lace cap, 1/6 plate in case with oval and leaf design, c. 1850.. **25.00**

Portrait, stocky man in his 30s, formal dress, 1/6 plate in Eichmeyer leather "band" case, c. 1855................ **25.00**

Portrait, 40-year-old woman in black dress, 1/6 plate in "Two Lilies" case, c. 1850.............................. **20.00-25.00**

Portrait, woman in her 30s wearing white dress, 1/6 plate in "Delicate Roses" variant case, c. 1844........... **25.00-30.00**

Portrait, young boy and girl, ¼ plate cased, Cincinnati, c. 1860............. **30.00**

Portrait, young man in black suit and vest, 1/6 plate in "Love Birds" case, c. 1851.............................. **20.00**

Portrait, young woman holding plump child, 1/6 plate in "Morning Glory"

| | |
|---|---|
| case, c. 1851...................... | **15.00-20.00** |
| Portrait, two pouting brothers dressed in identical white jackets, 1/6 plate in half case (slight tarnish at edges of image)... | **20.00** |
| Portrait, middle-aged gentleman, ¼ plate, in top-opening case with narrow paper mat, c. 1840.................. | **65.00-75.00** |
| Portrait, elegantly dressed young man wearing gold hoop earring in each ear and wearing a paisley vest and velvet collared jacket, 1/6 plate cased, hinge split. | **70.00-75.00** |
| Portrait, bearded, balding gentleman resting head against top of high back chair, 1/6 plate cased............... | **50.00-70.00** |
| Portrait, baby girl in large-skirt white dress, 1/6 plate tinted, in half case..... | **35.00** |
| Portrait, little girl cuddling her pet cat in her lap, 1/6 plate in half case......... | **60.00-75.00** |
| Portrait, bearded Western gentleman in fine suit, photographer identified as R. H. Vance, Premium Daguerrian Galleries, San Francisco, 1/6 plate in full case, hinge split.................... | **80.00-100.00** |
| Portrait, man in masonic apron holding rolled parchment in one hand, 1/6 plate tinted in half case................... | **75.00** |
| Portrait, two serious young brothers, cheeks tinted light pink, photographer identified as W. Germon, Philadelphia, 1/6 plate in case, hinge split........... | **40.00-50.00** |
| Portrait, young woman seated in front of mountain lake backdrop, 1/6 plate in half case......................... | **25.00-35.00** |
| Portrait, dark-eyed young woman in plaid dress, 1/9 plate in full case, hinge split .............................. | **25.00** |
| Portrait, "American Gothic"-style husband and wife, 1/6 plate matted....... | **20.00-30.00** |
| Portrait, little boy in a dress, cheeks tinted pink, 1/6 plate, half case........ | **35.00** |
| Portrait, mother and daughter in reverse painted passepartout, ¼ plate, marked | |

Bremen (Germany)................ **140.00**

Portrait, a gentleman, photographer identified as J. Gurney, New York, ¼ plate in half case................. **115.00**

Portrait, young girl, 1/6 plate in wooden frame............................ **25.00**

Portrait, young boy, 1/6 plate in full case............................. **30.00**

Portrait, man and wife identified as Dr. Jas. Anderson and wife No. 3, the doctor wearing a top hat and overcoat, wife wearing bonnet trimmed in lace, 1/6 plate in full case, hinge split.......... **50.00**

Portrait, man and wife in front of studio backdrop, 1/6 plate in full case, c. 1845. **50.00**

Portrait, young man with muttonchops identified as D. B. Johnson, ¼ plate in full case......................... **40.00-50.00**

Portrait of bearded man identified as E. Jacobs, New Orleans, ¼ plate in case... **50.00**

Portrait, two gentlemen, one man's arm around the other's shoulders, 1/6 plate cased, hinge split (some tarnish at edges of image)........................ **30.00**

Portrait, serious young man wearing wide-lapel jacket and holding book in hand, ¼ plate cased, hinge split....... **35.00**

Portrait, musician holding clarinet and rolled sheet of paper, 1/6 plate cased... **165.00**

Portrait, gentleman identified as William Shew of San Francisco, 1/6 plate in full case............................. **75.00-100.00**

Portrait, Jenny Lind wearing bonnet with long black veil, shawl, and gloves, possibly a copy of another image, 1/6 plate in Jenny Lind case, hinge repaired. **550.00-600.00**

Portrait, a European woman in black passepartout, ¼ plate (heavy tarnish at rim).............................. **85.00**

Portrait, young man in multi-patterned outfit, 1/6 plate in half case.......... **20.00-25.00**

Portrait, husband and wife, man wearing high starched white collar, woman with long drop earrings, 1/6 plate...... **15.00-25.00**

Portrait, schoolboy with his high, visored cap resting on a book on table, 1/6 plate in half case................. **25.00**

Portrait, long-faced gentleman, 1/6 plate in half case, original seal (part of image slightly solarized).............. **15.00-20.00**

Portrait, long-haired boy with dimpled chin, 1/6 plate in half case............ **20.00-25.00**

Portrait, peaceful-looking middle-aged woman, asleep in armchair with crochet cushion, 1/6 plate in full case with seal, image dated June 1846.............. **50.00-60.00**

Portrait, pretty young woman in nightdress lying against enormous pillow with Chippendale-style headboard visible behind her, 1/6 plate in half case....... **75.00**

Portrait, four men holding top hats, full plate in oval mask, uncased........... **400.00**

Portrait, young woman seated by table with flower pot, photographed by Southworth and Hawes of Boston, Mass., 1/6 plate uncased............ **800.00-900.00**

Portrait, mother and child, mother wearing fancy bonnet, photographed by Anson of New York City, ¼ plate matted and framed..................... **400.00**

Portrait, two girls, one reading book, photographed by Southworth and Hawes, Boston, Mass., 1/6 plate uncased............................. **800.00**

Portrait, gentleman in velvet-lapel coat and bow tie, photographed by Jeremiah Gurney of New York City, ½ plate matted and framed..................... **300.00**

Portrait, little girl sitting on table between her parents, ¼ plate in case, hinge repaired............................ **50.00**

Portrait, gentleman, photographer identified as Washington Gallery of

Hartford, Conn., 1/9 plate in full case. . **30.00**

Portrait, dead child lying in bed, 1/9 plate in case with newspaper clipping of obituary . . . . . . . . . . . . . . . . . . . . . . . . . . . **40.00**

Portrait, young girl, photographed by Anson of New York City, 1/6 plate in oval mat and case. . . . . . . . . . . . . . . . . . **150.00**

Portrait, young fair-haired boy, ¼ plate in passepartout. . . . . . . . . . . . . . . . . . . . . **65.00**

Portrait, heavy woman in satin dress, blue tinting added to ribbon at her throat, photographer identified as Knapp, 1/6 plate cased, hinge split. . . . . **25.00**

Portrait, American sailor in dress uniform, photographer identified as W. H. Lewis of New York City, 1/6 plate with tinting, cased. . . . . . . . . . . . . . . . . . **150.00**

Portrait, woman in plaid dress, photographer identified as M. A. Root of Philadelphia, Pa., ¼ plate cased. . . . . . . . . . **125.00**

Portrait, young madonna wearing bottle curls and heavy braid on her head, 1/6 plage in case, hinge split. . . . . . . . . . . . . **20.00**

Portrait, little girl seated in child-size captain's chair and wearing necklace, 1/6 plate tinted, cased. . . . . . . . . . . . . . . . **30.00**

Portrait, gentleman holding top hat, photographer identified as Robert H. Vance, San Francisco, ¼ plate cased, 1850s . . . . . . . . . . . . . . . . . . . . . . . . . . . **125.00-150.00**

Portrait, young woman wearing a ruffled bonnet trimmed with sprigs of flowers and fastened by a large taffeta bow, 1/9 plate in case, hinge split. . . . . . . . . . . . . . **15.00-20.00**

Portrait, young family with baby sprawling across parents' laps, photographer identified as R. N. Keely of Philadelphia, Pa., 1/6 plate cased. . . . . . . . . . . . **30.00**

Portrait of a handsome woman wearing bare-shouldered gown and velvet choker, long pendant earrings and bottle curls, 1/9 plate in full push-button case. **45.00**

Portrait, handsome gentleman wearing top hat and overcoat, 1/6 plate cased, hinge broken.................... 65.00

Portrait, young woman in print dress seated before mountain backdrop, 1/6 plate in half case.................. 35.00

Portrait, family with little boy leaning against his father, ¼ plate, some tinting, full case.......................... 50.00

Portrait, gentleman with his hair styled into an enormous curl, photographer identified as Collins of Springfield, Mass., 1/6 plate in half case.......... 30.00

Portrait, young man wearing a high-crowned felt hat tilted to one side, 1/6 plate in half case.................. 30.00

Portrait, pretty, brooding young woman in a striped dress and holding a daguerreotype case in one hand, 1/6 plate in half case......................... 30.00

Portrait, a genial young man finely dressed, 1/6 plate in case, hinge split.... 25.00

Portrait, grumpy-looking child with droopy socks sitting in a highchair, 1/6 plate in half case................... 25.00

Portrait, gentleman with a bowtie, photographer identified as Anson of New York City, 1/6 plate in half case (slight tarnish at top of mat).......... 25.00-35.00

Portrait, two almost identical women, one resting her hand on the other's shoulder, 1/6 plate in full case......... 25.00

Portrait, young man (probably a war veteran) wearing kepi and resting elbow on table while saluting, 1/9 plate cased, hinge split........................ 75.00

Portrait, inscrutable gentleman wearing a top hat and bundled in heavy overcoat, wearing leather gloves and holding a cigar, 1/9 plate, cased, hinge split (some light spotting of image).............. 25.00

Portrait, young couple, 1/6 plate in full case . . . . . . . . . . . . . . . . . . . . . . . . . . . . . . .     **30.00**

Portrait, old woman wearing a ruffled bonnet and shawl, 1/6 plate cased (some tarnish at edges). . . . . . . . . . . . . . . . . . . . .     **20.00**

Portrait, young man, 1/6 plate in half case . . . . . . . . . . . . . . . . . . . . . . . . . . . . . .     **20.00**

Portrait, schoolboy next to a table with book and his cap on it and a potted ivy wreth, photographer identified as W. Naumann, 1/6 plate in passepartout. . . .     **150.00**

Portrait, distinguished-looking gentleman with arm resting on table, ½ plate in carved gilt frame. . . . . . . . . . . .     **150.00-175.00**

Portrait, peevish little girl propped up against a pillow on a couch, photographer identified as Hagaman, Philadelphia, Pa. 1/6 plate in full case. .     **25.00-30.00**

Portrait, gentle woman wearing a pale dress sitting beside a basket of flowers, photographer identified as Van Loan and Ennis' Gellery of Philadelphia, Pa., 1/6 plate in case, hinge split. . . . . . . . . . .     **40.00**

Portrait, mother holding a smiling, fat baby in her lap, 1/6 plate in case, hinge split . . . . . . . . . . . . . . . . . . . . . . . . . . . . .     **25.00**

Portrait, three young girls in print dresses with tightly-fitted bodices and tiny waists, 1/6 plate, cased, hinge split.     **35.00**

Portrait, woman identified as "Aunt Anne Conover" wearing ringlets and braids, 1/6 plate cased, hinge split. . . . . .     **20.00**

Portrait, two boys dressed in matching white-collared dark suits, one sitting and the other standing, 1/6 plate in case, hinge split. . . . . . . . . . . . . . . . . . . . . . . . . .     **20.00-25.00**

Portrait, delivery coachman wearing heavy, long-sleeved black-closing duster over street clothes and holding a whip, 1/6 plate cased. . . . . . . . . . . . . . . . . . . . . .     **150.00**

Portrait, seated father and mother with

daughter standing behind them, identifying label on back dated 1856, 1/6 plate in carved wood frame..................  **125.00**

Portrait, gentleman wearing top hat and bushy gray hair, 1/6 plate tinted, in full case ...............................  **60.00**

Portrait, long-haired urban gentleman wearing spectacles, 1/6 plate in half case  **25.00**

Portrait, young woman, 1/16 plate in push-button case...................  **20.00**

Portrait, gentlewoman in white lace cap and plaid dress, 1/6 plate in case, (some tarnish at edges)....................  **50.00**

Portrait, little girl wearing pinafore, 1/6 plate with tinting, in half case.........  **30.00**

Portrait, a homley, smiling woman with her hands folded across her stomach, 1/6 plate in full case.................  **25.00**

Portrait, a gentleman holding a fancy cane, 1/6 plate cased, hinge split.......  **25.00-30.00**

Portrait, young woman wrapped in huge paisley shawl and wearing kid gloves, 1/6 plate in full case................  **45.00**

Portrait, black and white panting dog, 1/9 plate cased.....................  **60.00**

Portrait, young man with large floral bow tie, 1/6 plate cased, hinge split.....  **25.00**

Portrait, young woman in front of backdrop of trees and mountains, 1/9 plate in half case..........................  **30.00**

Portrait, young woman and little girl sitting ramrod stiff, tinting added to throat and wrist bows, 1/6 plate cased, hinge split ..............................  **25.00-35.00**

Portrait, gaunt woman with skinny bottle curls wrapped in shawl, 1/6 plate in half case..........................  **25.00**

Portrait, little child wearing dark feathered hat and tunic coat and holding buggy whip, 1/6 plate in full case, case damaged .........................  **45.00**

Portrait, middle-aged couple holding hands, 1/6 plate in half case........... 25.00

Portrait, a gentleman, photographer identified as C. D. Fredericks of New York, 1/6 plate cased, hinge split...... 36.00

Portrait, young woman wrapped in fringed shawl, photographer identified as E. Long of St. Louis, Mo., 1/6 plate cased, hinge split...................... 65.00

Portrait, woman in striped dress with white collar and starched cuffs, 1/6 plate in full case......................... 35.00

Portrait, young man with open book held up to camera, 1/6 plate in full case. 25.00-30.00

Portrait, young girl in short-sleeved dress, 1/6 plate tinted, cased, hinge split 35.00

Portrait, dapper gentleman with cigar in one hand, legs crossed, photographer identified as Atelier Photographique Harris's Portrait Rooms, Brighton, half plate in passeportout................ 150.00-200.00

Portrait, motherly-looking woman wearing spectacles, half plate cased, original seal................................... 85.00

Portrait of fat, jolly woman and skinny husband, ½ plate cased, hinge split.... 70.00

Portrait, gentleman resting arm on table, ¼ plate in passepartout studded with "jewels".......................... 85.00

Portrait, young girl holding flowers, 1/6 plate in passepartout................. 50.00

Portrait, family with mother and father each holding an infant, ¼ plate uncased 35.00

Portrait, gentleman holding walking stick, photographer identified as Victor Plumier, Photographe, Paris, 1/6 plate in passepartout (retaped)............ 80.00-95.00

Portrait, a Teutonic-looking gentleman, ¼ plate in black velvet passepartout (some tarnish at edges)............... 80.00

Portrait, young girl with hands in her lap, 1/6 plate in full case............. 20.00-25.00

Portrait, a woman, 1/6 plate cased, hinge split.......................... 20.00

Portrait, waifish young girl standing beside loveseat, 1/9 plate in half case... 20.00

Portrait, steely-eyed matron wearing lace mittens and a white cap, 1/6 plate in half case........................... 35.00

Portrait, family with father reading from open book to his wife and daughter, 1/6 plate in pale mauve leather case........ 250.00

Portrait, young woman with thick, bouncy ringlets, 1/6 plate in half case... 25.00

Portrait, tranquil young woman with freckles and hoop earrings, 1/6 plate in half case.......................... 20.00-25.00

Portrait, woman wearing bonnet, 1/9 plate cased, hinge split.............. 20.00-25.00

Portrait, dark-eyed woman with Jenny Lind-style hair, 1/6 plate cased, hinge split............................... 25.00-30.00

Portrait, little girl perched on highchair with lace and feather hat hanging to her right, 1/6 plate in full case........... 65.00

Portrait, man, 1/6 plate in half case.... 20.00

Portrait, long-haired young man wearing silk top hat and with legs crossed, 1/6 plate in full case................. 50.00-60.00

Portrait, freckle-faced boy, 1/6 plate tinted in half case................... 30.00

Portrait, dour-looking gentleman, 1/6 plate cased......................... 20.00-25.00

Portrait, young girl wearing a cape and holding a closed parasol in her lap, 1/6 plate uncased........................ 18.00-25.00

Portrati, stern-looking minister in his dark robes with white collar, ¼ plate cased, hinge split.................... 80.00

Portrait, woman wearing cameo at her neck on choker, 1/9 plate cased........ 15.00-20.00

Portrait, two young women, similarly dressed, holding hands, 1/6 plate in full case ............................... 25.00-35.00

Portrait, young woman with hands folded in her lap, 1/6 plate in half case..... **30.00**

Portrait, young couple with happy faces, 1/6 plate in full case (slightly worn)..... **30.00**

Portrait, young woman holding Bible partially open in her lap, 1/6 plate cased, hinge split......................... **35.00**

Portrait, young woman with short hair, 1/9 plate in half case................ **25.00**

Portrait, prissy middle-aged woman, 1/6 plate uncased...................... **15.00**

Portrait, beautiful woman with tight-fitting dress, 1/6 plate in full case...... **65.00**

Portrait, young soldier in high collared tunic, 1/9 plate in half case........... **35.00**

Portrait, six children, ¾ plate tinted, in leather case........................ **175.00**

Portrait, four young people, ½ plate (some spotting at bottom of image)..... **75.00**

Portrait, family of four, ½ plate in full case................................ **80.00**

Portrait, mother and children, ½ plate cased............................... **80.00**

Portrait, sailor wearing regulation blouse and holding a clasped album, ¼ plate uncased...................... **40.00**

Portrait, family of seven, ¼ plate lightly tinted, in full case.................. **55.00**

Portrait, young boy and his sister, ¼ plate.............................. **45.00**

Portrait, three children holding hands, 1/6 plate in full case................ **15.00-20.00**

Portrait, pensive young girl with tinted basket of flowers, 1/6 plate in full case.. **15.00-20.00**

Portrait, young man, 1/6 plate in case.. **25.00**

Portrait, middle-aged man, 1/6 plate in full case............................ **10.00-15.00**

Portrait, middle-aged woman seated in front of luxury backdrop, image signed "J. S. Old's, Newark, N.J.," 1/6 plate cased............................... **25.00-30.00**

Portrait, young man, 1/6 plate in "Lyre Motif" case, c. 1843 (some scratches at edges of image)...................... **35.00**

Portrait, man, 1/6 plate cased, c. 1843.. **20.00**

Portrait, man in dark jacket identified as Adam Gordon, ¼ plate cased, c. 1845.. **35.00**

Portrait, woman in flowered dress, 1/6 plate in "Curved Octagon with Scroll Center" case, c. 1845............... **15.00-20.00**

Portrait, balding minister, ¼ plate in "Delicate Roses" variant case, c. 1846.. **30.00-35.00**

Portrait, middle-aged man holding cane, 1/6 plate in "Delicate Roses" variant case, c. 1846....................... **20.00**

Portrait, old woman wearing glasses and a lace cap, 1/6 plate in Union case with medallion motif, c. 1850 (case cover missing)............................ **30.00**

Portrait, little boy wearing plaid pants and scarf, holding pony whip, ¼ plate in Union case with "jewels" on covers, c. 1855............................... **50.00**

Portrait, sleeping or dead baby, 1/9 plate in Union case with oval mat, c. 1855............................... **20.00**

Portrait, young girl by Knapp, 1/6 plate in "Little Gem" Union case, New York, 1857............................. **30.00-40.00**

Portrait, young woman, three-quarter view, 1/6 plate tinted, "Root's Gallery" studio legend embossed on plush lining, leather case........................ **75.00**

# AMBROTYPES

(Most of these images are by anonymous or little known photographers. Images by well known photographers are listed by name in the "Artist-Name Photographers" section.)

Top Left: Ambrotype photograph on velvet inside cover, 1/6 plate, full case c. 1864, $35. Top Right: Ambrotype, man in top hat. Full case, 1/6 plate, c. 1868l, $25-$30. Opposite: Ambrotype, unidentified man, 1/6 plate c. 1870, $20.

Group, three portraits, two of young men in oval gold metallic mats and frames, one of two women and a man, c. 1860..............................     25.00-30.00

Group, four portraits, three showing young women, one a young man in vest and tie, 1/6 plates cased, c. 1860.......     30.00-35.00

Group, two portraits, one showing two women and a small boy, the other an almost-tootless old woman seated at a table, 1/6 plates, c. 1860.............     25.00-30.00

Group, two portraits, one an oval image of a stern looking man and the other a seated woman with little boy, 1/16 paltes in double "Ornamental Circle Theme" case by Willard, c. 1862.............     25.00

Group, two portraits, one a middle-aged woman, the other an older man wearing large neck-scarf, 1/6 plates, c. 1855.... **15.00-20.00**

Outdoor, street scene showing row of carriages and a milk wagon beside the Boston Common, ¼ plate, late 1850s... **120.00**

Outdoor, Niagara Falls taken from Babbitt's Point, three small figures in foreground, ½ plate.................... **70.00-80.00**

Outdoor, two-story house with white wood fence in front, 1/9 plate in "Tangent Circle" case, c. 1857........ **30.00-35.00**

Outdoor, locomotive Amazon from Wm. Mason Builders, Taunton, Mass., Cutting's patent ambrotype of an engraving, probably used as salesman's display, 1/6 plate in half case.......... **65.00**

Outdoor, home with gingerbread porticos, sheds, etc., seen from an elevation with trees surrounding the home, 1/6 plate in ½ plate case (slightly damaged by attempted cleaning).............. **15.00**

Outdoor, unidentified building, possibly a college domitory, with several chimneys, ¼ plate in leather case...... **75.00**

Outdoor, buildings on a corner with white picket fence, one identified as New York's "J. Conklin Tavern," ½ plate in wooden frame..................... **200.00**

Outdoor, two-story house with wood fence and hitching posts in front, seven people, presumably a family, standing on porch, ¼ plate in floral case, c. 1857. **30.00-35.00**

Outdoor, two men in small horse-drawn cart with one man seated, the other standing and holding the reins, ¼ plate in "Bouquet of Flowers" case, c. 1858.... **60.00**

Portrait, man with goatee, vest and watch chain, 1/9 plate in "Angel Carrying Babies" Union case, New Haven, c. 1856................................ **25.00-35.00**

Portrait, young man with beard, wearing

vest, 1/9 plate in "Spray of Flowers" variant case inlaid with mother-of-pearl, c. 1860 . . . . . . . . . . . . . . . . . . . . . . . . . . .     **20.00-25.00**

Portrait, somber young woman wearing bonnet with veil and gown, 1/9 plate in "Catching Butterflies" Union case, c. 1861 . . . . . . . . . . . . . . . . . . . . . . . . . . .     **25.00**

Portrait, woman in elaborate dress with lace collar, 1/6 plate, double oval mat, c. 1854 . . . . . . . . . . . . . . . . . . . . . . . . . . .     **70.00**

Portrait, woman in dark patterned dress with lace collar and cuffs, 1/6 plate tinted, in case with floral motif, c. 1850 .     **20.00**

Portrait, young man with freckles and a cowlick, wearing coat, vest and bow tie, 1/9 plate in Union case with Medallion motif, c. 1860 . . . . . . . . . . . . . . . . . . . . .     **15.00**

Portrait, young man with beard, wearing bow-tie, 1/9 plate by C. E. Hawes in Union case with scroll motif, New Bedford, Mass., c. 1865 . . . . . . . . . . . . . . . . .     **25.00**

Portrait, young woman wearing earrings, ½ plate in black thermoplastic frame, c. 1855 . . . . . . . . . . . . . . . . . . . . .     **35.00-40.00**

Portrait, young woman wearing gold necklace and polka dot dress with lace collar, 1/9 palte cased, 1858 . . . . . . . . . .     **18.00**

Portrait, infant held in a woman's lap, 1/16 plate in leather case . . . . . . . . . . . . .     **10.00**

Portrait, two sisterly-looking women wearing similar dresses with lace collars and cuffs, 1/6 plate in "Fireman Saving Child" Union case, c. 1858 . . . . . . . . . . .     **15.00-25.00**

Portrait, unidentified Civil War Union officer in oval frame, full plate, c. 1865 .     **250.00-300.00**

Portrait, man and woman in striped dress, 1/6 plate, c. 1855 . . . . . . . . . . . . .     **15.00**

Portrait, woman in her early 30s in oval Union case, 1/9 plate, c. 1860 . . . . . . . .     **20.00**

Portrait, man and woman with three children, the man holding a large Bible, ½ plate, c. 1855 . . . . . . . . . . . . . . . . . . . . .     **30.00-40.00**

Portrait, middle-aged woman against a tropical scene backdrop, in "Chess Players" Union case, 1/9 plate, c. 1860.     **20.00**

Portrait, middle-aged man, 1/9 plate in Union case, c. 1860..................     **15.00**

Portrait, elderly woman, 1/6 plate in leather case, matted, Louisville, Ky., c. 1860s..............................     **18.00**

Portrait, woman with slight smile and dress with repeated pattern, oval 1/9 plate in "Catching Butterflies, variant Union case, tinted, Florence, Mass., c. 1860..............................     **20.00**

Portrait, two well-dressed men in top hats sitting in horse-drawn carriage in front of small-town shops, 1/6 plate, c. 1855..............................     **40.00**

Portrait, eight-year-old boy dressed as soldier in white stocking, pantaloons, coat and cap, holding small sword, 1/6 plate in Eichmeyer-style case, c. 1856...     **30.00**

Portrait, middle-aged man wearing striped bow tie in imitation tortoise-shell case, c. 1860......................     **20.00**

Portrait, small boy standing on chair beating a drum hanging from his neck on a cord, 1/6 plate cased, c. 1865........     **20.00**

Portrait, young girl in calico dress with dog on chair next to her holding a small basket by its handle in his mouth 1/6 plate in case with geometric pattern, c. 1865..............................     **30.00-35.00**

Portrait, small boy, by Kimball, 1/9 plate in "Wheat Sheaves" Union case, New York, c. 1860s.................     **20.00-30.00**

Portrait, Dickens-like man with tall beaver hat, greatcoat and vest 1/9 plate in Union case with floral design, c. 1860s     **30.00**

Portrait, middle-aged man with short white beard wearing dark suit and tie, full plate in wood frame, c. 1855.......     **75.00-100.00**

Portrait, two little girls dressed in identical plaid dresses with a little boy in a collarless jacket, 1/6 plate in "Medallion of George Washington" variant case, c. 1855 ................................ **30.00-35.00**

Portrait, man with a woman with folded hands, 1/9 plate in Union case with floral motif, c. 1860s ................ **20.00**

Portrait, middle-aged woman with brooch fastening lace collar, 1/9 plate in "Union Forever" Union case, c. 1860s .. **20.00**

Portrait, woman in off-shoulder dress, 1/9 plate in "Sunburst Motif" Union case, New Haven, c. 1860s ............ **20.00**

Portrait, woman in oval gilt frame, 1/16 plate in Union case, New Haven, Conn., 1857 ................................ **20.00-28.00**

Portrait, woman with plaid dress and ribbon tied in hair, 1/9 plate in Union case with floral motif, c. 1865 ......... **20.00**

Portrait, woman with braided hair, 1/9 plate in octagonal Union case, New Haven, Conn., 1855 ................. **25.00**

Portrait, young couple, the woman wearing a very wide skirt, 1/6 plate in Union case, c. 1865 ................. **15.00**

Portrait, young man with large fringed cravat around neck, 1/9 plate in Union case with church window design, New Haven, Conn., c. 1860s .............. **15.00**

Portrait, young boy seated on table with feet on a chair, 1/6 plate in octagonal Union case, New York, 1860s ......... **20.00-25.00**

Portrait, seated man in European military dress uniform with cap and sword, 1/6 plate in full case .......... **40.00**

Portrait, bearded man seated at table with pen and paper in hand, ¼ plate by Boston photographer Bowdoin, with his imprint, in leather case .............. **70.00**

Portrait, two men leading a bull, 1/6 plate in leather case ................. **40.00-50.00**

Portrait, woman and son, boy holding a closed image case, woman displaying a photograph (perhaps her husband), 1/6 plate in (worn) leather case........... **20.00**

Portrait, young girl standing and leaning on table with backdrop of mountains and trees, 1/6 plate in half leather case.. **18.00-22.00**

Portrait, family group of man, woman and girl with ringlets, ½ plate in gilt frame, c. 1855...................... **15.00**

Portrait, stern-looking woman in black dress and shawl, with furn bonnet, standing near table holding a cup, ¼ plate in geometric-decorated case, tined, c. 1856 **22.00**

Portrait, woman in black taffeta dress wearing brooch and long earrings, 1/6 plate in case with urn and leaf border, tinted, c. 1856...................... **15.00**

Portrait, sleeping baby held in a woman's arms, 1/6 plate in geometric-decorated case, tinted, c. 1856......... **15.00**

Portrait, baby lying in crib, 1/6 plate cased, c. 1858...................... **15.00**

Portrait, little girl, 1/9 plate in "book" case, tinted, c. 1858................. **15.00**

Portrait, middle-aged man seated, 1/6 plate by J. Timms, cased, London, 1850s **20.00**

Portrait, young man sitting at table, painted landscape backdrop, 1/6 plate cased, c. 1850s.................... **15.00**

Portrait, man with muttonchop sideburns wearing suit, 1/6 plate in "Thistle Motif" case, c. 1860.......... **23.00**

Portrait, young sea captain, 1/9 plate cased, c. 1860...................... **15.00**

Portrait, three well-dressed men, one bearded, all seated, ¼ plate in "Forget Me Not" case, tinted, c. 1865......... **18.00-20.00**

Portrait, Civil War soldier in Union uniform and hat, 1/9 plate in "Circle Motif" variant case, c. 1861.......... **35.00**

Portrait, two bearded men, possibly brothers ¼ plate in floral decorated case, c. 1865...................... 25.00

Portrait, two young men in hats, coats and gloves, one with fur muff, 1/6 plate in "Mixed Flowers" variant case, c. 1868 15.00

Portrait, two little girls, one freckle-faced, holding hands, in floral case, 1/6 plate, c. 1865...................... 15.00

Portrait, two Union officers seated, both wearing bummer's caps, ¼ plate, 1860s (minor peeling of backing)............ 45.00

Portrait, Union sergeant posing with his wife in formal dress, ¼ plate cased, 1860s............................. 50.00

Portrait, Union soldier with his wife at his side, soldier wearing jacket and holding musket, ¼ plate uncased...... 80.00

Portrait, Union officer with sword, identified as Capt. George H. Otis, N.Y. Volunteers, wearing eagle buckle, 1/6 plate (slight rim solarization).......... 80.00

Portrait, soldier from Virginia, seated wearing a large plumed Hardee Hat and holding a militia sword, 1/6 plate uncased............................. 70.00

Portrait, Confederate soldier wearing uniform of Richmond Lt. Infantry Blues, seated next to table, 1/6 plate (slight solarization at edges)........... 50.00

Portrait, Confederate soldier in full uniform, wearing old militia hat, cross belt, cap box, with pistol in holster, bowie knife on side, holding musket, 1/6 plate uncased...................... 110.00

Portrait, Union soldier wearing long jacket and kepi, 1/6 plate............. 20.00-30.00

Portrait, two hunters standing in front of house with large dog next to them, one hunter holding a rifle, ¼ plate, uncased............................. 75.00

Portrait, butcher in plaid apron, sharpening a knife, 1/6 plate uncased...     50.00

Portrait, unidentified Union soldier wearing frock coat, eagle buckle, with Colt in his belt and holding a Sharps carbine and calvary saber, 1/6 plate.......     130.00

Portrait, Confederate soldier wearing grey jacket with high collar, 1/9 plate uncased...........................     60.00

Portrait, young boy wearing nine-button coat and identified as member of Ninth Mass. Vols., 1/6 plate................     20.00

Portrait, Union soldier, identified, wearing jacket, oval buckle, cap, pistol in belt, 1/6 plate......................     70.00

Portrait, bare-chested man, 1/6 plate on ruby glass, uncased (some spots).......     20.00

Portrait, Southeast Asian boy and his mother the child dressed in missionary school clothes, the woman wearing a sarong, 1/6 plate in (battered) case.....     75.00-95.00

Portrait, unidentified woman, on unusual quarter-inch-thick black way backing, 1/6 plate cased.............     35.00

Portrait, two young boys seated at table playing game of checkers, 1/6 plate in full case (slight mat scratches)........     40.00

Portrait, young man in Revolutionary War clothes, wearing a false beard and holding rolled parchment in one hand, 1/4 plate in full case.................     75.00

Portrait, washerwoman at work on the porch of a house, her tub set on a chair next to water pump, 1/4 plate uncased...     100.00

Portrait, young soldier wearing blue jacket and kepi, 1/6 plate matted and framed............................     40.00

Portrait, Union private with kepi, eagle buttons and metal epaulettes, from Ambrotype Studio of Porter, Milford, N.H. (identified on card on back), 1/9 plate in patriotic mat.......................     35.00-40.00

Portrait, soldier identified as Henry L. Johnson, 16th N.H. Regiment, wearing kepi, name etched on back of the frame, 1/9 plate in patriotic case (minor brush marks due to attempted cleaning)...... 30.00-35.00

Portrait, Civil War musician wearing a nine-button musician coat, standing next to a chair, 1/9 plate................. 25.00-30.00

Portrait, Confederate soldier wearing home-made grey shirt and suspenders, 1/6 plate tinted..................... 50.00-60.00

Portrait, two unidentified Confederate soldiers wearing Jefferson Davis hats and holding bayonetted muskets and other military gear, 1/6 plate in full case 175.00-200.00

Portrait, two women seated in a boat by the seaside, 1/6 plate in full case and frame............................. 38.00

Portrait, elegantly dressed mother with her child, 1/6 plate in half case with mat and frame......................... 10.00

Portrait, girl holding cat in her lap, 1/9 plate in half case................... 25.00-30.00

Portrait, gentleman holding cigar and wearing top hat, 1/9 plate in half case (slight scratches at edge of image)...... 15.00

Portrait, dead man on pillow in white cap and covering, 1/6 plate in half case. 25.00

Portrait, Union corporal, waist-up pose, wearing shoulder scales and kepi, 1/6 plate, 1860s........................ 35.00

Portrait, middle-aged gentleman, signed "Hawes" (ambrotypist from New Bedford, Mass.) ¼ plate in full case....... 35.00-45.00

Portrait, gentleman holding adze, dressed in suspenders, 1/6 plate in full case.. 50.00-60.00

# TINTYPES

Tintype, 1/6 plate, Civil War Sargeant, gutta percha case, c. 1863, $85.

Group, uncut pair of CDV-size tintypes, group portrait...................... 15.00

Group, uncut gem-size strip of five identical portraits of a boy................ 10.00

Group, uncut gem-size tintype strip of six identical portraits of a man........ 15.00

Group, 27 fashion portraits of women, all wearing interesting dresses, bow ties, jackets, jewelry and hairstyles reflecting the times, 1/6 plates, some in paper frames, c. 1870....................... 25.00

Group, 41 portraits of men, mostly young, some in elaborate painted rustic landscape backgrounds, 1/6 plates and smaller, 20 in paper frames, 1870-80... 25.00

Group, 100 tintypes of men, mostly adults, some family groups and couples, some in front of elaborate painted backgrounds, 1/6 plates and smaller, 40 in paper frames, c. 1870................ 60.00-70.00

Group, four tintype portraits, a serious young boy, an old woman, an old man with beard, a young man in military cadet uniform, ½ plates (one extensively retouched), c. 1870.................. 40.00

Group, four tintype portraits, two of

sleeping babies, 1/6 plates, two in "Two Lilies" cases, c. 1855 ................. 40.00

Group, two tintypes of sleeping or dead infants, one tinted with chemical overlay to produce ethereal effect, 1/6 plates in cases, c. 1865 ...................... 20.00

Group, 28 tintype portraits, mostly of women, some men and children, in paper frames, 1870-80 ............... 10.00-15.00

Group, 84 portraits of women, mostly in their 30s, some in elaborate dresses and jewelry, mostly 1/6 plates, some smaller, 45 in paper frames, c. 1870-80 .. 40.00-50.00

Group, four portraits of workingmen including two men in overalls and two men with a horse, 1/6 plates, one in paper frame, c. 1870-1900 ................. 15.00

Group, 26 portraits including 22 1/36 plates and four 1/24 plates, all matted in cards, c. 1870 ...................... 20.00

Outdoor, large white house with white picket fence and trees, brook in foreground shows reflection of scene, ½ plate (slightly bent) ................. 20.00

Outdoor, Horticultural Hall, Centennial Exhibition of 1876, set into pressed metal belt buckle with stars around edge, 1/6 plate, c. 1876 (some flaking of emulsion) ............................... 40.00

Outdoor, Genesee Falls Mills, Genesee Fall, N.Y., including mill, several people, buggy and horse, people in window, with name of company appearing in reverse on building, ½ plate .......... 75.00

Outdoor, picnic with ten people around table under trees, dog on ground, 1/8 plate (slightly dark) ................. 8.00-10.00

Outdoor, Santa Monica Beach, Calif., with woman seated in front of beach, 1/6 plate ......................... 5.00-7.00

Outdoor, young woman wearing flowered hat and holding reins of a horse in the countryside, 1/6 plate in geometric design case, c. 1870.................. 15.00

Outdoor, winter scene with two horses and two sleighs and seven people, 1/4 plate................................. 20.00

Outdoor, scene including a man holding dog and a lady with a basket, 1/2 plate (trimmed)......................... 15.00

Outdoor, group of 28 people outdoors, 1/2 plate (some scratches).............. 10.00

Outdoor, U.S. Army hospital (Union) with flagpole and flag, ambulance to side, various people and soldiers in scene, 1/4 plate..................... 75.00-100.00

Portrait, baby wearing white nightdress, 1/6 plate in "Musicians" Union case, c. 1860.............................. 10.00-15.00

Portrait, young woman in calico dress with white lace collar, 1/9 plate in jeweled Union case, c. 1860............... 10.00-15.00

Portrait, young girl in black dress with hair in ringlets, sitting in a high black chair, 1/4 plate cased, c. 1865.......... 15.00

Portrait, Rev. Buckner Abernathy of Pittsburg, Tex. (identified), 1/8 plate in Union case with hexagon design, New Haven, Conn., c. 1855............... 20.00

Portrait, young girl in fancy dress, seated, 1/9 plate in Union case, 1857... 15.00

Portrait, woman with earrings and brooch at her neck, 1/9 plate in oval Union case with floral motif, New Haven, Conn., 1860s................. 15.00

Portrait, woman, 1/16 plate in large 1/6 plate Union case, c. 1860s............. 20.00

Portrait, three young men in Union Army uniforms, one wearing a cap, 1/6 plate in "Eagle at Bay" Union case, c. 1862................................. 40.00-50.00

Portrait, young black woman in checked dress with plain white collar, 1/6 plate in Union case, c. 1858.................. 10.00

Portrait, seated elderly woman with hair in ringlets, whole plate in wooden frame, tinted, c. 1870 . . . . . . . . . . . . . . . . . . . . . .  **20.00**

Portrait, woman's head and shoulders, ½ plate by Purdy's, Boston, matted and framed, with photographer's imprint on mat, c. 1880 . . . . . . . . . . . . . . . . . . . . . . :  **15.00**

Portrait, seated woman wearing elaborate dress and necklace, full plate tinted and matted, in gilt wooden frame, c. 1870 . . . . . . . . . . . . . . . . . . . . . . . . . . . .  **35.00**

Portrait, young man in Union Army uniform, full plate framed, tinted, c. 1865 . .  **50.00**

Portrait, a young couple, ½ plate tinted, c. 1870 . . . . . . . . . . . . . . . . . . . . . . . . . . .  **15.00**

Portrait, three men in overcoats and hats, one seated on stump, in cardboard frame, c. 1870 . . . . . . . . . . . . . . . . . . . . . .  **5.00**

Portrait, young man wearing coat and ascot, whole plate tinted, c. 1880 . . . . . . .  **5.00**

Portrait, child, ¼ plate tinted, matted and glazed, c. 1870 . . . . . . . . . . . . . . . . .  **8.00**

Portrait, 20-year-old man wearing hat with bulky overcoat, 1/6 plate tinted, c. 1860 . . . . . . . . . . . . . . . . . . . . . . . . . . . . .  **3.00**

Portrait, woman with large hat posed on a turn-of-the-century automobile, 1/16 plate, c. 1900 . . . . . . . . . . . . . . . . . . . . . .  **2.00**

Portrait, bathing beauty, 1/6 plate, 1880s . . . . . . . . . . . . . . . . . . . . . . . . . . . . .  **3.00**

Portrait, man looking through a photograph album, CDV-size . . . . . . . . . . . . .  **8.00-10.00**

Portrait, montage tintype showing large number of crying black babies, titled "I'se Sleepy," 1/9 plate (tintype of a lithograph) . . . . . . . . . . . . . . . . . . . . . . . .  **20.00**

Portrait, fireman wearing helmet, 1/6 plate uncased . . . . . . . . . . . . . . . . . . . . . .  **15.00**

Portrait, young man in leather apron holding a mallet and long stick, 1/6 plate uncased . . . . . . . . . . . . . . . . . . . . . . . . . . . .  **5.00-10.00**

Portrait, two little boys holding live white rabbits, ¼ plate uncased....... **20.00**

Portrait, Chinese gentleman in native dress, long braids wrapped around his head, wears satin jacket, 1/6 plate...... **30.00-40.00**

Portrait, small Mexican boy riding a horse in front of brick building, ¼ plate **25.00-30.00**

Portrait, two gentlemen playing cards with drinks and cigars in hands, 1/6 plate................................. **30.00**

Portrait, young man with shoulder-length hair, dressed in fringed leathers and holding a rifle, 1/6 plate.......... **25.00**

Portrait, man on horse-drawn buggy, ¼ plate, 1860s......................... **30.00**

Portrait, two baseball players, each holding a bat and wearing high socks, 1/6 plate........................... **35.00-40.00**

Portrait, policeman wearing shield badge and hat, 1/9 plate, c. 1870 (minor flaking).............................. **25.00**

Portrait, four joking soldiers, three of them pretending to thrust bayonets into fourth companion, 1/6 plate, 1860s.... **30.00**

Portrait, two Union soldiers, each holding musket and wearing kepis, 1-1/6 plate, 1860s........................ **60.00**

Portrait, soldier with NCO sword, wearing brass belt with breastplate, kepi and sash, 1/6 plate, 1860s............... **65.00-70.00**

Portrait, cavalry soldier wearing Hardee hat with crossed swords, jacket and belt, wearing a Colt pistol, 1/6 plate in patriotic mat (some emulsion flakes in corner)............................. **65.00**

Portrait, standing Union soldier in full dress with musket by his side, ¼ plate.. **40.00-45.00**

Portrait, three Union soldiers, all wearing long jackets, ¼ plate, 1860s........ **25 .00**

Portrait, standing Union soldier in full dress, holding musket, ¼ plate (somewhat dark image).............. **30.00**

Portrait, standing Union officer wearing rectangular eagle buckle, holstered weapon and holding a cavalry sword, 1-1/6 plate...................... 40.00

Portrait, two cavalry soldiers holding cavalry sabers and wearing Colt revolvers in their belts, 1/6 plate....... 70.00

Portrait, armed Negro soldier in jacket holding a bayonetted musket, 1/6 plate cased ............................ 150.00

Portrait, musician with Hardee hat and cavalry brass, 1/6 plate.............. 30.00

Portrait, federal soldier in four-button coat and wearing an oval buckle, 1/6 plate................................ 30.00

Portrait, Naval Admiral with wife, man wearing double buttoned jacket, epaulettes and sword, post-Civil War image in Victorian setting, 1/6 plate........... 30.00-40.00

Portrait, seated Union soldier holding NCO sword across his chest, 1/6 plate.. 45.00

Portrait, Union soldier reading book, wearing brass shoulder boards, with NCO sword, 1/6 plate.............. 50.00-55.00

Portrait, Union soldier holding kepi, 1/9 plate in full case.................... 25.00

Portrait, Union soldier, wearing kepi, in front of patriotic backdrop of flags and tents, ¼ plate...................... 35.00

Portrait, soldier with kepi and rain cover, seated, 1/6 plate cased......... 30.00

Portrait, soldier wearing metal shoulder boards, cap and carriage box and bayonet in belt, holding musket, 1/6 plate................................ 40.00

Portrait, child with metal-wheeled toy, ¼ plate cased...................... 30.00

Portrait, gentleman with his high-wheel bicycle, 1/6 plate................... 35.00

Portrait, musician holding violin and bow, 1/6 plate.................... 15.00

Portrait, three children and dog, ½ plate     **7.00**

Portrait, two musicians, one playing accordian and the other a violin, ½ plate..     **20.00-25.00**

Portrait, Union soldier wearing four-button frock coat, oval buckle, holding Springfield musket with bayonet attached, ¼ plate in mat and frame, uncased..     **40.00**

Portrait, standing Union soldier wearing kepi and nine-button coat, with pistol sticking out of his belt, ¼ plate matted.     **45.00**

Portrait, seated Federal Cavalry private wearing regulation shell jacket with piping, 1/6 plate......................     **20.00**

Portrait, Union infantry private with coat and cap, hand tucked in jacket Napoleon style, 1/6 plate.............     **20.00**

Portrait, Union artilleryman with his two daughters, soldier holding Colt in his hand, girl holding a doll with china head, 1/6 plate, 1860s..............     **75.00**

Portrait, eight soldiers and a civilian posed in 1880-era studio, soldiers wearing military jackets and hats, 1/6 plate matted and framed, uncased..............     **20.00**

Portrait of soldier wearing jacket and coat, 1/6 plate tinted.................     **25.00**

Portrait, Union private, (identified) wearing badge on chest, 1½6 plate in half case, 1860s....................     **30.00**

Portrait, Union cavalry soldier seated holding a Smith breechloading carbine and cradling a cavalry sword, with rare Whitney Navy revolver on table next to him, 1/6 plate......................     **60.00-75.00**

Portrait, Union soldier wearing US belt buckle and holding a Springfield musket with bayonet attached, backdrop showing tents and camp scene, 1/6 plate in mat and frame (image slightly dark)....     **25.00**

Portrait, militia soldier standing and wearing a jacket, 1/6 plate...........     **25.00**

Portrait, Confederate soldier with musket by his side, 1/6 plate..........  **50.00**

Portrait, sailor wearing cap and jacket, image signed "Child's Art Gallery, Taunton," 1/9 plate.................  **15.00**

Portrait, man in apron with broom, holding bucket in his hand, foot resting on box, CDV-size in paper frame......  **25.00**

Portrait, black and white dog posed on draped chair, 1/16 plate.............  **4.00**

Portrait, two coal miners smoking pipes and wearing miner's hats with oil lamps lit, 1/6 plate......................  **40.00**

Portrait, two boys with snoozing dog, 1/6 plate uncased...................  **6.00**

Portrait, young couple in horse and buggy stopped on a farm road with old farm house in background, 5x3½" un-framed...........................  **15.00**

Portrait, baseball player wearing uniform with brass rectangular buckle, soft hat, holding bat, 1/6 plate matted and framed, c. 1880.................  **45.00-50.00**

Portrait, Indian squaw with long braided hair and wrapped in a ceremonial robe or blanket, 1/6 plate.................  **175.00-200.00**

Portrait, attractive seated young man with bow tie and frock coat, full plate tinted, in gilt and black wood oval frame, c. 1868......................  **35.00**

Portrait, bust of woman, 1/9 plate in geometric Union case with medallion and scroll motif, c. 1857.............  **25.00**

Portrait, bare-shouldered young woman with flowing hair, pearl necklace, shown with a bearded man, full plate, California, late 19th-century (shellacked to preserve the print)..................  **20.00**

Portrait, small girl with basket, leaning on stuffed chair, 1/9 plate...........  **2.00**

Portrait, man and woman in open automobile, 1/6 plate...................  **3.00**

Portrait, painter in overalls and hat, paint-splattered and holding bucket of paint and brush, 1/6 plate............ 20.00

Portrait, woman, 1/9 plate in paper mate with label reading "Fernando Dessau's Photograph and Ferrotype Gallery, 145 Eighth Ave., New York".. 4.00

Portrait, Henry Stanley and David Livingston, by London Stereoscopic Co., 1880............................. 60.00-90.00

# CDVS

Left: CDV of Civil War Soldier, c. 1865, $15. Bottom Left: CDV of Unidentified Soldier, c. 1963, $8.50. Bottom Right: CDV, Ulysses S. Grant, c. 1964, $17-$20.

CDV, Sailor, c. 1885, $3.

CDV, Unidentified woman and girl, c. 1890, $1.00.

View of the reading of the execution order for the conspirators against President Lincoln, July, 1965, by Alexander Gardner. Albumen print, very rare, $800.

Outdoors, scene showing loaded stage-coach, by M. Chandler .............. 25.00

Outdoors, scene of Cunard Royal Mail Steam ship "Scotia," possibly from a painting ........................... 10.00

Outdoors, scene showing Fort Snelling and the Valley of the Minnesota, by Whitney, St. Paul .................. 7.00

Outdoors, a church, by O. C. Barnes, Middlebury, Vt.................... **4.00**

Outdoors, scene showing Cunard Royal Mail Steam Ship "Russia," schematic of interior on reverse................... **10.00**

Outdoors, scene showing a church, by Charles Pringle, Fredonia, N.Y........ **4.00**

Outdoors, woman walking in snow, labeled "Blizzard of 1888"............ **5.00**

Outdoors, scene showing State Capitol Building at Hartford, Conn., by U.F. Ney .............................. **6.00**

Outdoors, scene showing a dog lying in stage prop hay, by Townsend, Willimantic, Conn.......................... **4.00**

Outdoors, scene showing a horse identified as "Harry Knox" with pedigree on reverse, dated 1876................. **4.00**

Outdoors, scene showing Peace Jubilee Coliseum, Boston, 1872............. **12.00-15.00**

Portrait, Washington Irving, published by Anthony from Brady negative...... **15.00**

Portrait, Gen. Robt. Anderson by Lewis, New York (some foxing)........ **10.00**

Portrait, Ulysses S. Grant, one hand gripping handle of his sword, by Bringham Bishop....................... **35.00**

Portrait, woman seated in chair with album and a stereo viewer with card on table, 1860s........................ **12.00**

Portrait, Longfellow's daughters, tinted **8.00**

Portrait, couple in a two-horse shay, stamp on reverse dated 1866.......... **12.00**

Portrait, Oliver Wendall Holmes (inventor of hand-held stereoscope) with one hand resting on back of chair, by Anthony from a Brady negative.......... **25.00-30.00**

Portrait, Edwin Booth, side bust view by Gurney .............................. **15.00-20.00**

Portrait, Gen. Quincy Adams Gillmore (from an engraving)................. **5.00**

Portrait, William Cullen Bryant with beard, by Anthony from Brady negative     **20.00**

Portrait, Gen. Winfield Scott, three-quarter pose, noted as "Taken Evacuation Day, Nov. 1865," copyright by Gurney ..........................     **20.00-25.00**

Portrait, Joseph Jefferson with tousled hair, by Sarony & Co................     **8.00**

Portrait, Gen. William Rosecrans with one hand inside his coat, by Anthony from Brady negative................     **22.00**

Portrait, Gen. Horatio Wright, retouched (some foxing)....................     **8.00**

Portrait, Napoelon and daughter (from a painting).........................     **5.00**

Portrait, Gen. John Wool, by Anthony from Brady negative................     **20.00-25.00**

Portrait, Gen. Joseph Hawley in civilian clothing...........................     **20.00**

Portrait, Gen. Joseph Hooker, by Anthony from Brady negative (foxed).....     **5.00-10.00**

Portrait, Cardinal de Bonald, Archbishop of Lyon, by Desderi & Co., Paris     **15.00**

Portrait, Jefferson Davis standing with hand resting on book, by Anthony from Brady negative, New York, c. 1860.....     **20.00-25.00**

Portrait, Mrs. Henry Ward Beecher, by Rockwood, N.Y....................     **10.00**

Portrait, Mary Todd Lincoln, by Anthony from Brady negative, New York, c. 1861.............................     **20.00-25.00**

Portrait, firemen and their water cart outside firehouse, by R. Newell, Philadelphia, 1865......................     **15.00**

Portrait, Waugh Bunj, chief of Delaware Indians, in full ceremonial attire standing with hand on shoulder of white man, c. 1870s.....................     **15.00-20.00**

Portrait, a Zouave from Pennsylvania wearing sash and turban and holding musket.............................     **15.00**

Portrait, three officers wearing 17th Corps (Vicksburg) badges . . . . . . . . . . . .  **10.00**

Portrait, soldier in vest and three-button frock coat and wearing army medal . . . .  **5.00**

Portrait, Union soldier with four-button coat . . . . . . . . . . . . . . . . . . . . . . . . . . . . .  **5.00**

Portrait, seated Union soldier by Stowe, Louisville, Ky. . . . . . . . . . . . . . . . . . . . . .  **5.00**

Portrait, standing Union soldier in four-button frock coat . . . . . . . . . . . . . . . . . . .  **5.00**

Portrait, Prince Napoleon with cane in hand, by Anthony from Brady negative, (minute marks on image) . . . . . . . . . . . .  **20.00**

Portrait, Gen. McPherson . . . . . . . . . . .  **20.00**

Portrait, Gen. Sherman surrounded by vignettes of battles . . . . . . . . . . . . . . . . . .  **12.00**

Portrait, seated Union soldier wearing 17th corp badge . . . . . . . . . . . . . . . . . . . .  **5.00**

Portrait, Horace Greeley, by Fredericks (minute foxing) . . . . . . . . . . . . . . . . . . . . .  **8.00**

Portrait, Seth Kinman (California hunter and trapper) in fringed buckskin jacket with powder horn and bear claw pouch, leaning against Kentucky rifle, image by Brady . . . . . . . . . . . . . . . . . . . .  **45.00-50.00**

Portrait, Pauline Cushman (famous Union spy) holding an American flag and a derringer, by Miller and Rowell, Boston . . . . . . . . . . . . . . . . . . . . . . . . . . .  **25.00**

Portrait, Lincoln and family (copy print of a montage) . . . . . . . . . . . . . . . . . . . . . . .  **4.00**

Portrait, John Wilkes Booth, three-quarter pose with one hand in his coat pocket . . . . . . . . . . . . . . . . . . . . . . . . . . . .  **12.00**

Portrait, presidents of the U.S. from Washington to Johnson, dated 1866 . . . .  **12.00**

Portrait, Lincoln and his Cabinet (copyright) . . . . . . . . . . . . . . . . . . . . . . . . . . . . .  **15.00**

Portrait, Andrew Johnson, by M. O'Brian, Chicago . . . . . . . . . . . . . . . . . . .  **5.00**

Portrait, U.S. Grant and his family . . . . .  **15.00**

| | |
|---|---:|
| Portrait, Gen. U.S. Grant statue........ | **5.00** |
| Portrait, Gen. George B. McClellan.... | **5.00** |
| Portrait, Gen. Fitshugh Lee (from an engraving).......................... | **5.00** |
| Portrait, Tom Thumb with his wife and child............................... | **5.00** |
| Portrait, James Fiske Jr. (financier) wearing uniform.................... | **4.00** |
| Portrait, three South American Indians wearing ponchos.................... | **8.00** |
| Portrait, L.J.M. Daguerre posed in chair with one hand supporting his head (retouched photograph from a daguerreotype by Silver & Gieseke, New York)... | **85.00** |
| Portrait, little boy on a pony, by J. Loeffler, Staten Island, N.Y............... | **15.00** |
| Portrait, Gen. Mansfield, by Anthony from Brady negative................. | **12.00** |
| Portrait, Cpt. Lee, Comm. Dupont and Porter, by Charles Fredricks, New York | **10.00** |
| Portrait, Gen. Lyons with sword in hand, by Anthony................... | **15.00** |
| Portrait, Col. Ellsworth, by Anthony from Brady negative............... | **20.00-25.00** |
| Portrait, unidentified officer with arm in coat, by Matthew Brady............. | **10.00** |
| Portrait, Gen. Burnside, by Appleton.. | **15.00** |
| Portrait, Lt. Gen. Grant seated, by Morse Gallery of the Cumberland, Nashville, Tenn. (slight soiling of image. | **15.00** |
| Portrait, Gen. Fremont, by Anthony from Brady negative (slight foxing)..... | **15.00-20.00** |
| Portrait, three slave children wrapped up in flags, by Paxson, New York......... | **25.00** |
| Portrait, Rebecca, a slave girl from New Orleans, by Charles Paxson, New York. | **25.00** |
| Portrait, Gen. Burnside in civilian clothing with hand in coat, by Anthony from Brady negative (minor foxing).... | **15.00** |
| Portrait, Confederate Gen. Richard Ewell, by Anthony.................. | **20.00-25.00** |

| | |
|---|---:|
| Portrait, Gen. Leonidas Polk, by Anthony from Brady negative............ | **25.00** |
| Portrait, unidentified officer with sword in hand, by Pearce of Providence, R.I... | **10.00** |
| Portrait, John L. Burns at Gettysburg (copy of a photo by Tipton).......... | **10.00** |
| Portrait, midget Dudly Foster, by Charles Eisenmann (minor foxing)..... | **10.00** |
| Portrait, a fat (about 400 pounds) boy, by Smith...................... | **8.00** |
| Portrait, midget Anton Roubal, by Wetherby ......................... | **10.00** |
| Portrait, unidentified actor holding a knife, by Gurney................... | **8.00** |
| Portrait, Cyrus Westfield, by Mathew Brady............................. | **15.00** |
| Portrait, midget Adams Sisters of Massachusetts, by Eisenmann............. | **10.00** |
| Portrait, poet Tennyson, by Anthony... | **12.00** |
| Portrait, Irish giant Hugh Murphy (7′11″), by Eisenmann (slight foxing)... | **15.00** |
| Portrait, chemist Benjamin Silliman, by Anthony..................... | **8.00** |
| Portrait, politician Shyler Colfax, by Whitehurst ........................ | **10.00** |
| Portrait, Edwin Booth, copy of original by Gurney........................ | **10.00** |
| Portrait, composer Arthur Rubinstein, by Sarony, N.Y..................... | **8.00** |
| Portrait, Queen Victoria, by Disdiri & Co., Paris........................ | **8.00** |
| Portrait, Edward Everitt, by Tracy and Gray, Oswego, N.Y................. | **8.00** |
| Portrait, writer Charles Dickens, by Chappuis............................ | **10.00** |
| Portrait, Rob Roy (J. Magregor, Esq.) holding an oar with other boating items behind him, by Chappuis............ | **15.00** |
| Portrait, writer Thomas Carlyle, by Watkins............................ | **15.00** |

Portrait, Sarah Bernhardt holding flower to her face, by J. Tourtin Aine, Paris ............................... 20.00

Portrait, Hon. B. Disraeli, by W. & D. Downey........................... 15.00

Portrait, Don Carlos, by Le Jeune...... 10.00

Portrait, M. Lesseps, designer of Suez Canal, by London Photo Co......... 12.00

Portrait, gentleman viewing stereoviews while the salesman sneaks a hug from gentleman's wife, (minor foxing)....... 10.00

Portrait, seated gentleman missing his left hand, by Gurney................ 8.00

Portrait, Judge Roy Bean (copy of a photograph) ........................ 10.00

Portrait, unidentified girl, by Anthony from Brady negative................ 3.00

Portrait, two actresses, by Howell, New York ............................... 3.00

Portrait, actress Lucy Clinetof reclingin on couch, by Gurney & Son........... 6.00

Portrait, unidentified gentleman with "afro" hairdo and wearing a costume, by Eisenmann...................... 8.00

Portrait, heavyset Negro woman holding a dog on her lap.................... 20.00

Portrait, Abraham Lincoln with son Tod 10.00

Portrait, Mary Todd Lincoln in her Inaugural gown, by Anthony from Brady negative, c. 1862.................... 20.00

Portrait, actress Jenny Lind........... 8.00

Portrait, unidentified Civil War officer. 7.00

Portrait, P. T. Barnum.............. 20.00

Portrait, Confederate soldier wearing rebel coat....................... 15.00

Portrait, two identified Union soldiers with arms interlocked............... 10.00

Portrait, Gen. Wool, by Anthony from Brady negative..................... 15.00

Portrait, Robert E. Lee wearing three

stars on collar...................... 15.00

Portrait, Gen. Philip Kearny, by Anthony from Brady negative........... 20.00

# CABINET CARDS

Left: Cabinet Card, bicyclists, c. 1900,
$10. Below: Cabinet card, $5.

Group, seven cabinet photos by
Newsboy, New York, including Pres.
Wm. McKinley and other public figures. 40.00

Group, 31 cabinet photos including portraits of men, women and children,
mostly in Scottish studios, c. 1890...... 30.00

Group, 11 cabinet photos of European
and American actors and actresses, by
Sarony, Gehrig and others, c.
1880s-1890s......................... 20.00

Group, 5 cabinet photos, views of New
York City, by Underwood & Underwood, c. 1875....................... 20.00

Group, 18 cabinet photos including portraits and scenery and Pres. and Mrs.
Garfield, c. 1880-1890............... 18.00

Group, 15 cabinet photos of Matthew Brady's National Portrait Gallery including one woman and 14 men, mostly politicians, Washington, D.C., c. 1865-75 ............................. **30.00-40.00**

Group, 15 cabinet photos including views and portraits by Taber, Fry, Hirshberg and two views by Frith, c. 1860-90 ........................... **20.00-30.00**

Outdoor, panorama of Denver, Colorado, taken from Union Depot, by W. H. Jackson....................... **20.00**

Outdoor, scene showing Lawrence St., Denver, Colo., with buggies in street, by W. H. Jackson..................... **20.00**

Outdoor, ruins of a large fire in Elizabeth, N.J., showing people but no firefighting equipment, by Hill........ **12.00**

Outdoor circus scene showing monkey pumping handcart around raised track while small dog sits up on hind legs nearby with trainer, by Drum, Kansas City, Kans............................... **25.00**

Outdoor, canoes on beach with South Sea Islander standing bare chested and holding an oar..................... **8.00**

Outdoor, large buildings seen through tall, bare trees, possibly a college campus, by W. Notman................. **4.00-8.00**

Outdoor, longhaired man in fringed buckskin vest pointing a revolver at a cowboy-hatted head protruding from a pile of rocks, by J. E. Jeffres, York, Pa. **25.00**

Outdoor, long four-story brick building, possibly a school dormitory, with two men sitting in doorway, by W. Notman. **5.00**

Outdoor, flag-draped girl with bicycle and an "S.F. banner on the handlebars, by R. C. Houser, Michigan City, Ind... **7.00**

Outdoor, Gettysburg battlefield, from Little Round Top looking over Valley of Death, by Tipton.................. **8.00-10.00**

Outdoor, Rhone Toll Road, Mesa City, Colo. (view down dirt road) . . . . . . . . . . 7.00

Outdoor, Chimney Rock, Green River, UPRR, by George C. Mellen, Colorado Springs, Colo. . . . . . . . . . . . . . . . . . . . . . 10.00

Outdoor, Cape Cod beach houses and children playing, by Nickerson, Provincetown, R.I., 1880s . . . . . . . . . . . . . . 12.00

Outdoor, Chatham Light, Cape Cod, by Nickerson, Provincetown, R.I. . . . . . . . . 12.00

Outdoor, four family bicycle performers, each with a high-wheel bicycle at his side (identified as the Metrone Family), by Baker, Columbus, Ohio, 1880 . . . . . . . . . . . . . . . . . . . . . . . . . . . . . 20.00

Outdoor, Cape Cod view across small harbor from Railroad Wharf, by Nickerson, Provincetown, R.I. (slight foxing). 10.00

Outdoor, scene showing Frank and Albert Lauderbaugh each wearing a sidearm and cartridge belt . . . . . . . . . . . 30.00

Outdoor, Cape Cod with rooftops, homes, church and streets, by Nickerson, Provincetown, R.I., 1880s . . . . . . . . 10.00

Outdoor, drydocked double masted ship 5.00

Outdoor, paddlewheel steamboat Crystal Wave, 1870s . . . . . . . . . . . . . . . . 7.00

Outdoor, railroad crew putting down railroad ties with trestle in background, sepia toned . . . . . . . . . . . . . . . . . . . . . . . 8.00

Outdoor, Cape Cod overview showing city and harbor, by Nickerson, Provincetown, R.I., 1880s . . . . . . . . . . . . . . 15.00

Outdoor, farmer with pair of oxen, buggy in background . . . . . . . . . . . . . . . . 6.00

Outdoor, ruins of the World Columbian Exposition of 1893, image measuring 10x8″ . . . . . . . . . . . . . . . . . . . . . . . . . . . 10.00

Outdoor, scene showing the paddlewheeler "Newport," side view, by Seaside Views . . . . . . . . . . . . . . . . . . . . . 10.00

| | |
|---|---|
| Outdoors, scene showing the crew of the ill-fated battleship "Maine".......... | **20.00-25.00** |
| Outdoor, three Indians wearing white man's clothing, posed in front of a horse | **35.00** |
| Outdoor, scene showing a cowboy standing in the desert next to three organ-pipe cacti, by E. A. Bonine, Pasadena, Calif............................... | **30.00** |
| Outdoor, passengers and conductors posed around a Locomotive at Royal Gorge, Colo., by W. H. Jackson....... | **35.00** |
| Outdoor, the "Highland Light," a Cape Cod lighthouse, with cliff and boats, by Nickerson, Provincetown, R.I., 1880s.. | **12.00** |
| Outdoor, scene showing Russian peasants by a row of rundown log houses, by W. Carrick, St. Petersburg, 1870s.............................. | **10.00-20.00** |
| Outdoor, scene showing a steam engine after it rammed another railcar with wreckage on tracks.................. | **8.00-10.00** |
| Outdoor, unidentified three-span bridge | **3.00** |
| Outdoor, Cape Cod "from Centre Church East," lincluding sailing vessles in harbor, by Nickerson, Provincetown, R.I............................... | **12.00** |
| Outdoor, canyon view identified as "Tenny Falls No. 362, North Cheyenne Cannon," Colo., by J. L. Clinton, Colorado Springs, Colo................. | **15.00** |
| Portrait, Gen. James William Forsyth in uniform............................ | **20.00** |
| Portrait, Sioux Indian chief Sitting Bull, autographed, by Bailey, Dix & Mead, Fort Randall, D.T., 1882............. | **75.00** |
| Portrait, cross-eyed man with barefooted gentleman holding an umbrella.. | **3.00** |
| Portrait, statesman Roscoe Conkling... | **3.00** |
| Portrait, Edwin Booth, unsigned, dressed in shirt and jacket................. | **6.00-8.00** |
| Portrait, Capt. Thomas B. Weir and | |

Agnes Bates, in full military dress with sword............................. **20.00**

Portrait, unidentified freak with grotesquely oversize feet, by Wendt, New York **20.00**

Portrait, black midget George Williams from Arkansas, by Wendt, New York.. **15.00**

Portrait, musician W. E. Locke........ **12.00**

Portrait, Martha and George Washington, (copy from an engraving). **3.00**

Portrait, midget Gen. Tom Thumb and his wife, by Bogardus, New York...... **8.00**

Portrait, unidentified men in uniforms, one with a sword in his belt, another wearing hat and badge.............. **4.00**

Portrait, white dog seated next to a gentleman with a lady seated at a sewing machine, by Shackford, New Hampshire **5.00**

Portrait, William Jennings Bryan (copy of a drawing) addressed to W. R. Hearst on back, by Campbell, New Jersey..... **8.00**

Portrait, midgets Princess Ida and Gen. Totman, by Boston Photogravure Co... **8.00**

Portrait, President Grover Cleveland... **4.00**

Portrait, group of five midgets, by Butman, Mass......................... **10.00**

Portrait, 18-year-old midget Major Atom, by Eisenmann, New York...... **8.00**

Portrait, unidentified girl holding a cymbol, by Ogden...................... **2.00-3.00**

Portrait, girl on horse being led by silk-hatted black man, by Rushworth, Delaware................................ **6.00**

Portrait, unidentified monk........... **6.00**

Portrait, young carpenter posing with eight tools, Freeman, Mass........... **10.00**

Portrait, highwheel bicycle rider posed atop his bicycle...................... **20.00**

Portrait, Chauncey Moorlano and wife (each weighing over 525 pounds, by Wendt.............................. **10.00**

Portrait, Big Bow, chief of the Kiowa Indians, and two of his braves, one with a pistol tucked in his belt, with large buffalo head on floor, by Bennett & Brown, Santa Fe, N.M......................... 65.00

Portrait, lady holding a parrot on her arm, by H.J. Whitlock, Birmingham, England............................. 10.00

Portrait, "Bearded Lady" Annie Jones, by Eisenmann...................... 15.00

Portrait, Oliver Wendell Holmes, by Kirchner, New York................. 8.00

Portrait, William Cullen Bryant with beard, by Mora, New York........... 10.00

Portrait, Naval officer seated with sword and medals, by Lamson, Maine........ 10.00

Portrait, actor Edwin Forrest, by Sarony 7.00

Portrait, Gen. U.S. Grant with spectacles, taken three days before his death, 1885.............................. 25.00-35.00

Portrait, Syrian gentleman in a fez, by S. Hakin, Damascus, Syrie.............. 5.00

Portrait, female sharpshooter Georgie White wearing short skirt and looking down barrel of rifle, ready to shoot, by Kern Bros., New York.............. 20.00-25.00

Portrait, Mason standing in plumbed hat, sword at his side, by R. A. Hickox, Hiawatha, Kans...................... 5.00

Portrait, large black and white dog, mouth open, standing on a column, by W. T. Robinson, Parishville, N.Y...... 3.00

Portrait, Red Cloud, chief of the Oglalas and leader of Sioux and Cheyenne indians, holding peace pipe............. 45.00

Portrait, Running Antelope, Sioux Indian, by J. Pitcher Spooner, Stockton, Calif .............................. 40.00

Portrait, two spruced-up frontiersmen, each with double-barrel shotgun, by S. Shuster, Astoria, Ore................ 40.00

Portrait, Colorado cowhand wearing holster and cartridge belt, by L. McLean, Idaho Springs, Colo......... 40.00

Portrait, Nora Wren, a dwarf who performed at Ringling's in the 1880s, by Wendt............................. 5.00

Portrait, Long Dog, Nez Perce chief in full regalia, by J. Pitcher Spooner, Stockton, Calif.................... 45.00

Portrait, White Eagle Bill wearing a cowboy hat, by Eisenmann, New York.. 25.00

Portrait, the Lee Roys, a man holding a 140-lb. woman on a horizontal board by his hair, signed and autographed as "Wire hair marvels"................. 5.00

Portrait, young surveyor leaning on a surveyors' marker with his jacket on the floor, by Youker, Rockwell, Iowa...... 4.00-7.00

Portrait, three midgets posed in formal attire (identified as The Count, Countess and Baron Magri), by Swords Bros..... 13.00

Portrait, two boys, one holding a trumpet, the other standing next to a large bass drum, by Rickard, Michigan. 6.00

Portrait, The LaPearl's acrobatic team in pyramid pose..................... 8.00

Portrait, two Grosventure Indians, Swift Foot and Trail Dog, standing in full attire, by Huntington for Taylor's Gallery, St. Paul, Minn., 1870s.............. 25.00-30.00

Portrait, a freak named Chiquita Living Doll posed with a giant.............. 6.00-9.00

Portrait, chief Walking Mountain of the Salt Lake Utes, in full regalia, by C. R. Savage, Salt Lake City.............. 20.00-25.00

Portrait, young Indian woman wrapped in blanket and wearing a papoose carrier, by E. P. Butler, Nevada Art Gallery 35.00

Portrait, young man resting one hand on shoulder of Indian brave who wears long feathered headdress, by Thomas Sims, Kensington........................ 35.00

Portrait, a Moqui Indian boy wearing loin cloth and with body painted in snake design, by Parker, San Diego, Calif .............................. 20.00

Portrait, clown identified as George Sun Jr. of Sun Brothers show in typical clown costume, 1904................ 5.00-8.00

Portrait, four musicians posed with instruments, sepia toned.............. 6.00

Portrait, Indian brave wearing beads and bone necklace and holding a rifle, E. P. Butler, Nevada Art Gallery........ 40.00-45.00

Portrait, Big Hand, Sioux medicine man, holding a peace pipe in one hand, by S. Gilbert, Mandan, Dakota........ 55.00

Portrait, western gentleman wearing sombrero and holding a cigar, Shew's Photographic Art Studio, San Francisco, Calif...................... 35.00

Portrait, grinning cowboy, by F. W. Guerin, St. Louis, Mo............... 30.00

Portrait, John Link wearing leather chaps and a six-shooter and holding a clarinet, by Thomas Sims............ 30.00-40.00

Portrait, two children of Sioux chief Great Bear at Fort Sully, Dakota, 1882. 40.00-50.00

Portrait, five Ute Indian chiefs, one wearing the badge of the Indian police, by E. A. Wilder, Durango, Colo....... 100.00-125.00

Portrait, Spotted Eagle, Sioux chief, by Kelly and Odell, Pierre, Dakota........ 85.00-90.00

Portrait, Jim Bebb wearing a rough skirt and kerchief around his neck, by Thomas Sims, Kensington............ 35.00-40.00

Portrait, Sgt. Jim of Gen. Crook's Indian Scouts while on the Geronimo campaign, by Carter & Lamb, Fort Wingate, N.M. ............................... 75.00

Portrait, Apache Chief Geronimo, by Carter & Lamb, Fort Wingate, N.M.... 85.00-90.00

Portrait, Union soldier with his family, the group seated outside a tent, c. 1870.. 16.00

Stereoview of waterfall by F. Jay Haynes, official photographer of Yellowstone National Park, 1876-1916, $2.

Stereoview of tightrope walk above Niagra River, late 1880s or early 1900s, by George Barker, sold by Underwood & Underwood, $2-$3.

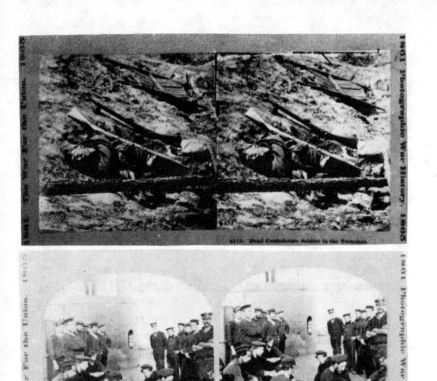

Stereo cards such as these Civil War scenes from the 1865 "The War For The Union" series generally sell for about a half dollar or less, although some antique dealers have peddled them for considerably more than that.

Portrait, Steps, a Nez Perce Indian who fought with Sitting Bull, by Bailey, Fort Randall, Dakota, 1882.............. 40.00

Portrait, Indian brave wearing leather shirt with silver tooling and porcupine quill vest, by G. W. Parsons, Pawhuska, Okla., 1880s...................... 75.00

# STEREO VIEWS

Group, 120 stereoviews, 40 in color, some by E. & H. T. Anthony, some by Geo. M. Lovell of Southridge, Mass., showing views of U.S. and some foreign scenes .......................... 50.00-60.00

Group, 230 glass stereo slides of Europe tour taken by New Jersey family c. 1905, mostly historic and scenic views, printed by Otto Perutz, Munchen, Germany.... 200.00

Group, 33 stereoviews, some western scenes, some exhibitions, some misc., including Japanese troops in 1904........ 60.00

Group, 8 stereoviews, outdoor scenes showing points of interest in eastern U.S., such as "Catskill Mountains" and "View of the Hudson River" with London Stereo Co. blind stamp........... 25.00-35.00

Group, 4 outdoor scenes of California towns or houses, Watkins' New Series.. 10.00

Group, 3 views of Yosemite, by E. & H. T. Anthony....................... 10.00

Group, 2 views of Colorado, one showing Gray's Peak, the other a horse team in Georgetown, by Collier, Central City, Colo................................ 5.00

Group, 4 views of mining operations in Pennsylvania, by E. M. Beckworth, Plymouth, Pa...................... 15.00

Group, 35 stereoviews of buildings, parks, panoramas and groups of people, all Eastern U.S. states, including two hand-tinted views of Boston's Faneuil Hall and Hunnewell's Grounds, 1880s-1900 . . . . . . . . . . . . . . . . . . . .             25.00

Group, 31 stereoviews of suspension and footbridges including 17 of Niagara spans, several by George Barker and George E. Curtiz, 1870s-1900. . . . . . . . . .             30.00

Group, 36 stereoviews of Montreal, Quebec, Nova Scotia and western mountain ranges, by J. G. Parks and others, 1880s-1900 . . . . . . . . . . . . . . . . . . . . . . . .             25.00

Group, 30 stereoviews of cemeteries including Mt. Auburn, Greenwood, Mt. Hope, Albany Rural, and Woodlawn, 1870s-1880s. . . . . . . . . . . . . . . . . . . . . . .             15.00

Group, 5 stereoviews of dirigibles including the Graf Zeppelin in Lakehurst (N.J.) hanger, by Keystone and Underwood & Underwood, 1917-1928 . . . . . . . .             20.00

Group, 65 stereoviews of English countryside, 1850s-1900. . . . . . . . . . . . .             20.00-25.00

Group, 50 stereoviews of seashore scenes in England, 1850s-early 1900s. . . . . . . . .             20.00-25.00

Group, 16 stereoviews of English castles and manor houses, 1860s to early 1900s.             10.00-20.00

Group, 36 stereoviews of Italy, including several of the Vatican and a view of Vesuvius erupting in March 1865, by J. Andrieu, Paris, 1860s-early 1870s. . . . . .             20.00-25.00

Group, 65 stereoviews of posed comic scenes, several in series with captions, many scenes with courting and hunting humor, late 1880s-1900. . . . . . . . . . . . . .             20.00-30.00

Group, 38 stereoviews of France, including several of the Paris Exhibition of 1900, 1880s-1900. . . . . . . . . . . . . . . . . . .             20.00-30.00

Group, 53 stereoviews of the Middle East including scenery, groups, and Biblical sites, 1890s-1900. . . . . . . . . . . . . .             30.00-35.00

Group, 53 stereoviews of France, trom Alps to port at Le Havre, 1850s-1880s. .             35.00-40.00

Group, 75 stereoviews of turn-of-the-century comic series, mainly marriage, courting and "illicit affairs" scenes 1890s-1900s........................ **30.00-35.00**

Group, 55 stereoviews of posed situation comdey scenes, mostly marriage, court-ship or city slicker vs. country bumpkin, 1890s-1900s........................ **20.00-30.00**

Group, 77 stereoviews of humourous posed scenes, mostly courtship and mar-riage, 1880s-1900s.................. **25.00-35.00**

Group, 46 stereoviews of interiors and exteriors of Massachusetts landmarks, mid 19th-early 20th centuries.......... **30.00**

Group, 65 stereoviews of posed comic and melodramatic scenes including several in series, racial jokes and mar-riage humor, 1890s-1900s............. **30.00-35.00**

Group, 25 stereoviews of historical sites and residences in New England, in-cluding serveral groups of people, 1870s-1880s........................ **25.00-30.00**

Group, 82 stereoviews of the Holy Land and various Biblical sites, 1890s-1900s.. **30.00-35.00**

Group, 7 stereoviews of the Mississippi River including three from American Scenery series, c. 1880s.............. **10.00-12.00**

Group, 5 stereoviews of Tennessee by J. B. Linn, including Lookout Mountain, part of 44-view set.................. **10.00-15.00**

Group, 24 stereoviews of the Holy Land including views by Francis Frith, Charles Bierstadt, and others, 1858-74......... **30.00-35.00**

Group, four miscellaneous outdoor scenes including Niagara Falls by Soule, Boston............................ **4.00**

Group, 5 views along Camden turnpike, by Mills, Camden, N.J.............. **6.00**

Group, 7 glass plate stereoviews of Euro-pean cities including four panoramas, c. 1880-90s ......................... **15.00-20.00**

Group, 27 glass plate stereoviews of Greece, 1895-1900 . . . . . . . . . . . . . . . . . .    **15.00-20.00**

Group, 28 glass plate stereoviews of the Isle of Wight, 1850s-early 1900s . . . . . . . .    **20.00**

Group, 27 glass plate stereoviews of assorted subjects including railroad trains, Irish countryside, Colorado and New England, by W. B. Kilburn, Littleton, N.H., 1870s . . . . . . . . . . . . . . . . .    **30.00-40.00**

Group, 23 glass plate stereoviews of Italy including scenes and groups of people, 1870s . . . . . . . . . . . . . . . . . . . . . . . . . . . . .    **20.00**

Group, 23 stereoviews of rivers and Trenton Falls, by Robert J. Moore, Jamestown, N.Y., 1870s . . . . . . . . . . . . .    **20.00**

Group, 78 stereoviews of New England, including Nantucket, Connecticut, Vermont, 1860s-1900 . . . . . . . . . . . . . . . . . .    **35.00-45.00**

Group, 45 stereoviews of New England states and New York, some showing horse and buggy traffic, including two views by W. E. Vaughn, 1960s-1880s . . .    **25.00-30.00**

Group, 31 stereoviews of New Hampshire, 1860s-1900 . . . . . . . . . . . . . . . . . .    **20.00**

Group, 36 stereoviews of New Hampshire including mountain scenes, by Kilburn Bros., late 1880s . . . . . . . . . . . . .    **35.00-40.00**

Group of 54 stereoviews of New York spas including the Adirondacks, including some by D. Barnum, C. W. Woodward, McIntosh & Baldwin and others, 1860s-1900 . . . . . . . . . . . . . . . . .    **30.00-40.00**

Group, 19 stereoviews of New York published by Julius M. Wendt, including scenes around Albany, early 1900s . . . . .    **15.00-20.00**

Group, 23 stereoviews of Philadelphia, 19 showing scenes from Centennial Exhibition, 1860s-1900 . . . . . . . . . . . . . . . .    **20.00-30.00**

Group, 28 stereoviews of New York, by Leo Daft, Troy, N.Y., 1880s . . . . . . . . . .    **15.00-20.00**

Group, 18 stereoviews of Niagara Falls including 10 from the Canadian side and one of Stephen Peer crossing on tightrope, seven by George Barker, 1870s-1902 ........................ **20.00-40.00**

Group, 14 stereoviews of Utah, several from American Scenery series, other by Pond, Savage & Bierstadt, 1870s-1900s. **20.00-30.00**

Group, 5 paper stereoviews with colored backing sheets from the series Siege de Paris 1870-71, showing doll-like figures in battle scenes, several prints scored or pin-pricked for color effects, published by B. K., Paris, c. 1872 .............. **20.00-25.00**

Group, 23 stereoviews of Philadelphia sites and landmarks, by James Cremer, Philadelphia, Pa., 1870s .............. **20.00**

Group, 35 stereoviews of Swiss scenery, 1870s-1880s ........................ **15.00-20.00**

Group, 58 stereoviews of battlefields of Spanish-American War (Cuba and the Philippines) by Keystone and others, 1898-1899 ........................ **35.00-45.00**

Group, 33 stereoviews of statues and monuments from 19th-century exhibitions, 1860s-1880s .................. **15.00-25.00**

Group, 11 stereoviews of Rochester and Troy, N.Y., by Union View Co., 1880s. **10.00-20.00**

Group, 39 stereoviews of Paris including tourist attractions, 1870s-1880s ........ **15.00-20.00**

Group, 32 stereoviews of Vermont towns and scenery, 1860s-1904 .............. **15.00-20.00**

Group, 30 stereoviews of Virginia landmarks, two hand-tinted, 1860s-1900s... **15.00-20.00**

Group, 46 stereoviews of Wales, including scenery and people, 1850s-early 1900s .............................. **25.00-35.00**

Group, 14 stereoviews of Washington, D.C., by F. H. Bell, 1867-1871 ........ **25.00-35.00**

Group, 22 views of halls and rooms in the White House and other Washington, D.C., buildings, 1860s-1900 ........... **20.00-40.00**

Group, 11 stereoviews of Wisconsin sites, 10 by H. H. Bennett, 1870s....... **15.00-20.00**

Group, 40 stereoviews of Yellowstone Park by Keystone, 1897-1904......... **40.00-50.00**

Group, 64 stereoviews of World War I battlefield scenes, Keystone and Underwood & Underwood, 1914-1918........ **40.00-50.00**

Group, 39 stereoviews of White House, inside and outside, 1860s-1902......... **35.00-45.00**

Group, 6 stereoviews of the Boston Fire by J. P. Soule, 1872................. **15.00-20.00**

Group, 2 views of Boston Navy Yard... **5.00-6.00**

Group, 2 stereoviews of Alaska Gold Rush by Kilburn and one Keystone vies, "Bound for Chilkoot"............... **10.00-12.00**

Group, 8 stereoviews of the Johnstown Flood by Kilburn................... **15.00-25.00**

Group, 13 stereoviews of New England published by S. F. Adams, New Bedford, Mass., 1869-1870.............. **15.00-20.00**

Group, 50 stereoviews of dirigibles and other aeronautic subjects, Keystone View Co., Meadville, 1934........... **40.00-50.00**

Group, 33 stereoviews of sites in Belgium, 1850s-1900............... **20.00-30.00**

Group, 10 stereoviews depicting black people in various activities in southern U.S., the northern states and Africa, by Underwood & Underwood, Webster & Albee, Keystone View Co. and others, c. 1900.......................... **20.00-35.00**

Group, 12 stereoviews of bridges, c. 1880-1910......................... **10.00-15.00**

Group, 34 stereoviews of Boston historical sites, two by C. Seaver Jr., 1872-1906...................... **40.00-50.00**

Group, 8 stereoviews of suspension bridges and railroad trestles, late 19th century........................ **10.00-15.00**

Group, 17 stereoviews of the Brooklyn-Greenwood cemetery, 1870s-1880s..... **15.00-20.00**

Group, 15 stereoviews of California sites including turn-of-the-century scenes in

Los Angeles and San Francisco, 1865-1900s ........................ **20.00-25.00**

Group, 11 stereoviews of the Sierra Nevada mountains in California, three by C. L. Pond, three by C. E. Watkins, 1860s-1905 ........................ **20.00-30.00**

Group, 60 stereoviews of Canadian sites and natural wonders, by Notman, Underwood & Underwood, E. & H. T. Anthony, Parks, and others, c. 1890-1905 ........................ **50.00-60.00**

Group, 11 stereoviews of Chicago and the Midwest, by A. C. Falor, Gates, Liebich and others, c. 1890 ........... **8.00-10.00**

Group, 18 stereoviews of northern California sites including two by C. E. Watkins of Farallones Island sea lions, 1860s-1906 ........................ **30.00-35.00**

Group, 15 stereoviews of early San Francisco, 1860s-1915 .................. **25.00-35.00**

Group, 15 stereoviews of Chicago landmarks, 1860s-1898 .................. **10.00-15.00**

Group, 10 stereoviews of wreckage caused by Chicago Fire, by P. B. Greene, J. H. Abbott, H. Reeves, and others, 1871. **15.00-20.00**

Group, 37 stereoviews of Cuba, mostly by Underwood & Underwood, some by H. C. White, Griffith & Griffith, 1899-1902 ........................ **15.00-25.00**

Group, 27 stereoviews of Colorado scenery, c. 1875 .................... **25.00-30.00**

Group, 15 stereoviews of Connecticut, two hand-tinted views by E. T. Whitney, 1860s-1880s ........................ **15.00-20.00**

Group, 15 stereoviews of giant Redwood trees in California, including some by E. & H. T. Anthony, John P. Soule, C. E. Watkins, Thos. Houseworth and others, 1860s-1870s ........................ **30.00-40.00**

Group, 21 stereoviews of comedy scenes, by Liberty Brand Stereo Views and others, c. 1890 .................... **10.00-15.00**

Group, 27 stereoviews of cotton processing, by Keystone View Co., H. C. White,
Underwood & Underwood, and others,
1900-1910 . . . . . . . . . . . . . . . . . . . . . . . .    **10.00-15.00**

Group, 11 stereoviews of the Dakotas,
including six published by Hamilton &
Hoyt and three by W. R. Cross, late
1800s . . . . . . . . . . . . . . . . . . . . . . . . . . . .    **15.00-20.00**

Group, 21 stereoviews of English man-
sions, published by London Stereoscopic
Co., 19 hand-tinted, 1850s-1860s. . . . . . .    **20.00-25.00**

Group, 20 stereoviews of disasters from
Italy; Galveston, Tex.; Martinique, etc.,
by Underwood & Underwood, Keystone
View Co., and others, c. 1895-1910 . . . . .    **15.00-25.00**

Group, 21 stereoviews of English art
works and European scenery, c. 1890. . .    **15.00-25.00**

Group, 57 stereoviews of monuments
and sites in England, by J. Davis Burton,
B. W. Kilburn, J. F. Jarvis and others, c.
1865-early 1900s. . . . . . . . . . . . . . . . . . .    **20.00-30.00**

Group, 31 stereoviews of Florida including some by E. & H. T. Anthony, J.
F. Mears, George Pierron, C. Seaver Jr.,
1860s-1880s. . . . . . . . . . . . . . . . . . . . . . .    **20.00-30.00**

Group, eight stereoviews of the Holy
Land and Egypt by Francis Frith (including three from his first series of
1856), London, 1856-1859 . . . . . . . . . . .    **40.00-50.00**

Group, 13 stereoviews of Georgia sites,
1860s-1900s. . . . . . . . . . . . . . . . . . . . . . .    **10.00-20.00**

Group, 25 stereoviews of English countryside, including some by J. R. Sawyer,
R. E. Mosely, J. Dutton, John Beattie,
1860s-1880s. . . . . . . . . . . . . . . . . . . . . . .    **20.00-25.00**

Group, 16 stereoviews of Greek ruins
(one photographed by Alexander Flury),
1870s-1900 . . . . . . . . . . . . . . . . . . . . . . .    **15.00-20.00**

Group, 43 stereoviews of comedy scenes,
by William McAllister and others, 27
tinted, c. 1860-1880. . . . . . . . . . . . . . . . .    **25.00-35.00**

Group, 6 stereoviews of Illinois including two of Chicago Exhibition displays, by Copelin, J. A. W. Pittman and others, 1870s-1890s.............    6.00-10.00

Group, 7 stereoviews of Grinnel tornado, Iowa, by D. H. Cross and J. S. Lovell, 1882......................    15.00-20.00

Group, 70 stereoviews of Irish farm life and other scenes, by Underwood & Underwood, Keystone View Co., James M. Davis and others, c. 1890-1905......    20.00-30.00

Group, 5 stereoviews of Yellowstone by W. H. Jackson, 4x7″, Denver & Washington, c. 1870-1875...........    60.00-70.00

Group, 5 stereoviews, mostly Eastern states scenery, by Langenheim, published by American Stereoscopic Co. of Philadelphia, 1858..................    50.00-60.00

Group, 27 stereoviews of European scenery and views of International Exhibition of 1862 and other exhibitions, 1850s-1870s......................    30.00-40.00

Group, 27 stereoviews of mines and miners, by Robert M. Davis, Keystone View Co., C. L. Pond, Underwood & Underwood, and others, c. 1890-1900s..    25.00-35.00

Group, 11 stereoviews of Minnesota, by R. N. Fearon, W. H. Illingworth, Charles A. Zimmerman and others, 1870s-1880s......................    10.00-20.00

Group, 87 stereoviews of the Near East, mostly Palestine, including Biblical sites, by Roberts & Fellows, B. W. Kilburn and others, 1898-1915...............    25.00-40.00

Group, 31 stereoviews of New Hampshire sites, some with people boating, hiking, etc., 1870s-1900s.............    20.00-30.00

Group, 13 stereoviews of New Hampshire by Kilburn Bros., late 19th century    10.00-20.00

Group, 13 stereoviews of New Jersey, including 10 of Atlantic City beaches, bathers and boardwalk, 1880s-1900....    10.00-15.00

Group, 21 stereoviews of Catskills, New York, eight by J. Loeffler, 1860s-1870s. **15.00-25.00**

Group, 21 stereoviews of Maine sites, 1860s-1870s......................... **15.00-20.00**

Group, 33 stereoviews of Adirondacks, New York, 1860-1900s.............. **15.00-20.00**

Group, 25 stereoviews of the Hudson River, New York, 1860s-early 1900s.... **15.00-25.00**

Group, 22 steroviews of North Africa, 1880s-1900 ....................... **10.00-20.00**

Group, 14 stereoviews of Lake George, N.Y., including ruins of Fort Ticonderoga, several by G. S. Irish, 1860s-1880s. **15.00-20.00**

Group, 40 stereoviews of Niagara Falls scenery, including one tinted view by Beckel Bros., 1860s-1900s............ **20.00-25.00**

Group, 20 stereoviews of Niagara Falls scenery by Charles BIerstadt, 12 with Bierstadt's imprint as winner of Silver Medal and Vienna Medal for 1873, 1870s **20.00-30.00**

Group, 93 stereoviews of Norway, late 19th-century-20th century........... **15.00-20.00**

Group, 20 stereoviews of Ohio cities and sites, 1860s-1900s................... **20.00-25.00**

Group, 26 stereoviews of Oregon, 1880s-early 1900s................... **15.00-20.00**

Group, 10 stereoviews of Johnston Flood, Penn., 1889................. **15.00-20.00**

Group, 7 stereoviews of President and Mrs. Warren Harding touring U.S., 1923-24 .......................... **15.00-20.00**

Group, 80 stereoviews of railroad subjects, by Underwood & Underwood, Keystone View Co. and others, 1890-1905 ......................... **30.00-40.00**

Group, 37 stereoviews of risque women with various undergarments revealed, by E. W. Kelly, Langley-Orr Co., Griffith & Griffith, Underwood & Underwood, and others, c. 1900.................. **30.00-45.00**

| | |
|---|---|
| Group, 60 stereoviews of the San Francisco Bay Area, by Oliver Enders, late 1920s.............................. | **20.00-30.00** |
| Group, 38 stereoviews of San Francisco earthquake damage, two of them original stereograms, 1906............ | **20.00-40.00** |
| Group, 36 stereoviews of ships and boats, by E. & H. T. Anthony, Griffith & Griffith and others, 1880s-1890s..... | **20.00-35.00** |
| Group, 10 stereoviews of abbeys, bridges, and other sites in England, by W. Russell Sedgefield, c. 1858......... | **8.00-12.00** |
| Group, 63 stereoviews of U.S. Navy ships and weapons, by Keystone View Co., Stromeyer & Wyman, Griffith & Griffith and others, c. 1900.......... | **20.00-25.00** |
| Group, 11 stereoviews of Virginia, including four 4x7″ stereograms from Anderson & Ennis catalog, 1860s-1870s. | **10.00-18.00** |
| Group, 15 stereoviews of Wisconsin sites, 1880s-1890s................... | **10.00-20.00** |
| Group, 57 stereoviews of interiors and exteriors of Washington D.C. sites, including the Capitol, several by E. & H. T. Anthony, 1860s-1890s............. | **20.00-30.00** |
| Group, 16 stereoviews of San Francisco and other western cities, by C. W. Carter, F. E. Rogers and others, 1870s-1880s........................ | **20.00-40.00** |
| Group, 58 stereoviews depicting men, places and carnage of World War I, by Keystone View Co. and Underwood & Underwood, c. 1918................. | **20.00-40.00** |
| Group, 300 stereoviews of World War I by Maj. Joseph M. Hanson, published by Keystone View Co., 1928........... | **100.00-125.00** |
| Group, 57 stereoviews of Yellowstone, by H. C. White, 1901-1905............ | **20.00-30.00** |
| Group, 36 stereoviews of Yellowstone Park including 10 by I. W. Ingersoll and three by W. I. Marshall, 1870s-1900.... | **20.00-25.00** |

Group, 8 stereoviews of Yosemite including views by John P. Soule, Charles Bierstadt, M. M. Hazeltine, L. Nesemann and B. W. Kilburn, 1870s-1890s...................... 20.00-35.00

Group, 49 stereoviews of Burma, Buddhist rituals, and Asian sites, Underwood & Underwood, 1903-1907....... 40.00-60.00

Group, 76 stereoviews of China, Underwood & Underwood, early 1900s...... 35.00-45.00

Group, 17 stereoviews of Civil War scenes, including several of paintings of battles at Gettysburg and Vicksburg, 1860s-1903 ...................... 20.00-30.00

Group, 45 stereoviews of Yosemite Valley, by C. L. Pond, Buffalo, N.Y., 1860s ............................ 80.00-90.00

Group, 36 stereoviews of Civil War scenes, including eight by Mathew Brady, published by E. & H. T. Anthony 100.00-150.00

Group, 84 stereoviews of the 1876 Centennial Exhibition in Philadelphia, published by E. L. Wilson and W. I. Adams' Centennial Photographic Co., Philadelphia, Pa., 1876.............. 90.00-125.00

Group, 20 stereoviews of San Francisco earthquake and fire, most published by Griffith & Griffith, c. 1906............ 30.00-35.00

Group, 29 stereoviews of Sears, Roebuck Co. Chicago offices, workrooms, clerks, etc., 1890s......... 15.00-25.00

Group, 22 stereoviews of Southern states, including a panorama of Savannah, by Nat W. Taylor, W. T. Robertson and others, 1860s-1880s........... 20.00-30.00

Group, 35 stereoviews of South Africa and the Boer War, early 1900s........ 25.00-35.00

Interior, Fort St. Augustine, Fla., by Ryan, Savannah, showing cannons, ammunition, etc....................... 3.00

Interior, church in Delaware, by Maybin, Wilmington................. 2.00

Interior, entrance to Principle Room at Great Metropolitan Sanitary Fair, published by E. & H. T. Anthony...... 5.00

Interior, tent with furnishings and with a stereoviewer resting on a table in foreground, location identified as Martha's Vineyard campground.......... 4.00

Interior, a printer at work with a press, a sample of his work pinned on the wall, by W. L. Hall, Trumansburg, N.Y..... 6.00

Outdoor, Washington Monument, Richmond, Va., by Anderson, Richmond, Va.................................. 3.00

Outdoor, Chicago Tribune Building after Chicago Fire, by Mountford...... 5.00

Outdoor, Chicago Court House after Chicago Fire....................... 5.00

Outdoor, large fallen orange tree in California with people on top of it and standing nearby, from Anthony's American Views.................... 4.00

Outdoor, scene showing dam that supplied Philadelphia city water, photographer unknown................... 3.00

Outdoor, scene showing Vermillion River near Hastings, Minn., by Zimmerman, Minneapolis................... 4.00

Outdoor, Spanish Cathedral in St. Augustine, Fla..................... 2.00

Outdoor, botanical garden's entrance in St. Louis, Mo., by Boel & Koenig...... 3.00

Outdoor, Unity Church after Chicago Fire............................ 4.00

Outdoor, buildings at the Rock Island Arsenal, Ill. one of a series by Western View Co........................... 6.00

Outdoor, bridge at Mauch Chunk, Pa... 2.00

Outdoor, entrance to mine shaft in New Mexico, by F. E. Evans, Las Vegas (Mine identified on reverse).......... 8.00-10.00

Outdoor, Niagara Falls in Winter scene

from the Canadian side, Clifton House in distance, published by E. & H. T. Anthony............................................... 3.00

Outdoor, city street in Medford, Mass., by Wilkerson...................... 2.00

Outdoor, "Burnt Porcupine Island," by Bradley Brothers, East Eden, Maine.'... 2.00

Outdoor, paddlewheeler "Newport", by Seaside Views...................... 5.00

Outdoor, paddlewheeler on Hudson River at sunset, by Griffin & Griffin.... 2.00

Outdoor, "Red River near the Dam," from the Gems of Kentucky Scenery series, by Mullen.................... 2.00

Outdoor, glass stereoview showing Niagara Falls in Winter, by Langenhem Bros, 1854........................ 40.00-50.00

Outdoor, a photographer's outdoor studio, by Reed, Georgetown, Mass.... 10.00

Outdoor, street scene with two-horse sleigh in foregound and side reading "... rean Gallery" in distance, by T. G. Richardson, St. Alban, Vt............. 6.00

Outdoor, five Indian chiefs posed in front of a teepee, from Stereoscopic Views series......................... 10.00-15.00

Outdoor, Fort Sumter after the first bombardment in 1861, by G. N. Barnard, Charleston, S.C................ 10.00-15.00

Outdoor, coal mining operations in Pennsylvania, by E. M. Beckworth, Plymouth, Pa......................... 5.00

Outdoor, Court House in Pittsburgh, Pa., by W. T. Purviance.............. 3.00

Outdoor, football game between U. of Penn. and Harvard, with thousands of spectators, by Griffith & Griffith...... 5.00

Outdoor, birdseye view of Philadelphia from Girard College, by M. P. Simins.. 3.00

Outdoor, Chicago, Michigan Ave. north from 21st St., by Lovejoy & Foster, 1871 series............................. 3.00

Outdoor, Chicago Water Works after Chicago Fire................... 3.00

Outdoor, castle on lake with sailboat... 2.00

Outdoor, village scene with three men in foreground, moon shining in sky....... 4.00

Outdoor, Swiss mountain scene with two people and a balloon aloft........... 8.00-10.00

Outdoor, Paris with cathedral tower and buildings and a balloon aloft with lights on it............................ 10.00-15.00

Outdoor, moon rising over mountain and valley......................... 3.00-5.00

Outdoor, moon rising over Lake Geneva 5.00-8.00

Outdoor, two men watching a volcano erupting............................ 10.00

Outdoor, old funnel stack locomotive at station, by G. R. Wheeldon, Maine.... 4.00

Outdoor, "Bay during Regatta, 4th of July, N.J.," by E. & H. T. Anthony.... 5.00

Outdoor, humorous pose with cameraman and a couple, Underwood & Underwood, 1898................... 3.00

Outdoor, Central Park, N.Y., view from terrace, by E. & H. T. Anthony, 1866... 4.00

Outdoor, construction on Buckport to Bangor railroad line with locomotive, by A. G. Webster, Maine, 1871........... 8.00

Outdoor, oil regions of Pennsylvania, Woodward Culvers Railroad Bridge.... 7.00

Portrait, Abraham Lincoln, bust pose with floral bouquet, by John Soule, Boston, c. 1870s.................... 20.00

Portrait, Charles Dickens, by J. Gurney 15.00-20.00

Portrait, Queen Victoria.............. 5.00-10.00

# ARTIST-NAME PHOTOGRAPHS

Images in this section include daguerreotypes, ambrotypes, silver prints, gravures and other types of photographic images, but they are valued primarily because of the photographer's name or as works of art rather than because they represent pioneer photographic processes. This is **not** an exhaustive list of well known photographers, but rather a fairly representative sampling. We have tried to list a variety of images by each artist, focusing on the type of photographs readily available from dealers or available from time to time at auction. No effort has been made to list the artist's "best" works, and many highly popular images are not included due to space limitations or lack of accurate recent market data.

Dimensions are in inches, height before width, rounded off to the nearest inch. Except where defects are noted, images are presumed to be in good to very good condition.

| | |
|---|---|
| Abbott, Berenice, portrait of Eugene Atget, silver print, 13x10, 1926 | 500.00-600.00 |
| Abbott Berenice, "Flower Seller," silver print, 8x6 print made from negative by Eugene Atget | 400.00-500.00 |
| Adams, Ansel, "Sculpture of a Buddha, San Francisco Museum of Art," silver print, 8x5, signed, 1920s | 350.00-500.00 |
| Adams, Ansel, "Golden Gate before Erection of Golden Gate Bridge, San Francisco," silver print, 7x10, signed, 1932 | 1,000.00-1,500.00 |
| Adams, Ansel, "White Gravestone, Laurel Hill Cemetery, San Francisco," silver print, 14x10, signed, 1933 | 800.00-900.00 |
| Adams, Ansel, portrait of Carolyn Anspacher, silver print, 13x10, signed and dated, 1933 | 900.00-1,100.00 |

Berenice Abbott, portrait of Eugene Atget, see page 227.

Ansel Adams, "Monolith, the Face of Half Dome, Yosemite National Park" see page 232.

Ansel Adams "Grand Tetons and Snake River, Wyoming" see page 232.

Ansel Adams "Clearing Storm, Mt. Williamson from Manzanar, Sierra Nevada, California" see page 232.

Ansel Adams ''Moonrise, Hernandez, N.M.'' see page 232.

Ansel Adams ''Clearing Winterstorm, Yosemite National Park''
see page 232.

230

Above: Ansel Adsams "Sunrise, Dunes, Death Valley National Monument" see page 232.

Right: Ansel Adams "Self-Portrait, Monument Valley, Utah" see page 235.

Adams, Ansel, "Half Dome, Orchard Winter, Yosemite National Park," silver print, 15x19, signed 1933 . . . . . . . . . . . . **2,000.00-3,000.00**

Adams, Ansel, "Museum Storeroom, San Francisco," silver print, 9x11, signed and dated, 1936 . . . . . . . . . . . . . . . . . **500.00-600.00**

Adams, Ansel, "Grand Tetons and Snake River, Wyoming," silver print, 15x19, signed, 1942 . . . . . . . . . . . . . . . . . **6,000.00-8,000.00**

Adams, Ansel, "Clearing Storm, Mt. Williamson from Manzanar, Sierra Nevada, Calif.," silver print, 15x19, signed, 1944 . . . . . . . . . . . . . . . . . . . . . **4,000.00-5,000.00**

Adams, Ansel, "Redwoods, Bull Creek Flat, Calif.," silver print, 16x19, signed . **1,000.00-2,000.00**

Adams, Ansel, "Moonrise, Hernandez, N.M.," silver print, 15x20, signed, 1944 **12,000.00-13-,000.00**

Adams, Ansel, "Moonrise, Hernandez, N.M.," silver print, 10x13, signed, 1944 **6,000.00-8,000.00**

Adams, Ansel, "Clearing Winterstorm, Yosemite National Park," silver print, 16x20, signed, 1944 . . . . . . . . . . . . . . . . . **8,000.-10,000.**

Adams, Ansel, "Mt. McKinley and Wonder Lake, Alaska," silver print, 16x19, signed, 1947 . . . . . . . . . . . . . . . . . **3,500.00-4,000.00**

Adams, Ansel, "Fresh Snow, Yosemite Valley, Calif.," silver print, 16x19, 1947 **1,000.00-1,250.00**

Adams, Ansel, outdoor scene showing a church, silver print, 9x7, signed, 1948 . . . **500.00-600.00**

Adams, Ansel, "Sunrise, Dunes, Death Valley National Monument," silver print, 18x15, signed, 1948 . . . . . . . . . . . . **8,000.00-9,000.00**

Adams, Ansel, "Alders, Prarie Creek Beach, Northern California," silver print, 15x19, 1949 . . . . . . . . . . . . . . . . . **2,000.00-2,500.00**

Adams, Ansel, "Sundown, the Pacific," silver print, 18x15, signed . . . . . . . . . . . . **2,000.00-2,500.00**

Adams, Ansel, "Monolith, the Face of Half Dome, Yosemite National Park," silver print, 11x8, signed, 1927 . . . . . . . . **10,000.-12,000.**

Ansel Adams "Aspens, Norther New Mexico" see page 235.

Adams, Ansel, "Winter, Sunrise, Sierra Nevada from Lonepine," silver print, 16x20 ............................... **7,000.00-8,500.00**

Adams, Ansel, "Nevada Fall, Yosemite National Park," silver print, 20x15, signed, 1950 ........................ **1,000.00-1,500.00**

Adams, Ansel, "White Branches, Mono Lake, Calif.," silver print, 19x15, signed, 1950 ............................ **4,000.00-6,000.00**

Adams, Ansel, portrait of Adlai Stevenson, silver print, 9x7, 1952 ............ **2,000.00-2,500.00**

Adams, Ansel, "Rails and Jet Trails, Roseville Calif.," silver print, 14x10,

Left: Thomas Annan, "High Street, Glasgow", see page 235.

Below: Diane Arbus, "Rudolf Nureyev and Erik Bruhn", see page 233.

signed, 1953......................**4,000.00-5,000.00**

Adams, Ansel, "Self-Portrait, Monument Valley, Utah," silver print, 14x9, signed, 1958......................**5,000.00-6,000.00**

Adams, Ansel, "Forest and Stream, Northern California," silver print, 16x19, 1959......................**3,000.00-3,500.00**

Adams, Ansel, "Stream, Sea, Clouds, Rodeo Lagoon, Marin County, Calif.," silver print, 19x16, signed, 1962........**3,000.00-4,000.00**

Adams, Ansel, "Cross, Cemetery, Mission San Xavier, Tucson, Ariz.," silver print, 8x7, signed, 1951.............. **400.00-500.00**

Adams, Ansel, "Road, Nevada Desert," silver print, 9x7, signed, 1951.......... **600.00-700.00**

Adams, Ansel, "Aspens, Northern New Mexico," silver print 19x16, signed, 1958 **1000.00-5000.00**

Adam-Salomon, A.S., portrait of Charles Carnier, woodburytype, 1880s.. **300.00-500.00**

Alinari, Fratelli, view of Michelangelo's "Last Judgement," albumen print, 1870s............................ **30.00-35.00**

Annan, thomas, outdoor scene showing High St., Glasgow, carbon print, 15x12, 1868-1899......................... **300.00-400.00**

Annan, Thomas, outdoor scene showing Low Green St., Glasgow, photogravure, 1868............................... **60.00-80.00**

Arbus, Diane, portrait of Rudolf Nureyev and Erik Bruhn, silver print, 8x8, 1963......................... **900.00-1,000.00**

Arbus, Diane, portrait of a circus fat lady and her dog named Troubles, silver print, 15x14, signed, 1964............. **800.00-1,000.00**

Arbus, Diane, "Identical Twins, Roselle, N.J.," silver print, 9x9, 1967... **300.00-500.00**

Atget, Eugene, portrait of a flower seller, silver print from Atget negative by Berenice Abbott, 8x6................ **300.00-400.00**

Atget, Eugene, outdoor scene showing Cour, Rue de Valence, silver print, from

Right: Eugene Atget "Portrait of a Flower Seller", see page 235. Below: Diane Arbus "Portrait of a circus fat lady", see page 235.

George Barker ''Niagara Falls'',
see page 238.

D.F. Barry ''Portrait of Sitting
Bull'' see page 238.

Atget negative printed by Berenice Abbott . . . . . . . . . . . . . . . . . . . . . . . . . . . . . . 300.00-400.00

Atget, Eugene, "Cathedrale d'Amiens, Stalles," silver print, 7x8, c. 1902 . . . . . . 900.00-1,000.00

Baldus, Edouard, outdoor scene showing Parisian streets, albumen print, 7x11, 1860-70 . . . . . . . . . . . . . . . . . . . . . . . . . 25.00-30.00

Barker, George, outdoor scene showing Niagara Falls from the American side, albumen print, 20x16, matted, 1880s . . . 300.00-400.00

Barraud, William, portrait of scientist John Tyndall, woodburytype, 9x7, 1899 25.00-35.00

Barraud, William, portrait of Maj. Gen. Sir Farncis Wallace Grenfill of the Egyptian Army, woodburytype, 9x7, 1889 . . . 20.00-30.00

Barry, D. F., portrait of Sitting Bull, gelatin print, 10x7, signed, 1890s . . . . . . . 150.00-175.00

Barry, D. F. (studio), portrait of Chief Rain-in-the-Face and D. F. Barry, gelatin print, 7x5, 1890s . . . . . . . . . . . . . 150.00-175.00

Barry, D. F. portrait of Chief Gall, gelatin print, 7x6, 1890s . . . . . . . . . . . . . 100.00-150.00

Baumgaertel, Karl A., "San Francisco Skyline," silver print, 13x10, 1930 . . . . . 75.00-100.00

Bayer, Herbert, "Standing Objects," silver print, 14x9, signed and dated, 1936, printed in 1960s . . . . . . . . . . . . . . 600.00-700.00

Beaton, Cecil, portrait of fashion editor Carmel Snow, silver print retouched, 11x8, early 1930s . . . . . . . . . . . . . . . . . . . 200.00-300.00

Beaton, Cecil, fashion study for British Vouge, silver print, 10x8 . . . . . . . . . . . . . 100.00-200.00

Bedford, Francis, "Photographic Views of North Wales," 20 landscape views, albumen prints, 6x8, c. 1870 . . . . . . . . . . 85.00-135.00

Bernhard, Ruth, "Two Forms," silver print, 10x7, 1930s . . . . . . . . . . . . . . . . . . 350.00-450.00

Bisson, Louis and Auguste, outdoor scene showing climbers on Mt. Blanc, Switzerland, albumen print, 9x15, 1860s 150.00-300.00

Bisson, Louis and Auguste, outdoor

Mathew Brady "Portrait of two couples", see page 239.

scene showing facade of cathedral at
Rheims, albumen print, 14x7, c. 1860...    **200.00-300.00**

Bodine, A. Aubrey, "Thames Power
House," silver print, 16x14, signed, 1950    **100.00-200.00**

Bodine, A. Aubrey, "Two Nuns," silver
print, 15x11, signed, 1930s...........    **225.00-300.00**

Bodine, A. Aubrey, "Willow Basket
Maker," silver print, 17x14, signed,
1930s.............................    **100.00-200.00**

Brady, Mathew, portrait of two couples,
½ plate daguerreotype...............    **200.00-300.00**

Above: Mathew Brady. "Portrait of an elderly man", see page 248.

Right: Mathew Brady "Portrait of a young man", 1/2 plate. See page 242.

Above: Mathew Brady, "Portrait of a father and son". See page 242.

Right: Mathew Brady, "Portrait of a man", 1/6 plate. See page 248.

Mathew Brady, "Portrait of a woman", 1/2 plate. See page 243.

Brady, Mathew, portrait of a boy, ¼
plate in case........................ **150.00-250.00**

Brady, Mathew, portrait of a young
man, ½ plate daguerreotype cased..... **400.00-500.00**

Brady, Mathew, portrait of a man, 1/6
plate cased......................... **200.00-250.00**

Brady, Mathew, portrait of a father and
his son, ½ plate daguerreotype cased... **200.00-300.00**

Brady, Mathew, portrait of an uniden-
tified man, ¼ plate daguerreotype cased **200.00-300.00**

Brady, Mathew, portrait of a middle-
aged man, ½ plate daguerreotype cased
(slight spotting)..................... **200.00-300.00**

Brady, Mathew, portrait of an elderly

man with spectacles, ½ plate daguer-
reotype, cased.............................. 450.00-500.00

Brady, Mathew, portrait of a man,
three-quarter figure, ¼ plate daguerreo-
type cased.............................. 200.00-300.00

Brady, Mathew, portrait of a woman,
1/6 plate daguerreotype cased.......... 100.00-150.00

Brady, Mathew, portrait of a woman, ½
plate daguerreotype, tinted, in leather
case.............................. 300.00-400.00

Brady, Mathew, portrait of a middle-
aged couple, ½ plate ambrotype, tinted,
matted, cased.............................. 200.00-300.00

Mathew Brady "Portrait of man and wife" oval gilt mat. See
page 247.

Left: Mathew Brady "Portrait of a middle aged man" 1/4 plate daguerreotype.

Below: Mathew Brady "Portrait of a man", full plate ambrotype. See page 247.

Above: Mathew Brady, "Portrait of a middle aged woman". See page 248. Right: Mathew Brady, "Portrait of a young woman". See page 247.

Julia Margaret Cameron, "Portrait of George Frederick Watts". See page 251.

Lewis Carroll "Portrait of Quintin F. Twiss". See page 253.

Clarence Sinclair Bull "Portrait of Greta Garbo. See page 251.

Brady, Mathew, portrait of man and his wife seated, ½ plate ambrotype, tinted, matted, cased...................... **200.00-300.00**

Brady, Mathew, portrait of a man, full plate ambrotype, tinted, matted, cased.. **300.00-400.00**

Brady, Mathew, portrait of a man, three-quarter figure, full plate ambrotype, tinted, cased.................. **250.00-300.00**

Brady, Mathew, portrait of a brother and sister, full plate ambrotype, tinted, cased........................... **250.00-300.00**

Brady, Mathew, portrait of a young woman, full plate ambrotype, cased.... **300.00-500.00**

Brady, Mathew, portrait of a child identified as F. G. King, ½ plate ambrotype, matted, uncased.................. **50.00-75.00**

Brady, Mathew, portrait of a middle-aged woman, ½ plate ambrotype, tinted, cased...................... 125.00-200.00

Brady, Mathew, portrait of two gentlemen seated, ¼ plate ambrotype, in leather case....................... 75.00-125.00

Brady, Mathew, portrait of Gen. Sheridan and his staff, albumen print, matted, c. 1863..................... 20.00-30.00

Brady, Mathew, portrait of Abraham Lincoln, CDV, published by E. and H. T. Anthony, 1865................... 200.00-300.00

Brady, Mathew, view of Navy Ordinance Yard, albumen print, mounted on cardboard with photographer's credit and June 1866 date printed on mount... 300.00-400.00

Brady, Mathew, portrait of Abraham Lincoln, 8x10 mounted on cardboard, dated Feb. 1861..................... 350.00-450.00

Brady, Mathew, portrait of a standing gentleman, full-plate ambrotype, cased, 1854.............................. 250.00-400.00

Brady, Mathew, group of 14 Civil War views mounted on black cardboard..... 100.00-175.00

Brady, Mathew, portrait of a middle aged man, ¼ plate daguerreotype, tinted, cased .......................... 150.00-250.00

Brady, Mathew, portrait of Chester Arthur on a fishing trip, albumen print.... 60.00-70.00

Brady, Mathew, portrait, of Kate Chase Sprague, albumen print, matted, c. 1864 150.00-250.00

Brady, Mathew, portrait of two young girls, full-length figures, full-plate ambrotype, tinted, cased............. 175.00-275.00

Brady, Mathew, portrait of a little girl, ¼ plate ambrotype, in leather case, hinge damaged..................... 20.00-35.00

Brady, Mathew, portrait of an elderly man, full-plate, ambrotype, cased...... 200.00-250.00

Brady, Mathew, portrait of a man, head and shoulders, 1/6 plate ambrotype, cased ............................. 25.00-35.00

Brady, Mathew, portrait of German Division officers including Gen. Blenker, albumen print, matted, c. 1861     **35.00-45.00**

Brady, Mathew, outdoor scene showing photograher's van in front of a posted bridge, albumen print, matted, 1863...:     **30.00-45.00**

Brady, Mathew, outdoor scene showing the locomotive "General", albumen print, matted, c. 1865..............     **40.00-75.00**

Brady, Mathew, group of three photographs of Union troops, albumen prints, mounted, matted, 1861-62...........     **150.00-200.00**

Brady, Mathew, group for four photographs of Civil War subjects including Headquarters of Gen. Banks and the portrait of Gen. Burnside and Anderson by J. C. Browne, albumen prints, matted, 1865................     **150.00-175.00**

Brady, Mathew, outdoor scene showing camp headquarters of Graham's Brigade, albumen print, mounted, matted, 1860s........................     **150.00-175.00**

Brady, Mathew, outdoor scene showing First Maine Infantry, albumen print, matted, 1861.....................     **150.00-200.00**

Brady, Mathew, outdoor scene showing Camp Griffin, Va., albumen print, mounted, matted, 1862..............     **100.00-150.00**

Brady, Mathew, unidentified Civil War officer seated with sword, CDV, 1860s..     **15.00-20.00**

Brandt, Bill, portrait of Pablo Picasso at Cannes, silver print, 13x11, signed, 1956     **300.00-400.00**

Brassai, "Maxim's, Paris," silver print, 12x8, 1949.......................     **300.00-500.00**

Brassai, "Le Chat de Grasse," silver print, 12x9, 1938..................     **200.00-400.00**

Brassai, "Fernand Leger dans Son Atelier," silver print, 12x9, signed, 1953, printed later......................     **300.00-400.00**

Brassai, "Braque dans son Ateleier a Paris," silver print, 12x9, signed, 11953, printed later......................     **200.00-300.00**

Brassai, "Portrait of George Rouault," silver print, 12x9, c. 1955 . . . . . . . . . . . .    **250.00-300.00**

Brassai, "Ecce Homo," silver print, 12x9, signed, 1946, printed in 1960s . . . .    **200.00-250.00**

Breitenbach, Josef, portrait of Bertolt Brecht, silver print, 14x11, signed, 1939.    **200.00-300.00**

Wynn Bullock "Kay, 1958". See page 251.

Right: Bill Brandt "Pablo Picasso at Cannes". See page 249.

Bruehl, Anton, portrait of Marlene Dietrich, silver print, 14x11, 1930s..... **100.00-150.00**

Bruguiere, Francis, portrait of Ruth St. Denis as Radha, silver print, 13x10, c. 1911.............................. **250.00-350.00**

Bruguiere, Francis, portrait of a nun, silver print, 10x9, 1922.............. **100.00-150.00**

Bruguiere, Francis, "Cathedrals," intended double exposure of cathedrals, silver print, 13x9, 1931, printed later.... **200.00-300.00**

Bruguiere, Francis, still life, silver print, 9x8, signed, 1930s, printed later........ **150.00-200.00**

Bull, Clarence Sinclair, portrait of Greta Garbo, silver print, 12x9, 1939......... **100.00-150.00**

Bullock, Wynn, "Broken Tree," silver print, 8x7, signed and dated, 1972...... **300.00-400.00**

Bullock, Wynn, "Half an Apple," silver print, 7x9, signed and dated, 1953...... **800.00-1,000.00**

Bullock, Wynn, "Kay, 1958," silver print, 7x9, signed, 1958.............. **600.00-700.00**

Cameron, Julian Margaret, portrait of two children kissing, albumen print, 10x8, 1860s....................... **500.00-600.00**

Cameron, Julia Margaret, portrait of George Frederick Watts, albumen print, 5x4, 1864.......................... **400.00-500.00**

Cameron, Julia Margaret, portrait of Virginia Woolf's mother, silver print, 1867............................1,500.00-3,000.00

Cameron, Julia Margaret, portrait of a young woman, albumen print, 11x8, late 1860s.............................. **400.00-700.00**

Cameron, Julia Margaret, portrait of Mrs. Herbert Fisher, albumen print, 13x10, signed and dated, 1867......... **500.00-600.00**

Cameron, Julia Margaret, portrait of unknown sitter, albumen print, 14x11, c. 1870.............................. **300.00-400.00**

Cameron, Julia Margaret, portrait of Rachel Gurney, albumen print, 15x12, early 1870s....................... **500.00-600.00**

Above: Imogen Cunningham, "Alfred Steiglitz". See page 254.

Right: Henri Cartier Bresson, "Outdoor Scene-Fireworks in China". See page 253.

Below: Imogen Cunningham, "Portrait of Martha Graham". See page 254.

Cameron, Julia Margaret, portrait of a Neopolitian, albumen print, 11x8, matted, c. 1860...................... 200.00-300.00

Callahan, Harry, "Providence," silver print, 5x7, signed, c. 1976............ 500.00-600.00

Caponigro, Paul, "Tree Stump and Pale Mist, Redding Woods, Conn.," silver print, 8x13, signed and dated, 1968..... 300.00-400.00

Caponigro, Paul, portfolio of eight silver prints (ranging from 7x9 to 10x13), mounted and signed, 1957-70......... 1,000.00-1,250.00

Caponigro, Paul, "Window," silver print, 7x9, mounted, signed.......... 300.00-400.00

Carjat, Etienne, portrait of Emile Zola, woodburytype, mounted, matted...... 75.00-125.00

Carjat, Etienne, portrait of Charles Baudelaire, woodburytype, 9x7........ 150.00-200.00

Carjat, Etienne, portrait of Alexander Dumas pere, woodburytype, 9x7....... 200.00-250.00

Carjat, Etienne, portrait of Victor Hugo, woodburytype, 3x4, 1870s...... 50.00-75.00

Carroll, Lewis, portrait of Quintin F. Twiss, albumen print, 6x5, 1858....... 600.00-700.00

Cartier-Bresson, Henri, "Under Water Swimmer," silver print, 14x10, signed.. 250.00-350.00

Cartier-Bresson, Henri, "Bali," silver print, 9x14, signed, 1950............. 250.00-350.00

Cartier-Bresson, Henri, "Mt. Aso, Japan," silver print, 9x14, signed, 1965. 300.00-350.00

Cartier-Bresson, Henri, "Children Playing in Ruins, Spain," silver print, 7x12, 1933, printed later................. 400.00-500.00

Cartier-Bresson, Henri, outdoor scene showing fireworks in China, silver print, 12x8, 1948....................... 500.00-600.00

Coburn, Alvin Langdon, "The Rudder," halftone gravure from Camera Work 21, matted, 1908........ 75.00-100.00

Coburn, Alvin Langdon, outdoor scene showing the Park Row Building, photogravure, 8x6, 1910................. 100.00-200.00

Coburn, Alvin Langdon, outdoor scene showing El Capitan and Yosemite Valley, gum and platinum print, 13x15, 1911 . . . . . . . . . . . . . . . . . . . . . . . . . . . . . **1,000.00-1,300.00**

Coburn, Alvin Langdon, group of five portraits including Augustus John, Anatole France and Jacob Epstein, collotypes, 1922 . . . . . . . . . . . . . . . . . . . . . **175.00-250.00**

Crawford, Henry E., "The Cajon Pass," pigment print, 14x11, 1935 . . . . . **100.00-200.00**

Cunningham, Imogen, "Two Callas lilies," silver prints, 14x11, 1929 . . . . . . . **500.00-800.00**

Cunningham, Imogen, "Magnolia Blossom, 1925," silver print, 11x8, 1925 **400.00-600.00**

Cunningham, Imogen, portrait of Alfred Steiglitz, silver print, 9x7, 1934 . . **800.00-900.00**

Cunningham, Imogen, portrait of a young boy, silver print, 7x6, 1952 . . . . . . **200.00-300.00**

Cunningham, Imogen, "Unmade Bed," silver print, 9x12, 1957 . . . . . . . . . . . . . . **650.00-750.00**

Cunningham, Imogen, "Imogen! Imogen Cunningham Photographs, 1910-1973" (University of Washington Press, 1974), exhibition catalog including an original photography by Cunningham, silver print, 6x6 . . . . . . . . . . . . **500.00-600.00**

Cunningham, Imogen, "The Supplicant", silver print, 13x10, signed and dated, 1910, printed later . . . . . . . . . **500.00-600.00**

Cunningham, Imogen, "Agave Design 2," silver print, 9x7, signed and dated, 1920, printed later . . . . . . . . . . . . . . . . . **500.00-600.00**

Cunningham, Imogen, portrait of Martha Graham, silver print, 7x9, signed and dated, 1931, printed later . . . . . . . . . . . . **500.00-600.00**

Curtis, Edward S., "The North American Indian," (Cambridge 1907-30), complete set of 20 elephant folios each with about 36 photogravures (total of 722) measuring 12x16 (This book holds Curtis auction record; it was auctioned at

Left: Edward S. Curtis. "Portrait of Alden Sampson"

Below: Edward S. Curtis, "Outdoor scene—mounted Apache scout". See page 255.

Sotheby Parke Bernet, New York, in May 1976 for ($60,000)
**35,000.-55,000.**

Curtis, Edward S., outdoor scene showing three Pigean Indian chiefs, silver print, 16x20......................**1,100.00-1,300.00**

Curtis, Edward S., outdoor scene showing mounted Apache scout, orotone, 10x13, signed and framed.............**1,700.00-1,800.00**

Curtis, Edward S., outdoor scene titled "The Vanishing Race" showing mounted Indians riding down path, orotone, 10x13, signed and framed . . . . . **1,100.00-1,300.00**

Curtis, Edward S., portrait of Alden Sampson, platinum plate, 8x5, mounted, c. 1910 . . . . . . . . . . . . . . . . . . . . . . . . . . . . . **300.00-400.00**

Curtis, Edward S., six photogravures from "The North American Indian," tissue . . . . . . . . . . . . . . . . . . . . . . . . . . . . . **200.00-300.00**

Curtis, Edward S., "The North American Indian, Folio I: Navaho, Apache, Jicarilla," 39 photogravure plates . . . . . . . . . . . . . . . . . . . . . . . . . . . . **1,000.00-2,000.00**

Curtis, Edward S., "The North American Indian, Folio 5: Mandan, Arikana, Atsina," 36 photogravure plates . . . . . . . . . . . . . . . . . . . . . . . . . . . . **2,000.00-2,500.00**

Curtis, Edward S., "The North American Indian, Folio 13: Klamath, Yurok, Karok, Hupa, Tolowa," 36 plates on vellum . . . . . . . . . . . . . . . . . . . . **500.00-800.00**

Doisneau, Robert, outdoor Parisian scene, silver print, 9x12, c. 1945 . . . . . . . **150.00-200.00**

Druet, E. portrait of Rodin in the pose of Balzac, platinum print, 11x6, 1914 . . . **600.00-700.00**

Dupont, Aime, portrait of a society matron, silver print, early 1900s . . . . . . **150.00-200.00**

Eakins, Thomas, portrait of three male models dressed in Greek costume, albumen print, 4x5, mounted, 1883 . . . . **900.00-1,250.00**

Eakins, Thomas, portrait of two male models in classical Greek costume posed in front of "The Three Fates" statue, albumen print, 4x4, c. 1883 . . . . . . . . . . **4,000.00-5,000.00**

Eakins, Thomas, portrait of three nude males in an art studio, albumen print, 4x5, c. 1883 . . . . . . . . . . . . . . . . . . . . . . **3,000.00-4,000.00**

Eakins, Thomas, portrait of three male nudes, two of them seated, albumen print, 4x5, c. 1883 . . . . . . . . . . . . . . . . . . **2,000.00-3,000.00**

Eakins, Thomas, two female nudes wearing blindfolds, one standing, the other reclining, albumen print, 4x5, c.

Thomas Eakins, "Two Models in Greek Costume" Note plaster casts in backgroung. See below.

1883 . . . . . . . . . . . . . . . . . . . . . . . . . . . . .**4,000.00-5,000.00**
Eakins, Thomas, outdoor scene showing
male nudes, two of them boxing,
albumen print, 4x5, c. 1883 . . . . . . . . . .**3,000.00-4,000.00**
Eakins, Thomas, portrait of two male
models in classical Greek costume with
cast of Aphrodite statue, albumen print,
4x5, c. 1883 . . . . . . . . . . . . . . . . . . . . . . . .**3,000.00-3,500.00**
Eakins, Thomas, portrait of two male
models in classical Greek costume posed
against a wall with plaster casts, albumen
print, 4x5, c. 1883 . . . . . . . . . . . . . . . . . .**1,000.00-2,000.00**
Eakins, Thomas, outdoor scene showing
two male nudes, one holding a stick,
albumen print, 4x5, c. 1883 . . . . . . . . . .**2,000.00-3,000.00**
Eakins, Thomas, indoor scene showing a
dismembered horse's leg, albumen print,
4x5, c. 1883 . . . . . . . . . . . . . . . . . . . . . . . .**3,000.00-4,000.00**

Eakins, Thomas, outdoor scene showing male nudes in standing tug of war, albumen print, 4x5, c. 1883..........**4,000.00-5,000.00**

Eakins, Thomas, portrait of three female nudes, one shielding her eyes, albumen print, 4x5, c. 1883...........**3,000.00-5,000.00**

Eakins, Thomas, portrait of three female nudes, albumen print, 4x5, c. 1883.............................**6,000.00-8,000.00**

Eakins, Thomas, portrait of male nudes at a swimming hole, albumen print, 4x5, c. 1883...........................    **8,000.-10,000.**

Peter Henry Emerson "On the River Bure". See below.

Eakins, Thomas, portrait of two male models in classical Greek costume in low light, albumen print, 4x5, c. 1883......**3,000.00-5,000.00**

Eakins, Thomas, outdoor scene showing male nudes wrestling, albumen print, 4x5, c. 1883.......................**4,000.00-6,000.00**

Emerson, Peter Henry, outdoor scene "On the River Bure," platinum print, 5x9, 1886.........................    **300.00-450.00**

Emerson, Peter Henry, "Towing the Reed," platinum print, 9x11, 1866.....    **600.00-800.00**

Emerson, Peter Henry, "Cattle on the Marshes," platinum print, 7x12, 1886..    **350.00-550.00**

Emmons, Chansonetta S., outdoor scene showing strawberry plantation, silver print, 6x4, 1926...................    **50.00-100.00**

Emmons, Chansonetta S., portrait of two women with calf, silver print, 5x7, c.

Walker Evans "Wellfleet, Mass.,"
silver print. See page 260.

Walker Evans "Belle Grove Plantation,
White Chapel, Louisiana", see page
260.

| | |
|---|---|
| 1905 . . . . . . . . . . . . . . . . . . . . . . . . . . . . . | **75.00-100.00** |
| Emmons, Chansonetta S., portrait of a young woman, silver print, 6x3, 1915... | **40.00-80.00** |
| Ernst, Max, animal design, photogram from surrealist book by Rene Crevel, "Mr. Knife, Miss Fork," 7x5, 1931.... | **300.00-500.00** |
| Ernst, Max, "What is Death?" photogram, 7x5, from surrealist book by Rene Crevel, "Mr. Knife, Miss Fork," 1931.. | **400.00-500.00** |

Evans, Frederick, outdoor scene titled "Sark," platinum print, 3x4, 1902 . . . . . **250.00-350.00**

Evans, Frederic, outdoor scene showing old Parliament House, platinum print, 4x6, c. 1900 . . . . . . . . . . . . . . . . . . . . . . **375.00-400.00**

Evans, Walker, "Woman and Children, Havana," silver print, 5x10, signed, 1932 . . . . . . . . . . . . . . . . . . . . . . . . . . . **450.00-600.00**

Evans, Walker, "Portuguese Workman's Bedroom," silver print, 8x6, signed and dated, 1931 . . . . . . . . . . . **500.00-600.00**

Evans, Walker, "Belle Grove Plantation, White Chapel, Louisiana," silver print, 8x10, signed and dated, 1935 . . . . . **400.00-500.00**

Evans, Walker, "Goodwill Industries Billboard," FX70 print, 8x7, signed and dated . . . . . . . . . . . . . . . . . . . . . . . . . . **400.00-600.00**

Evans, Walker, "Auto Graveyard," silver print, 7x9, signed, 1930s . . . . . . . . **500.00-600.00**

Evans, Walker, "Wellfleet, Mass.," silver print, 6x5, signed, 1931 . . . . . . . . . . **300.00-400.00**

Evans, Walker, portrait of a man, silver print, 5x4, signed, 1930s . . . . . . . . . . . . . **400.00-600.00**

Evans, Walker, woman and child in subway, silver print, 5x7, 1938 . . . . . . . . . . . **400.00-500.00**

Evans, Walker, "Faces, Pennsylvania Town," silver print . . . . . . . . . . . . . . . . . **900.00-1,100.00**

Feininger, Andreas, "New York, 1940," silver print, 14x10, 1940 . . . . . . . . . . . . . **200.00-300.00**

Fenton, Roger, outdoor scene showing Tartar laborers, salt print, mounted, 1855 . . . . . . . . . . . . . . . . . . . . . . . . . . . **100.00-125.00**

Fenton, Roger, portrait of officers of the 4th light dragoons, salt print, 7x7, 1855 . **125.00-175.00**

Fenton, Roger, portrait of Brigadier Garrett and officers, salt print, 8x7, 1855-56 . . . . . . . . . . . . . . . . . . . . . . . . . **90.00-125.00**

Fenton, Roger, portrait of Nubian model reclining, salt print, 1858 . . . . . . . . **4,000.00-5,500.00**

Above Frances Flaherty. "Portrait of an old man", see below. Left: Frances Flaherty, "Portrait of a man", see below.

Flaherty, Frances, portrait of mother and child, silver print, 19x15, 1936..... 100.00-200.00

Flaherty, Frances, portrait of a man, silver print, 19x15, 1936.............. 150.00-200.00

Flaherty, Frances, portrait of an old woman, silver print, 19x15, 1936....... 150.00-200.00

Flaherty, Frances, portrait of an old man, silver print, 19x15, 1936........ 150.00-200.00

Flaherty, Robert J., portrait of Tooktoo, an Eskimo chief, photogravure, 7x7, c. 1921.................... 100.00-150.00

Frith, Francis, outdoor scene showing Monaco, albumen print, 6x8, 1870s.... 15.00-25.00

Frith, Francis, "Egypt, Sinai and Jerusalem: A Series of Twenty Photographic Views," (James S. Virtue, London, c. 1860), illustrated with 20 large albumen prints (about 15x20), 1858.... 18,000.-20,000.

Frith, Francis, outdoor scene showing the statues of Memnon, Egypt, albumen print, 6x9, 1857..................... 50.00-60.00

Frith, Francis, outdoor scene showing
the Valley of the Tombs of the Kings,
Egypt, albumen print, 6x9, 1857....... 50.00-60.00

Frith, Francis, portrait of a group of Indians, albumen print, 9x7, 1860s....... 30.00-40.00

Frith, Francis, portrait of a group of
Afghanis, albumen print, 9x7,
1860s-1870s....................... 20.00-25.00

Frith, Francis, outdoor scene, Japan,
albumen print, 1870s............... 15.00-20.00

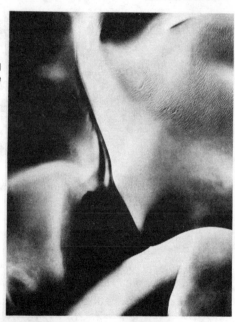

William A. Garnett, "Sand
Dune, Death Valley, Calif." see
page 263.

Arnold Genthe, "1906 Fire,
Chinatown, San Francisco".
See page 263.

Allan Grant, "Portrait of Marcel Duchanm". See page 264.

Frith, Francis, "Gems of Photographic Art, Selected by Francis Frith," a portfolio of 36 albumen prints of Switzerland, each 6x8, 1860s ................ **600.00-700.00**

Frith, Francis, outdoor scene showing Alps, albumen print, 6x10, 1870s ...... **20.00-40.00**

Garnett, William A., "Sand Dune, Death Valley, Calif.," silver print, 13x10, signed, 1954 ................ **300.00-500.00**

Genthe, Arnold, portrait of Mary Pickford, silver print, 14x11, 1920s ..... **200.00-300.00**

Genthe, Arnold, outdoor view of 1906 fire, Chinatown, San Francisco, silver print, 5x9, matted, 1906 ............. **250.00-300.00**

Genthe, Arnold, woman and child, Chinatown, San Francisco, silver plate, 7x3, 1905 ......................... **100.00-150.00**

Genthe, Arnold, portrait of two men,

Chinatown, San Francisco, silver print, 7x3, 1905 . . . . . . . . . . . . . . . . . . . . . . . . .  **100.00-150.00**

Genthe, Arnold, outdoor scene showing San Antonio Mission, Texas., silver print, 8x6 . . . . . . . . . . . . . . . . . . . . . . . .  **75.00-125.00**

Genthe, Arnold, outdoor scene showing Japanese countryside, silver print, 9x7, 1908 . . . . . . . . . . . . . . . . . . . . . . . . . . .  **125.00-150.00**

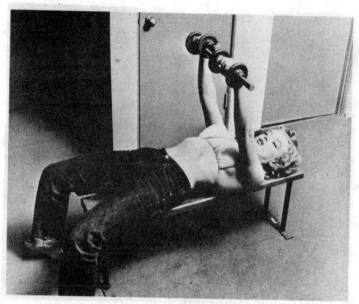

Philippe Halsman, "Portrait of Marilyn Monroe, lifting barbells." See page 265.

Genthe, Arnold, outdoor scene showing Japanese street, silver print, 7x9, 1908 . .  **75.00-100.00**

Gibson, Ralph, "Still Life," silver print, 12x8, signed and dated, 1974 . . . . . . . . .  **100.00-200.00**

Grant, Allan, portrait of Marilyn Monroe, silver print, 9x8, 1962 . . . . . . . .  **100.00-200.00**

Grant, Allan, portrait of Marcel Duchamp, silver print, 13x10, 1953 . . . . .  **200.00-400.00**

Greene, Milton, portrait of Marilyn Monroe, silver print, 20x16, signed, 1952  **300.00-400.00**

Halsman, Philippe, "Salvador Dali and Three Cats, Jumping," silver print, 11x13, 1940s . . . . . . . . . . . . . . . . . . . . . .  **400.00-500.00**

Right: Laton Huffman "Portrait of Young Crow Groom", see page 267.
Below: Lanton Huffman "Outdoor scene-Cowboys roping cattle." See page 267.

Halsman, Philippe, portrait of Marilyn Monroe lifting barbells, silver print, 11x14, 1952 . . . . . . . . . . . . . . . . . . . . . . .      **400.00-500.00**

Halsman, Philippe, portrait of Ansel Adams, silver print, 14x11, 1958 . . . . . .      **300.00-400.00**

Halsman, Philippe, portrait of Bob Hope jumping, silver print, 14x11, 1950s      **250.00-350.00**

Halsman, Philippe, portrait of Richard Nixon jumping, silver print, 14x11, 1969      **500.00-600.00**

Hausmann, Raoul, "Melanographie," silver print, 7x10, 1931 . . . . . . . . . . . . . .      **200.00-300.00**

Haynes, F. J. outdoor scene showing the Grand Canyon, albumen print, framed, 23x35 . . . . . . . . . . . . . . . . . . . . . . . . . .      **300.00-400.00**

Hesse, Edwin Bower, portrait of a seated nude, silver print, 1920s . . . . . . . . . . . . .      **100.00-200.00**

Hesse, Edwin Bower, portrait of a model, silver print, 16x13, 1920s . . . . . . .      **100.00-200.00**

Hessler, Alexander, portrait of Abraham Lincoln, albumen print, framed, printed in 1870s.................... 300.00-400.00

Hill, David, portrait of Kenneth Macleay, calotype, 6x4, matted, 1840s.. 800.00-1,200.00

Hillers, John, outdoor scene showing waterfall near Red Gate Utah, albumen print, 9x7, matted, 1880s............ 200.00-250.00

Hillers, John, outdoor scene showing Zuni transportation, albumen print, 7x9, matted, 1880s..................... 150.00-250.00

Hillers, John, outdoor scene showing

Yousuf Karsh ''Portrait of Albert Schweitzer'' see page 271.

John Hillers, ''Outdoor scene-Waterfall near Red Gate, Utah.'' See 267.

Moraine Lake, Utah, albumen print matted, 7x9, 1880s .................. **100.00-150.00**

Hillers, John, outdoor scene showing Winslow's Cascade, Utah, albumen print, 9x7, matted, 1880s ............ **100.00-150.00**

Hine, Lewis, group of 20 photographs of Ellis Island and child labor, each 5x7, 1910-11 .......................... **300.00-400.00**

Hine, Lewis, "The Empire State Building with Steel Workers," silver print, 7x9, 1931 ................... **125.00-200.00**

Hixon, Orval, portrait of Ruth St. Denis, silver print, 12x8, signed, 1918, printed in 1975 ..................... **100.00-150.00**

Hixon, Orval, portrait of woman with portrait bust, silver print, 14x11, signed, 1920, printed in 1970s .............. **100.00-150.00**

Hixon, Orval, portrait of Theda Bara, silver print, 14x11, signed, 1918, printed in 1975 ........................... **100.00-150.00**

Hope, E. O. portrait of Laurent Novikoff, silver print, 7x5, c. 1920 ..... **100.00-125.00**

Huffman, Laton, outdoor scene showing sheep flock next to Powder River, Montana, silver print, 19x27, 1890s .... **100.00-150.00**

Huffman, Laton, outdoor scene titled "Going to the Roundup," silver print, 11x20, 1898 ....................... **200.00-300.00**

Huffman, Laton, outdoor scene showing cowboys roping cattle, albumen print, 3x4, 1870s .................... **50.00-75.00**

Huffman, Laton, outdoor scene showing hunters skinning a bear, albumen print, 4x3, 1880s ................... **75.00-100.00**

Huffman, Laton, "Evening at the Roundup: Big Pumpkin Creek," collotype, 8x14, 1907 ......................... **40.00-60.00**

Huffman, Laton, portrait of Young Crow Groom, Fort Keough, collotype, 8x10, early 1900s ................... **40.00-60.00**

Izis, "Le roi de clowns," silver print, 12x9, signed, 1954 ................. **150.00-200.00**

Above: Yousuf Karsh, "Portrait of Winston Churchill." See page 271.

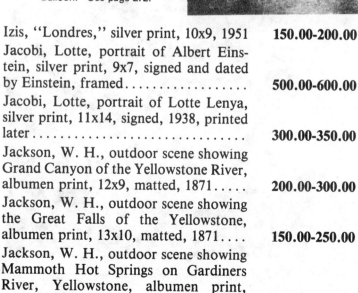

Right: Jacques Henri Lartique "Outdoor Scene-Large Balloon." See page 272.

| | |
|---|---|
| Izis, "Londres," silver print, 10x9, 1951 | **150.00-200.00** |
| Jacobi, Lotte, portrait of Albert Einstein, silver print, 9x7, signed and dated by Einstein, framed . . . . . . . . . . . . . . . . . | **500.00-600.00** |
| Jacobi, Lotte, portrait of Lotte Lenya, silver print, 11x14, signed, 1938, printed later . . . . . . . . . . . . . . . . . . . . . . . . . . | **300.00-350.00** |
| Jackson, W. H., outdoor scene showing Grand Canyon of the Yellowstone River, albumen print, 12x9, matted, 1871 . . . . . | **200.00-300.00** |
| Jackson, W. H., outdoor scene showing the Great Falls of the Yellowstone, albumen print, 13x10, matted, 1871 . . . . | **150.00-250.00** |
| Jackson, W. H., outdoor scene showing Mammoth Hot Springs on Gardiners River, Yellowstone, albumen print, 8x12, matted, 1871 . . . . . . . . . . . . . . . . . | **150.00-200.00** |

Jackson, W. H., view of **Palace Butte**, Yellowstone, albumen print, matted, 1871 . . . . . . . . . . . . . . . . . . . . . . . . . . . . .  **125.00-225.00**

Jackson, W. H., outdoor scene showing Mt. Harvard and the Valley of the Arkansas, Yellowstone region, albumen print, 17x22, matted, 1871 . . . . . . . . . . .  **300.00-350.00**

Jackson, W. H., outdoor scene showing Lake San Miguel, Colorado, albumen print, 17x22, matted, 1871 . . . . . . . . . . .  **300.00-400.00**

Jackson, W. H., outdoor scene showing Gray's Peak, Yellowstone region, albumen print, 17x22, matted, 1871 . . . .  **200.00-300.00**

Jackson, W. H., outdoor scene showing Ute Pass, Yellowstone region, albumen print matted, 21x16, 1880s . . . . . . . . . . .  **350.00-450.00**

Jackson, William Henry, "Grand Canyon of the Yellowstone," albumen print, 13x9, 1871 . . . . . . . . . . . . . . . . . . . . . . . .  **200.00-300.00**

Jackson, W. H., "Colorado Midland Railroad, Pike's Peak Route," albumen print from mammoth plate, 1870s . . . . . .  **200.00-250.00**

Lotte Jacobi, "Portrait of Lotte Lenya" see page 268.

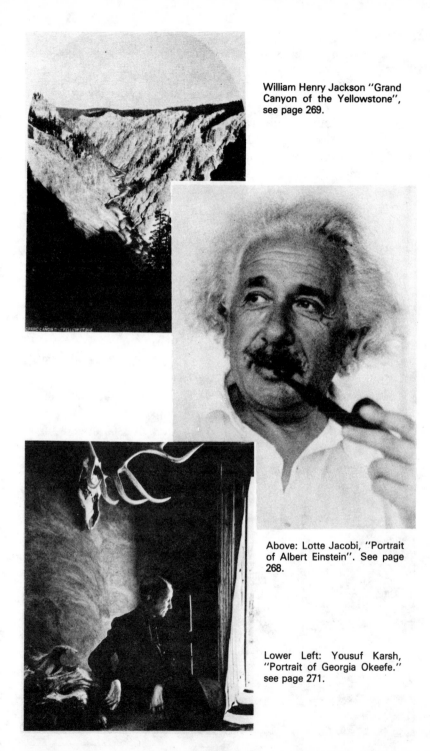

William Henry Jackson "Grand Canyon of the Yellowstone", see page 269.

Above: Lotte Jacobi, "Portrait of Albert Einstein". See page 268.

Lower Left: Yousuf Karsh, "Portrait of Georgia Okeefe." see page 271.

Karsh, Yousuf, portrait of Albert Schweitzer, silver print, 9x7, signed.... **500.00-600.00**

Karsh, Yousuf, portrait of Winston Churchill, silver print, 20x16, signed, 1941............................... **700.00-800.00**

Karsh, Yousuf, portrait of Georgia O'Keefe, silver print, 20x16, 1956...... **800.00-900.00**

Kasebier, Gertrude, portrait of woman and child, platinum print, 8x4, c. 1900.. **1,000.00-1,150.00**

Kertesz, Andre, "Reading, Esztergom (Hungary)," silver print, 8x10, 1915.... **130.00-150.00**

Kertesz, Andre, "Chez Mondrian," silver print, signed and dated, 1926, printed later....................... **900.00-1,200.00**

Kertesz, Andre, portrait of a dancer, silver print, 10x8, signed and dated, 1926, printed later.................. **400.00-500.00**

Kertesz, Andre, "Melancholy Tulip," silver print, 9x7, signed and dated, 1939, printed later....................... **300.00-400.00**

Kuehn, Heinrich, outdoor scene in Holland, gum print, 11x14, c. 1897..... **300.00-400.00**

Kuehn, Heinrich, outdoor scene, pigment print, 6x15, 1907.............. **300.00-450.00**

Andre Kertesz, "Chez Mondrian". See listing above.

Kuehn, Heinrich, portrait of a young girl, pigment print, 11x9, 1911........ 300.00-450.00

Lange, Dorothea, California FSA photo showing group of children at water pump, 8x10, 1930s................ 150.00-225.00

Lartigue, Jacques Henri, portrait of Women at Longchamps, silver print, 11x13........................... 300.00-400.00

Lartigue, Jacques Henri, portrait of man on a motorcycle, silver print, 11x13..... 250.00-300.00

Lartigue, Jacques Henri, portrait of cousin Andrea Haguet diving, silver print, 10x14, signed, early 1900s....... 300.00-500.00

Lartigue, Jacques Henri, outdoor scene showing early racing vehicle, silver print, 10x14, signed, early 1900s............ 300.00-400.00

Lartigue, Jacques Henri, outdoor scene showing large balloon, silver print, 14x10, signed, c. 1910............... 300.00-500.00

Lartigue, Jacques Henri, "Cousin Bichonade in Flight," silver print, 7x9, 1905, printed in 1970s............... 200.00-250.00

Lartigue, Jacques Henri, "The Famous Rowe Twins of the Casino," silver print, 7x9, 1929, printed in 1970s............ 400.00-500.00

Laughlin, Clarence John, "The Appearance of an Anonymous Man," silver print, 13x10, signed, 1949............ 200.00-300.00

Luckie, Dorothy, outdoor scene showing Los Angeles City Hall, silver print, 14x11, 1938....................... 50.00-75.00

Luckie, Dorothy, still life titled "Whole Wheat," silver print, 10x13, 1930s..... 100.00-150.00

Luckie, Dorothy, "Gothic Lines," silver print, 13x10, 1938................... 75.00-100.00

Lynes, George Platt, portrait of Maria Tallchief, silver print, 9x7, 1948....... 100.00-150.00

Macpherson, Robert, "The Capitol from the Piazza of the Ara-Coeli," albumen print, 10x16, late 1860s....... 75.00-125.00

Marcus, Eli, portrait of actress Lilli Darvas, silver print, 6x8, 1930s............ 100.00-150.00

Margrethe Mather "Open Door", see below.

| | |
|---|---|
| Marcus, Eli, portrait of Alfred Stieglitz, silver print, 10x8, 1944.............. | **200.00-300.00** |
| Mather, Margrethe, "Open Door," silver print, 9x7, 1928............... | **200.00-250.00** |
| Mather, Margrethe, outdoor scene showing Beverly Hills home, silver print, 8x9, 1927......................... | **150.00-200.00** |
| Meyer, Baron de, portrait of singer Eva Gauthier, silver print, 9x7, 1920s....... | **175.00-200.00** |
| Meyer, Baron de, portrait of a nurse, silver print, 9x7, c. 1925............. | **125.00-150.00** |
| Meyer, Baron de, profile portrait of a nurse, silver print, 9x7, c. 1925........ | **100.00-150.00** |
| Michaels, Duane, portrait of Robert Rauschenberg, silver print, 5x7, signed and dated, 1963..................... | **100.00-150.00** |
| Michaels, Duane, portrait of Henri Clouzot, silver print, 5x7, signed and | |

Baron de Meyer "Portrait of a Nurse." See page 372.

dated, 1968........................ **100.00-200.00**

Michaels, Duane, portrait of artist Claes
Oldenberg, silver print, 5x7, signed and
dated, 1971....................... **100.00-125.00**

Mock, J.E., portrait of Sadakichi Hart-
mann, silver print, 13x9, c. 1930....... **75.00-125.00**

Model, Lisette, portrait of woman with
veil, San Francisco, silver print, 15x19,
signed, 1950s..................... **150.00-250.00**

Moholy-Nagy, Lazslo, outdoor scene
showing marketplace in Finland, silver
print, 9x7, 1930s.................... **600.00-700.00**

Karl Moon, ''Portrait of The War Lord''. See page 277.

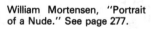

William Mortensen, ''Portrait of a Nude.'' See page 277.

Top: Eadweard Muybridge "Tutokanula, Valley of the Yosemite." See page 278.

Left: Herbert Ponting, "Portrait of Japanese Girl" see page 279.

Bottom: Timothy O'Sullivan "Canyon of the Colorado River". See page 279.

Moon, Karl, portrait of "The War Lord," Indian chief, silver print, 17x13, framed.......................... 400.00-600.00

Moon, Karl, portrait titled "Comasita," silver print, 16,10, early 1900s (slight stain)............................ 200.00-300.00

Moon, Karl, portrait of "The Scout," silver print, 13x17, framed, early 1900s. 300.00-500.00

Moon, Karl, outdoor scene showing Navajo silversmith at work outside his hogan, silver print, 16x12, framed, early 1900s............................ 600.00-700.00

Morath, Inge, portrait of Adlai Stevenson and Eleanor Roosevelt at the United Nations, silver print, 14x9, signed, 1950s 150.00-250.00

Mortensen, William, "The Crucifixion," from Cecil B. deMilles's "King of Kings," pigment print, 10x13, signed, 1930s...................... 500.00-600.00

Mortensen, William, portrait of "A Romany Maid," silver print, 7x6, 1930s. 60.00-80.00

Mortensen, William, portrait of a nude titled "Myrdith," bromoil transfer print, 13x10, c. 1927................ 500.00-700.00

Mortensen, William, portrait of a nude, silver print, 7x6, 1930s............... 100.00-150.00

Mortensen, Willia, "Obsession," silver print, 7x6, 1930s.................... 40.00-60.00

Mortensen, William, portrait of a nude with a peacock on a stand, titled "Mutual Admiration," silver print, 7x6, 1930s............................. 150.00-250.00

Mucha, Alphonse, study of a nude female model against Art Nouveau background, silver print, c. 1900 (poorly exposed in parts)..................... 600.00-1,000.00

Muray, Nikolas, "A Japanese Dancer," silver print, 10x8, signed and dated, 1924 100.00-200.00

Muray, Nikolas, portrait of Mrs. Wells Fargo Thomas, silver print, signed and dated, 1924........................ 100.00-200.00

Muybridge, Eadweard, "Tutokanula, Valley of the Yosemite," albumen print from mammoth plate, 1870s .......... **1,500.00-2,000.00**

Muybridge, Eadweard, sequential exposure of athlete jumping, (plate 158 from "Animal Locomotion"), collotype, 1887 ........................ **100.00-150.00**

Muybridge, Eadweard, sequential exposure of athlete throwing javelin, (plate 319 from "Animal Locomotion"), collotype, 1887 ..................... **150.00-250.00**

Muybridge, Eadweard, sequential exposure of woman turning (plate 231 from "Animal Locomotion"), collotype, 1887 ........................ **200.00-300.00**

Muybridge, Eadweard, sequential exposure of man riding a horse, (plate 616 from "Animal Locomotion"), collotype, 1887 ........................ **100.00-150.00**

Muybridge, Eadweard, sequential exposure of athlete lifting weights, (plate 321 from "Animal Locomotion"), collotype, 1877 ..................... **100.00-150.00**

Nadar, (Gaspard Felix Tournachon), portrait of Viollet de-Duc, woodbury-type, 9x7 ........................ **150.00-200.00**

Nadar, (Gaspard Felix Tournachon), portrait of Alexander Dumas, Pere, 1857 **15,000.-16,000.\***

Nadar (Gaspard Felix Tournachon), portrait of Sarah Bernhardt, albumen print (cabinet card) on Nadar's Rue d'Anjou studio mount, 1860s ......... **125.00-175.00**

Newman, Arnold, "David Hare," silver print, 9x7, signed and dated, 1952 ...... **100.00-150.00**

Newman, Arnold, "Milton Avery," silver print, 8x10, signed and dated, 1960, printed in 1970s ............... **100.00-150.00**

Newman, Arnold, "Kim Stanley," silver print, 12x10, signed and dated, 1963 .... **100.00-150.00**

\* Record for photographic image, 1979 SPBNY

Newman, Arnold, "I.M. Pei," silver print, 12x10, signed and dated, 1967.... **75.00-100.00**

O'Sullivan, Timothy, "Shoshone Falls, Snake River, Idaho," albumen print, 8x11, 1870s........................ **400.00-600.00**

O'Sullivan, Timothy, "Canyon of the Colorado River," albumen print, 8x11, 1873............................ **500.00-600.00**

O'Sullivan, Timothy, "Cooley's Park, Sierra Blanca Range, Ariz.," albumen print, 8x11, 1870s.................. **400.00-600.00**

O'Sullivan, Timothy, "Entrance to Black Canyon Colorado River," albumen print, 8x11, 1871............ **400.00-600.00**

Outerbridge, Paul Jr., "Chesterfield Pack and Lily," silver print, 7x9, 1934.. **800.00-1,000.00**

Plumbe, John Jr., portrait of young woman with braided hair, 1/6 plate daguerreotype in "Basket of Flowers" case, New York, c. 1845.................. **40.00-60.00**

Plumbe, John Jr., portrait of young man with wavy hair, 1/6 plate daguerreotype in "Plain Octagon" case, c. 1844............................. **25.00-40.00**

Plumbe, John Jr., building facades in New York City, 1/6 plate daguerreotype in "Grecian Urn" case, c. 1841 (image in poor condition with severe fading and slight scratches).................... **40.00-50.00**

Plumbe, John Jr., portrait of middle-aged woman, 1/6 plate daguerreotype in "Grecian Urn" case, c. 1850.......... **25.00-40.00**

Ponting, Herbert, portrait of Japanese girl writing a letter, silver print, 13x18, early 1900s....................... **350.00-450.00**

Ponting, Herbert, "Burmese Girls Leaving the Temple," silver print, 13x18, early 1900s......................... **200.00-300.00**

Ponting, Herbert, "The Tomb of Columbus," silver print, 13x18, early 1900s. **200.00-250.00**

Ray, Man, portrait of Gertrude Stein and Alice B. Toklas, silver print, 3x5,

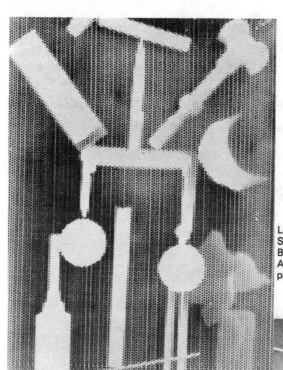

Left: Man Ray, "Rayograph". See page 282.
Below: M. P. Rice, "Portrait of Alexander Stephens". See page 282.

Charles Rosher. "Portrait of Mary Pickford in Tess of the Storm Country". See page 285.

F. A. Rinehart, "Portrait of Wah-be-Git", see page 283.

| | |
|---|---|
| 1923............................ | 2,000.00-3,000.00 |
| Ray, Man, indoor scene showing a gaudy mantlepiece decoration, silver print, 9x7, 1920s.................... | 200.00-300.00 |
| Ray, Man, "Rayograph," silver print, 9x7.............................. | 700.00-1,000.00 |

Ray, Man, "Rayograph of Two Manne-quins," silver print, 10x7, signed, 1971 .. 400.00-700.00

Ray, Man, "The Pony Express Museum," silver print, 8x10, 1940s ..... 400.00-600.00

Ray, Man, portrait of Paulette Goodard and Hurd Hatfield, silver print, 10x8, 1940s ............................ 350.00-450.00

Ray, Man, portrait of dancer Georgia Blaine, solorized silver print, 10x8, 1940s 400.00-600.00

Ray, Man, portrait of Ava Gardner, silver print, 4x3, signed, 1950 ......... 200.00-300.00

Ray, Man, portrait of Ruth Ford, silver print, 10x8, 1940s ................. 150.00-200.00

Rice, M. P., a meeting of Civil War of-ficers including Gen. Custer, platinum print probably from a Brady negative, signed and dated 1892, matted ........ 200.00-300.00

Rice, M. P., portrait of Alexander Stephens, possibly from an Alexander Gardner negative, signed and dated 1901 150.00-250.00

Rinehart, F. A., portrait of a group of Sioux Indians, platinum print, 7x9, mat-ted, 1898 ......................... 150.00-250.00

Rinehart, F. A., portrait of Oglalla Sioux named Broken Arm, platinum print, 9x7, 1899 ................... 60.00-100.00

Rinehart, F. A., portrait of Oglalla Sioux chief Little Wound, platinum print, 9x7, 1899 ................... 60.00-90.00

Rinehart, F. A., portrait of Arapaho, Little Chief, platinum print, 9x7, 1898.. 100.00-150.00

Rinehart, F. A., portrait of Freckled Face, an Arapaho Indian, platinum print, 9x7, 1898 ................... 100.00-150.00

Rinehart, F. A., portrait of Sioux Chief Goes-to-War and Chief Hollow Horn Bear, platinum print, 9x7, 1898 ....... 125.00-175.00

Rinehart, F. A., portrait of Chief American Horse and a Squaw, platinum print, 9x7, 1898 ................... 100.00-150.00

Rinehart, F. A., portrait of Yellow

Magpie, an Arapaho Indian, Platinum
print, 9x7, 1898..................... 100.00-150.00

Rinehart, F. A., portrait of Wah-be-Git,
a Ute Indian, platinum print, 9x7, 1899. 100.00-150.00

Robertson, James and Beato, Felice,
outdoor scene showing fountain in
courtyard of the Sulimanie, Constantin-
ople, albumen print, 11x9, c. 1854...... 200.00-300.00

Sanford H. Roth, "Portrait of
James Dean." See page 285.

Sandford H. Roth, "Portrait of
Pablo Picasso". See page 285.

Authur Rothstein, "Daughter of a participant in New York Land Use Project." See page 285.

August Sander, "Portrait of Chamber Music Quartet." See page 288.

Robertson, James, and Beato, Felice, outdoor scene showing Constantinople street scene, albumen print, 11x10, c. 1854 ............................. 200.00-300.00

Robertson, James, outdoor scene showing Russian General's hut, calotype, 8x11, 1955 ........................ 100.00-200.00

Rosher, Charles, portrait of Mary Pickford, in "Tess of the Storm Country," silver print, 8x9, 1922 ........... 150.00-200.00

Rosher, Charles, portrait of Mary Pickford in "Little Lord Fauntleroy," silver print, 9x6, 1921 ................ 100.00-200.00

Roth, Sanford, H., portrait of Triston Tzara, silver print, signed, 1950s ....... 100.00-150.00

Roth, Sanford H., portrait of Pablo Picasso, silver print, 13x11, signed, 1953 175.00-225.00

Roth, Sanford, H., portrait of Man Ray, silver print, 13x11, signed, 1950s ....... 150.00-250.00

Roth, Sanford H., portrait of Giacometti, silver print, 10x13, 1953 ............ 200.00-300.00

Roth, Sanford H., portrait of Utrillo, silver print, 13x10, signed, 1950s ....... 200.00-300.00

Roth, Sanford H., portrait of James Dean, silver print, 10x13, 1950s ........ 200.00-300.00

Roth, Sanford H., portrait of Marlene Dietrich, silver print, 14x10, signed, 1952 250.00-350.00

Rothstein, Arthur, "Daughter of a participant in New York Land Use Project," silver print, 10x7, FSA stamp, 1930s ............................. 100.00-200.00

Rothstein, Arthur, outdoor scene showing North Dakota farmer searching for rain clouds, silver print, 9x7, FSA stamp, signed, 1930s ................ 100.00-150.00

Rothstein, Arthur, outdoor scene showing North Dakota farm, silver print, 7x10, FSA stamp, signed, 1930s ........ 75.00-100.00

Rothstein, Arthur, portrait of young son of an Arkansas sharecropper, silver print, 8x10, FSA stamp, signed, 1930s .. 100.00-125.00

Upper left: Eugene W. Smith "Walk to Paradise Garden", see page 288. Upper right: Nealson Smith, "Portrait of Rudolph Valentino." See page 288.

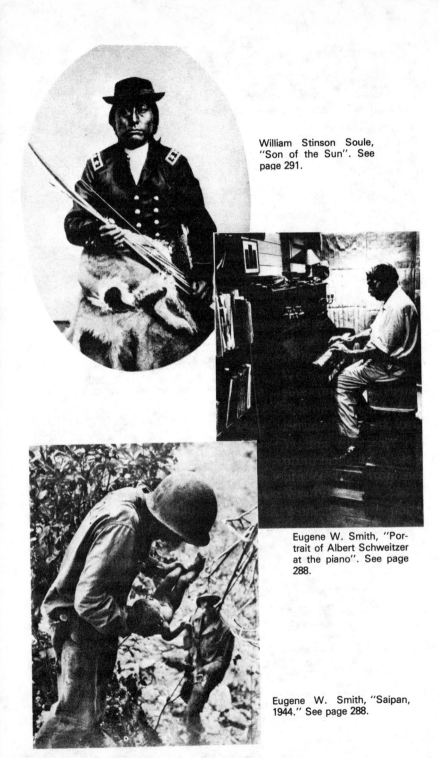

William Stinson Soule, "Son of the Sun". See page 291.

Eugene W. Smith, "Portrait of Albert Schweitzer at the piano". See page 288.

Eugene W. Smith, "Saipan, 1944." See page 288.

287

Sander, August, portrait of Dr. Sulsen, silver print, 11x9, 1931, printed in 1950s. **300.00-450.00**

Sander, August, portrait of chamber music quartet, silver print, 11x8, 1930s, printed later...................... **300.00-400.00**

Sander, August, portrait of actress Cilly Feindt, silver print, 11x9, 1927, printed in 1950s............................. **300.00-350.00**

Sarony, Napoleon, four portraits of Joseph Jefferson as Rip Van Winkle, each a carbon print contained in Washington Irving's "Rip Van Winkle" (G. P. Putnam & Sons)................. **75.00-125.00**

Saudek, Jan, "The Life," silver print, 11x8, signed, 1960s................. **200.00-225.00**

Scavullo, Francis, portrait of Gyneth Jones, silver print, signed............ **100.00-175.00**

Schenk, Charles, portrait of woman in diaphanous drapery, silver print, 4x6, 1902............................. **100.00-200.00**

Shaw, G., "The Pyramid," platinum print, 6x8, signed and dated, 1886...... **100.00-150.00**

Siskind, Aaron, "Mexico," silver print, 17x13, signed, 11955............... **150.00-175.00**

Slavin, Neil, "Entire Staff of the Statue of Liberty, New York," color print, 13x11, signed and dated, 1974........ **100.00-150.00**

Smith, Nealson, portrait of Rudolph Valentino, silver print, 10x13, 1920s.... **150.00-200.00**

Smith, W. Eugene, "Walk to Paradise Garden," silver print, 12,10, signed, 1946, printed later.................. **800.00-900.00**

Smith, W. Eugene, "Saipan, 1944," silver print, 18x15, signed, 1944, printed later.............................**1,200.00-1,500.00**

Smith, W. Eugene, portrait of Albert Schweitzer at the piano, silver print, 13x9, signed, 1950s................. **600.00-700.00**

Smith, W. Eugene, outdoor scene showing Welsh village, silver print, 6x12, signed, 1950........................... **500.00-700.00**

William Stinson Soule, "Paugh, Apache Medicine Man." See page 291.

Rosalind Solomon, "Doll's Face." See page 291.

William Stinson Soule, "Tosh A. Wah, Chief of the Penateka Comanches", see page 291.

William Stinson Soule, "Grey Leggings, Comanche Tribe." See page 292.

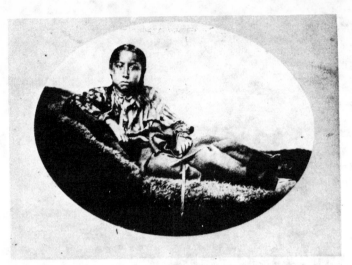

William Stinson Soule "Son of Little Raven, Arapaho Chief". See page 292.

| | |
|---|---|
| Smith, W. Eugene, portrait of black Jews in Harlem, silver print, 7x9, 1950s. | 700.00-900.00 |
| Solomon, Rosalind, "Doll's Face," silver print, 12x8.................. | 100.00-125.00 |
| Soule, William Stinson, "Son of the Sun," albumen print, 8x5, mounted, early 1870s...................... | 200.00-250.00 |
| Soule, William Stinson, "Stumbling Bear, Kiowa Chief," albumen print, 8x5, mounted, 1870s............... | 300.00-400.00 |
| Soule, William Stinson, "Kicking Bird, Kiowa Chief," albumen print, 8x5, mounted.......................... | 200.00-350.00 |
| Soule, William Stinson, "Paugh, Apache Medicine Man," albumen print, 8x5, mounted, 1870s................ | 250.00-350.00 |
| Soule, William Stinson, "Tosh-A-Wah, chief of the Penateka Comanches," albumen print, 8x5, mounted, 1870s.... | 200.00-300.00 |
| Soule, William Stinson, "Whirlwind, Cheyenne Tribe," albumen print, 7x5, mounted, 1870s...................... | 200.00-300.00 |
| Soule, William Stinson, "Lone Wolf, Kiowa Chief," albumen print, 7x5, mounted, 1870s.................... | 200.00-300.00 |

Soule, William Stinson, "Grey Leggings, Comanche Tribe," albumen print, 8x5, mounted, 1870s . . . . . . . . . . . . . . .   **200.00-300.00**

Soule, William Stinson, "Scalped Hunter near Fort Dodge," albumen print, 5x8, mounted, 1868 . . . . . . . . . . .   **200.00-300.00**

Soule, William Stinson, "Son of Little Raven, Arapaho Chief," albumen print, 6x8, mounted, 1870s . . . . . . . . . . . . . . .   **200.00-300.00**

Soule, William Stinson, "Portrait of Five Kiowa Braves," albumen print, 7x5, mounted, 1870s . . . . . . . . . . . . . . .   **200.00-300.00**

Steichen, Edward, "Moonlight: The Pond," photogravure from **Camera Work** 14, 1906 . . . . . . . . . . . . . . . . . . . .   **100.00-150.00**

Steichen, Edward, portrait of "E. Gordon Craig," photogravure from **Camera Work** 42/43, 1913 . . . . . . . . . . . . . . . .   **75.00-150.00**

Steichen, Edward, portrait of George Bernard Shaw, four-color halftone from **Camera Work** 22, 1908 . . . . . . . . . . . . . .   **100.00-200.00**

Steichen, Edward, "Autumnal Afternoon: The Poplars, Voulangis," three-color halftone from **Camera Work** 42/43, 1913 . . . . . . . . . . . . . . . . . . . . . .   **50.00-100.00**

Steichen, Edward, aerial photograph from World War I, 14x19 . . . . . . . . . . . .   **100.00-175.00**

Steichen, Edward, portrait of "Anatole France," photogravure from **Camera Work** 42/43, 1913 . . . . . . . . . . . . . . . . .   **80.00-90.00**

Steichen, Edward, fashion portrait "Jaeckal," silver print, 9x7, 1930 . . . . . .   **500.00-700.00**

Steichen, Edward, "The Man That Resembles Erasmus," photogravure from **Camera Work** 42/43, 1913 . . . . . . .   **150.00-200.00**

Steichen, Edward, portrait of Peggy Wood, silver print, 9x7, 1925 . . . . . . . . . .   **500.00-600.00**

Steichen, Edward, double exposure of Rockefeller Center, silver print, 9x7, mid 1930s . . . . . . . . . . . . . . . . . . . . . . . . . .   **500.00-600.00**

Steichen, Edward, "Dolor,"

Left: Alfred Stieglitz, "The Incoming Boat". See page 296.

Below: Alfred Stieglitz, "Portrait of Louis Kalonyme." See page 294.

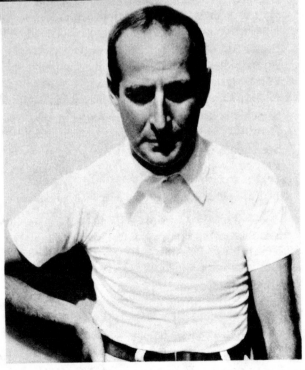

photogravure from **Camera Work** 2, 1903 . . . . . . . . . . . . . . . . . . . . . . . . . . . . . . 100.00-125.00

Steichen, Edward, portrait of actress Louise Brooks, silver print, 13x10, 1928, printed later . . . . . . . . . . . . . . . . . . . . . . . 400.00-600.00

Steichen, Edward, portrait of E. Gordon Craig, photogravure from **Camera Work**, 42/43, 1913 . . . . . . . . . . . . . . . . . 100.00-150.00

Steichen, Edward, "Lotus, Mount Kisco, New York," silver print . . . . . . . . 7,500.00-8,500.00

Steichen, Edward, "The Flat Iron Building, New York," colored halftone gravure from **Camera Work** 14, 8x6, 1906 . . . . . . . . . . . . . . . . . . . . . . . . . . . 300.00-400.00

Steichen, Edward, portrait of Henri Matisse, photogravure from **Camera Work** 42/43, 1913 . . . . . . . . . . . . . . . . . 100.00-150.00

Steichen, Edward, "Three Pears and an Apple," silver print, 10x7, signed and dated, 1921 . . . . . . . . . . . . . . . . . . . . . . . 3,000.00-4,500.00

Steichen, Edward, portrait of Peggy Wood for **Vogue**, silver print, 10x8, 1931 300.00-500.00

Steichen, Edward, fashion study for **Vogue**, silver print, 8x9, 1931 . . . . . . . . . 300.00-350.00

Steichen, Edward, "Nocturne— Orangerie Staircase, Versailles," silver print . . . . . . . . . . . . . . . . . . . . . . . . . . . . 9,000.-10,000.

Stieglitz, Alfred, outdoor scene in Switzerland, platinum print, 8x6, 1890s . . . . . 1,000.00-1,500.00

Stieglitz, Alfred, "The Flatiron Building," photogravure from **Camera Work** 4, 1903 . . . . . . . . . . . . . . . . . . . . . 300.00-400.00

Stieglitz, Alfred, "The Steerage," photogravure from **Camera Work** 36, 1911 . . . . . . . . . . . . . . . . . . . . . . . . . . . 800.00-900.00

Stieglitz, Alfred, "The Steerage," photogravure on tissue from deluxe edition of "291," 13x11, 1907 . . . . . . . . . . . 2,000.00-2,500.00

Steiglitz, Alfred, portrait of art critic Louis Kalonyme, silver print, 8x7, early 1920s . . . . . . . . . . . . . . . . . . . . . . . . . . . 1,000.00-1,250.00

Left: Paul Strand, "Iris Facing the Winter, Orgeval. See page 296.

Below: Paul Strand, A Portfolio of Eleven Photographs, 1914-1973, "On My Doorstep." See page 296.

Stieglitz, Alfred, "The Letter Box," photogravure, 8x6, 1897 . . . . . . . . . . . . . .     **200.00-400.00**
Stieglitz, Alfred, "Scurrying Home," photogravure, 7x6, 1897 . . . . . . . . . . . . . .     **175.00-350.00**

Stieglitz, Alfred, "The Incoming Boat," photogravure, 6x5, late 1890s ......... 250.00-350.00

Stieglitz, Alfred, "Excavating—New York," photogravure from **Camera Work** 36, 1911 ..................... 75.00-100.00

Stieglitz, Alfred, "The Swimming Lesson," photogravure from **Camera Work** 36, 1911 ..................... 100.00-125.00

Strand, Paul, "Telegraph Poles," photogravure from **Camera Work** 48, 1916 ............................. 100.00-150.00

Strand, Paul, "Photographs of Mexico" (published by Virginia Stevens, N.Y., 1940), complete portfolio of 20 photogravures, up to 8x10 ................. 1,700.00-2,000.00

Strand, Paul, "Ranchos de Taos Church, New Mexico," silver print ..... 3,000.00-4,500.00

Strand, Paul, "Rebecca, New York City," silver print, 8x9, 1922, printed in 1970s ............................. 1,200.00-1,400.00

Strand, Paul, "A Portfolio of Eleven Photographs, 1914-1973, On My Doorstep," (published by Michael Hoffman, N.Y., 1976), 11 silver prints up to 13x9, various dates ................. 6,000.00-8,000.00

Strand, Paul, "Iris Facing The Winter, Orgeval," silver print, 1973 ........... 1,200.00-1,400.00

Struss, Karl, "California Palm Shadows," silver print, 13x10, 1926 .... 150.00-200.00

Thomson, John, outdoor view of an old clothes shop with two ladies, woodburytype, 3x4, 1877 ..................... 200.00-300.00

Thomson, John, portrait of a shellfish seller, woodburytype, 3x4, 1877 ....... 150.00-200.00

Thomson, John, portrait of a dealer in fancy wares, woodburytype, 3x4, 1877 .. 200.00-300.00

Tice, George A., "Tree Study," platinum print, 7x10, signed ........... 200.00-300.00

Uelsmann, Jerry, untitled landscape, silver print, 14x10, signed and dated, 1970 ............................. 150.00-200.00

John Thomson, "Outdoor View of an old Clothes Shop with two Ladies." See page 296.

James Van Derzee, "Portrait of Kate and Rachel Van Derzee." See page 299.

Above Left: S. Uyida "Waterlilies." See below. Below Right:
Marion Post Walcott, "Outdoor scene showing horse team."
See page 300.

Uelsmann, Jerry, self portrait, silver
print, 10x13, 1965.................... 200.00-250.00

Ulmann, Doris, portrait of black woman
plowing field, photogravure, 8x6, 1930s. 75.00-125.00

Ulmann, Doris, black man eating lunch,
photogravure, 8x6, 1930s............ 50.00-75.00

Uyida, S., "Waterlilies," silver print,
12x12............................. 250.00-350.00

Uyida, S., "Hands in Shadow," silver print, 13x11, 1928.................... 250.00-300.00

Vamerson, group of portraits of North American Indians taken from life, 43 albumen prints, 8x6, mounted, Washington, D.C., 1859.............. 1,000.00-3,000.00

Van Derzee, James, portrait of Kate and Rachel Van Derzee, silver print, 7x6, 1908............................. 200.00-300.00

Vechten, Carl Van, portrait of George Gershwin, silver print, 10x8, 1933...... 100.00-200.00

Left: Eva Watson-Schutz "Woman holding an apple leaf." See page 300. Below: Carlton Watkins, "Outdoor Scene showing Columbia River, Oregon." See page 300.

Vechten, Carl Van, portrait of Charles Laughton, silver print, 10x9, 1940 . . . . . .    **50.00-75.00**

Vechten, Carl Van, portrait of actress Adele Addison, 12x9, 1955 . . . . . . . . . . .    **40.00-60.00**

Vishniac, Roman, "The Village Cheder," silver print, 10x11, signed and dated, 11938, printed later . . . . . . . . . . .    **75.00-100.00**

Walcott, Marion Post, outdoor scene showing horse team and farmer planting corn, silver print, 11x14, 1930s . . . . . . . .    **250.00-350.00**

Walcott, Marion Post, "Post Office in Blizzard, Aspen, Colo.," silver print, 8x11, signed, 1939, printed in 1978 . . . . .    **200.00-250.00**

Watkins, Carlton, outdoor scene showing Columbia River, Ore., albumen print, 16x21, mounted, c. 1868 . . . . . . .    **600.00-700.00**

Watkins, Carlton, outdoor scene showing Sentinel Rock, albumen print printed by I. W. Taber . . . . . . . . . . . . . . . . . . . . .    **250.00-350.00**

Watkins, Carlton, "Yosemite Valley, Three Sisters," albumen print from mammoth plate, 1866 . . . . . . . . . . . . . . .    **200.00-300.00**

Watson-Schutz, Eva, woman holding an apple leaf, platinum print, 6x4, 1897 . . . .    **150.00-200.00**

Watson-Schutze, Eva, outdoor scene with boat, platinum print, 8x6, 1900 . . . .    **150.00-200.00**

Watson-Schutze, Eva, portrait of a young woman, platinum print, 8x6, c. 1902 . . . . . . . . . . . . . . . . . . . . . . . . . . . . .    **100.00-200.00**

Webb, Todd, solarized portrait of Harry Callahan, silver print, 6x4, signed and dated, 1942 . . . . . . . . . . . . . . . . . . . . . . .    **150.00-200.00**

Webb, Todd, portrait of Harry Callahan, silver print, 6x5, signed and dated, 1942 . . . . . . . . . . . . . . . . . . . . . . .    **100.00-150.00**

Webb, Todd, "Michigan, 1942," silver print, 7x4, signed and dated, 1942 . . . . . .    **75.00-100.00**

Webb, Todd, "Cable Car, San Francisco," silver print, 11x14, signed and dated, 1955 . . . . . . . . . . . . . . . . . . . . . . .    **50.00-125.00**

Weegee (Arthur Fellig), portrait of Louella Parsons, silver print, 13x11 . . . .    **200.00-250.00**

Left: Edward Weston, "Portrait of a Young Woman", see page 304. Below: Brett Weston "White Sands", see page 302.

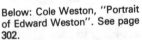

Below: Cole Weston, "Portrait of Edward Weston". See page 302.

Weegee (Arthur Fellig), "Harlem, Clothing Salesman, Easter Sunday," silver print, 13x10, 1940s............ 150.00-200.00

Weegee (Arthur Fellig), "Coffee Break by and with Weegee," silver print, 5x7, 1950s ............................. 200.00-300.00

Weegee (Arthur Fellig), "Self Portrait with Shoe," silver print, 8x9, 1950s..... 100.00-200.00

Weiner, Dan, portrait of Learned Hand, silver print, 10x7, 1952.............. 400.00-600.00

Weston, Brett, "Trees," silver print, 8x10, signed and dated, 1947......... 100.00-200.00

Weston, Brett, "White Sands," silver print, 8x10, signed and dated, 1946..... 150.00-250.00

Weston, Brett, "Tools," silver print, 8x10, signed and dated, 1951........... 100.00-150.00

Weston, Brett, "Sand Dunes," silver print, 9x7, signed and dated, 1934...... 200.00-300.00

Weston, Cole, portrait of Edward Weston, silver print, 7x10, signed and dated, 1946...................... 200.00-300.00

Weston, Edward, "Oceano," dye print by Cole Weston from a color transparency by Edward Weston, 8x9, 1948, printed later...................... 100.00-200.00

Weston, Edward, "Portrait of my Son," sepia-toned platinum print, 10x7, matted, c. 1923......................1,500.00-2,500.00

Weston, Edward, "D. H. Lawrence, Mexico, 1924," silver print, 9x7, signed and dated, matted, 1924, (creased through center).................... 600.00-800.00

Weston, Edward, "Pepper," silver print, 9x7, signed and dated, 1929......2,500.00-3,000.00

Weston, Edward, "Portrait of Harold Kreutzbert," silver print, 4x3, 1932..... 400.00-500.00

Weston, Edward, "Portrait of Zohmah Charlot," silver print, 5x4, dated and signed, 1933...................... 500.00-800.00

Weston, Edward, "Female Nude," silver print, 3x4, 1934...............1,300.00-1,500.00

Weston, Edward, "Ansel Adams' Darkroom," silver print, 7x10, signed and dated, 1938....................1,000.00-1,500.00

Weston, Edward, "Nude Buttocks," silver print, 5x3, 1930s............... 500.00-600.00

Weston, Edward, "Monument of Wilshire Boulevard," silver print, 9x7, signed and dated, 1936.............. 400.00-600.00

Weston, Edward, "Dunes, Oceano," silver print, 8x9, signed and dated, 1936. 5,500.00-6,500.00

Weston, Edward, "The Shell," silver print..............................6,000.00-8,500.00

Weston, Edward, portrait of a young woman, silver print, 9x5, signed, 1920s. 500.00-700.00

Weston, Edward, portrait of William Andrews Clark, Jr., platinum print, 9x7, signed, 1921........................1,500.00-2,000.00

Weston, Edward, "Monterey Cypress," silver print, 9x7, signed, 1929..........1,800.00-2,000.00

Weston, Edward, "Cabbage Leaf," silver print, 7x9, signed, dated, 1931....1,500.00-2,500.00

Weston, Edward, portrait of Brett and Erica, silver print, 9x8, 1945...........1,000.00-1,500.00

Weston, Edward, "Point Lobos," silver print made by Cole or Brett Weston, printed 1955 from negative by Edward Weston, 8x10......................2,000.00-2,500.00

White, Clarence, portrait of actress Mrs. Patrick Campbell, platinum print, 9x6, 1918s............................ 350.00-450.00

White, Margaret Bourke, "Kremlin, USSR," silver print, 7x13, signed, 1931. 100.00-175.00

Worth, Don, "Grass, Atasco Mountains, Arizona," silver print, 8x10, signed ..................... 100.00-200.00

Worth, Don, "Ferns and Skull in Rain, Elk, Calif.," silver print, 9x8, signed... 100.00-200.00

Yavno, Max, "San Francisco From Twin Peaks," silver print, signed, 1945. 200.00-250.00

Yavno, Max, portrait of Aaron Siskind, silver print, 13x19, signed, 1941........ 200.00-300.00

# GLOSSARY
## of Photographical Terms

**Abberation**: a distortion, usually blurring, caused by some optical defect in the camera lens.

**Accelerating buff**: a leather buff saturated with various organic materials used to polish the daguerreotype plate to produce brighter images.

**Accelerator**: a substance added to developing solution to hasten development process; also known as "quick."

**Albertype**: an early photographic process developed by Josef Albert to produce an image on a ground glass plate that could be used for printing purposes. Also known as a Collotype.

**Albumen process**: the use of glass covered with a thin film of albumen (made from the whites of eggs) together with light-sensitive chemicals to produce an image. First used in 1848.

**Albumen print**: a print on paper made using albumen obtained from egg whites to produce an even, glossy image, widely used before the turn of the century, most notably for stereo cards, cartes de visite, and studio portraits.

**Ambrotype**: a negative image on glass produced by an early wet-plate process. It was viewed as a positive when placed against a dark background. Ambrotypes were popular during the late 1850s and early 1860s.

**American film**: the type of factory-loaded film George Eastman invented and marketed along with the original Kodak camera in 1888.

**Anastigmat**: a type of lens introduced in 1889 by Zeiss, free of the optical defect of astigmatism.

**Aniline process**: patented in 1864, a process for photographic reproduction (without a negative) of drawings made on transparent paper. Similar to blueprinting process.

**Anthony's**: The E. & H.T. Anthony Co., founded in 1852, which became the nation's largest dealer in photographic equipment and supplies during the 1860s and 1870s and later. The firm widely marketed Mathew Brady wartime images in stereograph form.

**Aperture**: the lens opening on a camera, determining the amount of light reaching the sensitive materials. Size of opening is designated by the term f/stop.

**Aplantic lens**: a type of lens capable of defining well at a large aperture. It is corrected for spherical abberation.

**Arched print**: an image trimmed at the top so as to represent the curve of a Gothic window. Many cabinet cards and stereographs were so shaped.

**Archival processing**: a method of carefully processing photographs so as to preserve them from any future damage caused by chemical traces.

**Aristotype**: a gelatine-chloride print popular in the late 1800s.

**Astigmatism**: an aberration of the lens which prevents equal focus of mutually perpendicular points, such as a cross, on the same plane.

**Autographic**: Kodak trade name for process which enabled photographer to write with a metal stylus on undeveloped film still in the camera, thereby identifying and dating photos as they were taken. Kodak produced autographic cameras between 1914 and 1934.

**Barrel distortion**: the magnification of an image at its center.

**Belinograph**: a photograph transmitted by telephone lines using a system dependent on a point of light aimed at a revolving drum covered with photo-sensitive paper.

**Bellows**: a collapsible light-tight unit in a camera, enabling the lens to be moved toward or away from the camera back or film plane.

**Berline portrait**: a photographic image made on a piece of glass which, coarsely ground on the back, gives the image a soft fuzzy look considered flattering in portraiture.

**Boudoir**: a size of cabinet card popular around 1890, larger than the usual cabinet card. Boudoir size is usually about five by eight inches.

**Bromide paper**: light sensitive paper with a silver bromide emulsion, used for printing photographs.

**B setting**: mark on shutter setting ring indicating that the shutter will stay open while the shutter release remains depressed.

**Box camera**: a camera of the type George Eastman introduced in 1888 consisting of a light-tight box with lens, shutter and view-finder. Box cameras used film, not phates.

**Brewster viewer**: a kind of stereoscopic viewer which looks like a tapered box with a lens at the back and a slot at the top for insertion of stereo slide. Brewster viewers were popular in the 1850s.

**Brownie:** a simple rollfilm box camera first marketed in 1900 by Eastman Co.

**Burning-in:** a photomechanical process of giving additional exposure to areas of an image when printing in the darkroom.

**Cabinet card:** a 4½" x 6½" card with a mounted photograph slightly smaller than that, popular in the mid-1860s. Most cabinet cards were portraits, usually of celebrities of the day.

**Calotype:** a silver chloride print on paper made by a process invented by Englishman William Henry Fox Talbot. It involved producing a negative and then contact printing it onto a second sheet. Calotypes were made during the 1840s and early 1850s.

**Cameo print:** a carte de visite photograph with image raised in bas relief by an embossing process.

**Camera obscura:** an early optical instrument that consisted of either a room or a box in which an image entering through a small opening was projected two-dimensionally and inverted on the opposite wall. The camera obscura was the predecessor of the camera. In 1826 Niepce succeeded in capturing the image projected within the box thanks to the use of the lens and a photo-sensitive material.

**Carbon print:** a durable photographic print created by exposing a negative onto special carbon (in gelatin) tissue. The process dates from the 1850s, and was little used in the U.S.

**Carte de visite:** a 2½" x 4½" photograph mounted on a piece of cardboard and used as a calling card, popular in the 1850s and later.

**Carte de visite camera:** a special camera equipped with two to four lenses so it could take a number of photographs simultaneously, the images later to be cut apart.

**Case:** a decorative container, usually hinged, used to house daguerreotypes or ambrotypes. Leather and thermoplastic were most common materials.

**CDV:** Commonly used term for cartes de visite.

**Chemical toning:** the use of gold or compounds of their chemicals to preserve or color a photograph, usually with a reddish or brownish hue.

**Chloro-bromide paper:** a printing paper with a balance of silver chloride and silver bromide, introduce in 1883 and in use ever since.

**Coating box:** a wooden box containing chemical into which the polished daguerreotype plate was dipped to render it light sensitive.

**Collodion print**: a print made by collodion process introduced in 1851. The process is a wet-plate system in which a light-sensitive glass plate is created by coating glass with collodion containing potassium iodide, then bathing it in nitrate of silver just before exposing the dripping plate in the camera. This process, producing a negative on glass, made possible the first production of satisfactory paper prints in quantity. It was the dominant photographic process from the mid-1850s until the mid-1880s. Ambrotypes and tintypes were both produced using the wet collodion process.

**Collotype**: print made by any of the photo-gelatin methods for reproducing a photographic image on a glass plate which could be used for printing purposes. Colotypes were used extensively for book illustration until outmoded by photogravure.

**Combination print**: the print resulting from the use of two or more negative to create a single positive print on paper.

**Compound lens**: a lens system containing two or more elements

**Costume card**: a cabinet card depicting local costume of a foreign country, sometimes colored by hand, popular during the 1880s.

**Cyanotype**: popularly known as a blueprint, a white-on-blue photographic image using a process invented by Sir John Herschel in 1842. It was useful for low-cost permanent prints.

**Daguerreotype**: the first practical system of photography devised by Nicephore Niepce and J. L. M. Daguerre. A daguerreotype is a unique positive image produced directly on a silvered copper plate sensitized with iodine or bromine vapor or both, exposed, then developed in mercury vapor. Designations of size (full-plate, half-plate, etc.) are derived from the size of plate originally used by Daguerre—6½" x 8½". Popular mainly in the 1850s, daguerreotypes lost popularity after the negative-producing wet-plate collodion method was introduced, enabling many copies to be made.

**Detective camera**: a box-shaped dry-plate camera of a type used to photograph criminals, or any camera which was disguised as those concealed in satchels, books, and clothing.

**Develop**: to treat with chemicals to produce a visible image.

**Diaphragm**: that part of a camera which controls the amount of light allowed to pass through the lens. It is a variable opening measured in f/stops.

**Direct positive**: a positive obtained without use of an intervening negative.

**Dodging**: local control in photographic printing achieved by reducing the exposure to specific areas of the printing paper.

**Dry collodion**: collodion in the dry form, as in the dry collodion process developed in 1855 to supplant the messy wet-plate process.

**Dry mount**: a method of affixing a print to cardboard for display, using wax-coated paper which is heated after being sandwiched between print and board.

**Dry plate**: successor to wet-plate process, a light-sensitive glass or film-base sheet coated with already dried but still sensitized chemicals. It was loaded in the dark into a plate-holder then placed in the camera for the exposure.

**Edge fog**: the darkening at the edges of a photograph, either film or paper, because of the action of chemicals or of light.

**Emulsion**: a light-sensitive material that is coated on a suitable base to produce an image during exposure. Usually consists of silver halides suspended in gelatin.

**Ferrotype**: a direct positive made by the collodion process on tinned iron. The ferrotype became known erroneously as the "tintype," despite the fact that it is not on tin.

**Fixer**: the chemicals used in developing which remove the silver halide crystals not exposed to light.

**Flare**: a hole appearing in the photographic image caused by reflections of light inside the lens.

**Fixed Focus**: a camera which has no method of adjusting the focus of the lens.

**Focal Length**: The distance between the lens (strictly its rear nodal point) and the focal plane, when the camera is focused at infinity.

**Focal plane**: An image line at right angles to the optical axis passing through the focal point. This forms the plane of sharp focus when the camera is set on infinity.

**Focal plane shutter**: a shutter system devised to operate in the focal plane, or close to the film, usually as a rolling curtain with a slot in it to permit light to reach film as it passes across surface.

**F/Stop**: the numerical expression of the relative size of the lens opening. The focal length of the lens divided by the effective diameter of the lens.

**Folding camera**: A camera constructed for maximum compactness and minimum weight employing collapsible leather bellows between the lens at front and the film-holding section at back.

**Full-plate**: a daguerreotype size, about 8 x 10 inches, thus larger than the "whole" plate.

**Gelatin**: a medium made by boiling animal substances, used in sensitized emulsion for the suspension of the light-sensitive silver halides.

**Gelatin film**: a type of film initially manufactured by Eastman and used in the Kodak No. 1, introduced in 1888. It replaced the need for photographic plates.

**Gelatin paper**: a coated paper which produces a purplish brown image, such as the Aristotype introduced in 1888.

**Gem**: a tiny tintype, sometimes incorporated into a piece of jewelry such as a brooch. Such jewelry was popular in the mid 1860s to 1880s.

**Glass plate**: a wet-collodion plate.

**Graphoscope**: a viewing device providing a magnified image of a transparent photograph. The Kombi and Versacope cameras could be used as viewers of this kind.

**Gravure**: same as photogravure. An engraving produced by means of a photograph, or the printed copy of an original photograph from such an engraving.

**Gum print**: a type of highly controlled print created by either the gum-bichromate or gum-platinotype process. Starting in 1894, this process, based on discoveries by A. Poitevin in 1855, gave the photographer an opportunity for handwork to alter tonality, omit details or produce special effects.

**Gutta percha**: a substance derived from the tree of that name and used in photography experiments with collodion and used in the production of miniature cases.

**Half-plate**: a daguerreotype size which is larger than the quarter plate but not larger than 4¼" x 5½".

**Halftone**: a reproduction of a photograph by a mechanical process which simulates the photograph by using a finely patterned screen of dots for reproduction of the image.

**Heliograph**: the early process of Nicephore Niepce in which an image on a polished pewter plate was produced by slow exposure.

**Holmes-Bates**: a hand-held viewing device for looking at stereoscopic photographs. It was invented by Oliver Wendell Holmes in 1861.

**Hyalotype**: the name under which Frederick Langenheim secured his U.S. patent for the lantern slide in 1850.

**Hypo**: the popular name for hyposulfite of soda, the solution used to fix the photographic image.

**Iris diaphragm**: lens aperture continuously adjustable in diameter by means of interspersed moveable metal leaves or blades. It was invented by Nicephore Niepce.

**Kinetograph**: the Edison camera of c. 1891 for photographing motion, using flexible roll film passing a shutter that opened and closed rhythmically.

**Long-focus lens**: lens with focal length exceeding the length of the diagonal of the film format with which it is used.

**Lantern slide**: a transparent positive intended for projection, first developed by the Langenheim Bros. of Philadelphia c. 1850.

**Leaf shutter**: a concentric arrangement of overlapping metal plates which, when activated, moves to admit light into the camera. Also called diaphragm shutter.

**Lithoprint stereograph**: a card stereograph produced in color and in black and white in the late 1890s and early years of this century, usually showing travels or humorous scenes.

**Magazine camera**: a camera capable of storing a number of plates (or pieces of cut film) and containing a mechanism for shifting the plate following each exposure, usually by dropping the plate to the bottom of the camera.

**Magic Lantern**: early name for a projection device incorporating an oil lamp (later electicity) to project an image on a glass slide through a lens to a screen or wall, a common parlor entertainment among Victorians.

**Mahoganytype**: a humorous term for an all-black picture, the result of forgetting to put the plate in the camera.

**Mat**: a cardboard frame or border used to isolate, hold and protect a photographic print.

**Matte**: an emulsion surface in a photographic paper which is dull and non-reflective, as opposed to glossy or shiny.

**Mascher viewer**: a folding stereo viewer patented by J. F. Mascher in 1852 as a case holding a pair of stereo images. The case lid held two lenses to permit the viewer to enjoy the illusion of depth.

**Medallion portrait**: a head-and-shoulders portrait enhanced by being enclosed in a contrasting circle or oval to produce the effect of a border.

**Medium Plate**: a daguerreotype size of plate, namely the sixth plate 2¾" x 3¼".

**Megalethoscope**: a large (nearly 5 foot long) parlor-type viewing device with a magnifying lens to permit daylight or artifical light magnification of views, especially travel views, in a three dimensional effect.

**Melainotype**: a kind of photograph produced in sheet metal, later known more widely as the tintype.

**Melanograph**: a collodion positive made directly on black paper.

**Mercury bath**: a slightly warmed bath of purified mercury whose fumes were used in the daguerreotype process to bring out the latent image.

**Meniscus lens**: a single-element lens, of glass or plastic, optically designed to throw an image to a plane surface. Meniscus lens were common on low-cost cameras.

**Mezzotint**: a photographic print with a softened effect obtained by interposing a sheet of glass, tissue or mica between negative and printing paper.

**Miniature camera**: any very small camera (some even used sensitized microscope slides), some of which were used as detective cameras.

**Miniature case**: an enclosure, usually hinged, designed to hold a photograph, usually a daguerreotype portrait, and intended as a keepsake. Size usually ranges from 3 or 4 inches down to about 1¾" x 2".

**Miniature photograph**: a paper image about 1-1/8" x 2" in size, or smaller, usually intended to be mounted in albums designed for them in the late 1800s.

**Monobath**: a single-bath processing system with one bath containing both developing and fixing agences (commonly used in direct-positive processes, such as found in street cameras).

**Mourning mat**: a mat of dark paper used in mounting daguerreotypes, usually portraits of the dead.

**Multiple photograph**: a number of images made separately on a single plate.

**Multiplying camera**: a type of camera with more than one lens, capable, with two or more exposures, of producing a number of pictures from just one pose. The first multipliers were sold by Simon Wing of Waterville, Maine.

**Mutoscope:** a hand-cranked "peep show" device dating from 1895 in which card photographs mounted on a reel slip by to recreate an action sequence.

**Ninth plate:** the roll film invented by Rev. Hannibal Goodwin in 1887 and later improved by Eastman. The type of roll film in use to this day.

**Opalotype:** a positve made on an opaque white glass, producing what was called an "opal picture" (one of clear glass is called a transparancy).

**Palladium print:** a print on paper made with salts of palladium as a substitute for platinum, usually with a delicate gray image. Palladium prints were produced mostly during the World War I years.

**Passepartout:** a cut-out matting, as found under the glass framing a daguerreotype in a miniature case. The passepartout album contains slots into which photographs may be inserted.

**Photochromscope:** a type of camera invented in 1891 by Frederic Eugene Ives to take three positive transparencies which could later be superimposed to create a single three-color image.

**Photogram:** a photograph made by simply placing an object or objects on light-sensitive paper for a period of time, capturing their "shadow."

**Photographic jewelry:** popular in the 1860s, jewelry incorporating tiny photographs (usually tintypes) made for that purpose, often in the form of a brooch, pin, locket, or ring.

**Photogravure:** not a photograph, but a reproduction of one, in ink on paper, produced by an intaglio process. The process dates from 1879.

**Photo-jumelle:** a kind of detective camera, one of the first which was designed to be held at eye-level. Invented by Jules Carpentier in 1892, the camera had two identical lenses, one forming the image on the dry plate and the other on ground glass for viewing.

**Photomechanical process:** any process in which a printing surface is prepared from the action of light upon chemical substances.

**Photomicrograph:** a photograph taken through a microscope (not just any small photograph).

**Photo relief**: a Woodburytype using Walter B. Woodbury's process for photo mechanical printing in the late 1880s in which a metal mold was made from a gelatin image with photographically created depth.

**Pinchbeck**: a flexible, light, gilt-metal frame used to hold daguerreotypes in miniature cases or to preserve other small photographs. An alloy of copper and zinc, pinchbeck resembles gold.

**Pistol camera**: a single-lens miniature camera with fast lens invented in 1856 by Thomas Skaife. The word also refers to a hand-held camera with a grip like that of a pistol.

**Plate**: a smooth surface either glass or metal, on wich the photographic image is recorded, as in dry collodion plate or wet plate (both glass). The word also means a printed photograph in a book.

**Platinotype**: A durable photographic print with delicate tones and rich blacks with an overall soft silver-grey color, made on an uncoated paper rendered light-sensitive with salts of platinum.

**Platinum Print**: can refer either to the platinotype (above) or to more modern photograph prints by artists such as George Tice who revived platinum printing.

**Plumbeotype**: a hand-pulled copy of a daguerreotype rendered on a lithographic stone, produced by a method devised by John Plumbe.

**Pocket camera**: a camera small enough to be carried about conveniently in a man's coat pocket.

**Porcelain picture**: a photograph made on porcelain using the collodion wet-plate method.

**Publics**: the term cabinet photographer J. M. Mora applied to his collection of portraits of celebrities.

**Quarter Plate**: a daguerreotype size, 3¼" x 4¼", a popular size for both daguerreotypes and ambrotypes since it fit into a miniature case.

**Quick**: Alsso "quickstuff," the accelerator or chemical addition used in the daguerreotype process to speed exposure of images, especially portraits.

**Rapid rectilinear lens**: a type of lens introduced by J. H. Dallmeyer in 1866, having a miximum aperture of f/8. This type of lens was used on early Kodak cameras and other mass-produced cameras.

**Range finder**: an optical device to accurately determine distance from the observer to a distant point.

**Rayograph**: A photograph of the type made by Man Ray in 1922 by placing an object or objects directly on light-sensitive paper.

**Reflex camera**: a type of camera which incorporates a mirror affixed to the camera base to reflect the image onto a ground glass at the top of the camera, permitting the photographer to see his subject right up to time he takes picture. Thomas Sutton patented a reflex camera in 1861, but none was manufactured until 1884.

**Reticulation**: a defect in a print, such as wrinkling of the surface of a processed emulsion, usually as a result of temperature change or chemical actions.

**Rinhart**: after Floyd and Marion Rinhart, experts and authors of books on old photograph cases, the "Rinhart number" refers to the numbers they assigned to various miniature case styles in their books.

**Roll-film camera**: a camera of the modern kind which contains a device for winding film off one spool and onto another.

**Roll holder**: a device invented in 1884 which held film spools which could be turned by a key outside the camera. Usually mahogany, the holder could ordinarily be used interchangeably with the glass-plate holder.

**Rotogravure**: the reproduction of a photograph achieved by use of a photogravure plate on a rotary cylinder press, an adaptation which, after 1895, made possible rapid commercial printing of large editions of images.

**Salon print**: a photograph made in imitation of a painting, both in sentiment and composition, often by posing figures against a fanciful allegorical background.

**Salted paper**: paper made sensitive for printing by being immersed in a soluble chloride and then floated in a bath of silver nitrate.

**Screen**: a moveable surface employed by mid-19th-century photographs to provide background for a portrait.

**Sepia toning**: any of a number of processes used to convert a black silver print image to a brownish one.

**Series print**: one produced from the same negative as the original or vintage print but, due to the passage of time or differences in printing, differing at least slightly from the original.

**Shutter:** the shield between the light-sensitive material in a camera and the front of the lens, controlled at the moment of exposure.

**Silver bromide:** the most popular type of printing paper in use from 1880 onward.

**Silver chloride print:** a print on the kind of plain salted "writing" paper used by Fox Talbot for the calotype.

**Silver-copper plate:** the daguerreotype plate.

**Silver halide:** the combination of silver with halogen elements to create light-sensitive emulsions (bromide, iodide, or chloride).

**Silver intensification:** a method of restoring faded calotypes by supplementing the silver already present in the image.

**Silver print:** the most common form of paper photograph, made on plain salted paper, a method dating from Fox Talbot's calotypes. The image is not silver in tone, and is often pleasingly brownish.

**Single lens reflex:** a type of camera in which both the viewing and focusing are accomplished through the same lens. At the instant of exposure the position of a mirror is changed to permit the image to reach the film. William Sutton of England patented such a camera in the 1860s, but it was not widely manufactured until the late 1880s.

**Sixteenth plate:** a rarely used small daguerreotype size, about 1-3/8" x 1-5/8".

**Sixth plate:** a daguerreotype plate size, 2¾" x 3¼", also called the medium plate.

**Sliding box:** a simple type of camera popular between 1840 and 1865 in England, consisting of two open-ended boxes telescoped into each other to focus.

**Solarized print:** a photograph with tones reversed due to gross overexposure. A partial reversal (the Sabattier effect) may take place if negative is exposed to a strong darkroom light.

**Souvenir album:** a photographic album containing 10 or more commercial photographs, usually showing travel scenes, and particulary popular from 1890 to around 1910. Some fold out accordian style.

**Spy camera:** the same as a detective camera.

**Stanhope:** an optical novelty (named after Charles Stanhope) which consists of a tiny magnifying glass which magnifies an attached film positive about 1/8 inch across.

**Stereo**: term widely used for a stereograph or stereogram which is technically one of a pair of photographic prints designed to be viewed in tandem, side by side, to produce a surprisingly three-dimensional effect of depth.

**Stereoscope**: a device for viewing twin images which creates an illusion of depth.

**Stereoscopic camera**: a camera with twin lenses capable of taking two pictures simulatenously from two points, with a slight angle that corresponds to the space between human eyes. When viewed in a stereoscope, the twin images merge to produce a seemingly three-dimensional image.

**Studio portrait**: a commercially made portrait, usually larger than the carte de visite or cabinet cards that inspired studio portrature.

**Tableau vivant**: a posed photograph of a kind popular at the end of the 19th century, often featuring models posing to commemorate some special event or to illustrate a maxim.

**Talbotype**: another name for the calotype invented by Fox Talbot.

**Tax stamp**: A U.S. Government-required stamp that was affixed to commercial photographs between Sept. 1864 and Aug. 1866, now often helpful in dating images.

**Thermoplastic**: a substance invented (and patented) by Samuel Peck in 1854 and used in manufacturing extremely durable miniature photograph cases. The gutta-percha-like material could be molded into a variety of relief designs.

**Tint**: a light color applied to a photograph, as in the pink blush applied to cheeks in daguerreotypes, ambrotypes and tintypes.

**Tintype**: a photograph, usually a portrait, produced by the collodion process directly on japanned iron (not tin, despite the name; technically, its a ferrotype). Cheap to produce en masse, the tintype portrait was used as a keepsake, set into tombstones, used in jewelry and as campaign buttons, and sent through the mails as love tokens.

**Tombstone portrait**: a picture of the deceased, usually a tintype, mounted on his or her tombstone.

**Twin-lens camera**: a camera specially constructed to take stereoscopic pictures; or, a kind of reflex camera with two lenses, one for transmitting image to film, the other for viewing.

**Underwood set**: a set of stereographs manufactured and sold by the firm of Underwood & Underwood, usually 50 to 100 stereographs boxed.

**Union case**: a composition (thermoplastic) miniature case for holding small portrait photographs, usually daguerreotypes or ambrotypes but sometimes tintypes or even paper photographs. This type of case was popular in the 1850s and 1860s, contained either one or two photographs, usually with an ornate cover design.

**Varnished print**: a photograph which has been varnished after processing, as commonly done to cartes de visite.

**View camera**: a type of camera lacking automatic focusing, equipped with a viewing screen to enable the photographer to see his subject and check focus and composition.

**Viewfinder**: apparatus for compositing and sometimes focusing the subject. It can be either a direct vision viewfinder, an optical viewfinder, a ground glass screen or a reflex viewfinder.

**Vignette**: a photograph employing a printing technique in which the edges of the print are faded out at the corners or edges. Frequently seen in cartes de visite.

**Vintage print**: one made by the photographer himself or under his direct supervision, usually soon after the picture was taken, as opposed to later series prints.

**Wet-collodion print**: a print resulting from the use of a glass plate coated with collodion, sensitized with silver nitrate, placed in the camera while still wet, exposed, and quickly developed. The process dates from 1851 and was widely used until the 1880s, when dry plates appeared. The wet-collodion print is generally made on albumen paper.

**Wet plate**: a photographic negative made by the collodion process of 1851, popular until the appearance of the dry plate. Cameras of the period are called wet-plate cameras.

**Whole plate**: the largest standard size of daguerreotype plate, measuring 6½" x 8½".

**Woodburytype**: the earliest form of photo-mechanical print, widely used for book illustration in the late 1880s. The process uses continuous halftones in a relief mold for printing. Slightly purplish in color and lacking grain, the Woodburytype has a satisfying brilliance and sharpness of detail.